"John Paulk's story has the capacity to shock, amuse, encourage, and break the reader's heart all at once. Some will be outraged by his 'ex-gay' claims, but anyone interested in hearing the full spectrum of sexual and relational options inherent in the human condition will at least give this book a fair hearing."

— JOE DALLAS
Author, *A Strong Delusion: Confronting the Gay Christian Movement*

"The greatest cover-up in America has nothing to do with party politics, but with the politics of sex. The myth that many are forced to accept is that homosexuals can't change their orientation, and God help the person who says they can. In fact, God helps the person who wants to change and John Paulk is just one of many who has accepted that aid. In his book, *Not Afraid to Change*, you will find blessing and hope, especially if you are one who has been living in darkness, but longing to find the way to the light."

— CAL THOMAS
Nationally Syndicated Columnist

"John Paulk's riveting story is a hand grenade that blows away that myth that says, 'Once gay, always gay.' John's book points the way to freedom for anyone struggling with homosexuality. I can't recommend it highly enough."

— MARLIN MADDOUX
Host, *Point of View* Radio Talk Show

NOT AFRAID TO
CHANGE

THE REMARKABLE STORY OF HOW ONE MAN
OVERCAME HOMOSEXUALITY

NOT AFRAID TO
CHANGE

THE REMARKABLE STORY OF HOW ONE MAN
OVERCAME HOMOSEXUALITY

JOHN PAULK
WITH TONY MARCO

WINEPRESS WP PUBLISHING

Printed in the United States of America

Packaged by WinePress Publishing, PO Box 1406, Mukilteo, WA 98275. The views expressed or implied in this work do not necessarily reflect those of WinePress Publishing. Ultimate design, content, and editorial accuracy of this work is the responsibility of the author(s).

All events in this book are true. However, in some cases, names and other details have been changed to protect the identities of certain individuals.

All Scripture is taken from the New American Standard Bible, © 1960, 1963, 1968, 1971, 1972, 1973, 1975, 1977 by The Lockman Foundation. Used by permission.

ISBN 1-57921-150-X
Library of Congress Catalog Card Number: 98-60061

FOR TIMMY.
YOU ARE THE JOY OF MY LIFE.

Along unfamiliar paths I will guide them; I will turn the darkness into light before them and make the rough places smooth. These are the things I will do; I will not forsake them. (Isa. 42:16)

FOREWORD

Two gay men are standing on a street corner and a sexy, voluptuous woman walks by. One turns to the other and says, "It's moments like this that I wish I were a lesbian!"

This joke serves—besides getting people to read this foreword—to underscore a basic lesson of John Paulk's autobiography: The homosexual condition is not really about sexual preference; it's about gender-identity confusion. It is a convoluted way of seeing the world.

The basic reparative rule is: "We do not eroticize those with whom we are identified." Brotherly familiarity negates sexual arousal. The man who is fully identified with his gender will not fall in love with another man.

In this book, John Paulk's honesty and humility combine with the ability to vividly describe the events of his life. He is personal, passionate, and yes—very funny. In a style reminiscent of John Rechy's *City of Night*, he tells of his years in the gay world, accurately portraying the pathological personalities so commonly found (and so vehemently denied by homosexual apologists) to exist within that subculture.

Later chapters tell us of his healing, offering personal testimony to the critical issues of reparative therapy. Early on in the process, there is the shift in self-concept from "gay" to the new understanding, "I am a (still unactualized) *heterosexual* man." He tells of the shift in his perception of other men from sexual object to real person ("eros" to "philia"). He confronts his fear of giving up the familiar defensive detachment toward straight men so that he can receive from them the three A's—attention, affection, and approval—which are essential for the internalization of masculine identity. John's male mentors, Frank Worthen and Mike Riley, were strong and benevolent (salient) men, who consistently gave of themselves in a way that gay men, because of their narcissism, cannot.

Yet beyond a basic adherence to the principles of reparative therapy, John's healing followed an essentially religious path. The Bible offers a powerful model by which to live a fulfilling life. We see here the great value of religious community, which has the power to dissolve individual ego boundaries and expose our shared identity as men created in God's image. Yet the science of psychology remains unable to explain how religious faith can heal homosexuality. Can it be, perhaps, because a two-hundred-year-old science is still too young to explain a two-thousand-year-old faith?

If psychology did attempt to explain religious healing in terms of psychological principles, it would have to begin with the understanding that a gay identity is a false self—a self-deception. Gay is an "umbrella lie" that shelters many, many smaller lies about oneself and the world. Healing begins when the client is able to identify within himself the distinction between a false and a true mode of being.

At first the client may have difficulty making the distinction because, since early boyhood, he has been living within the false self. When he is able to distinguish between these two ways of being, he will discover that compelling homoerotic attractions arise only out of the false self. The remainder of the therapy consists of identifying what throws him into the false self and what he must do to return himself back to the true self.

For John, the personification of the gay deception was his alter ego, Candi. She represented not only his gender-identity confusion, but a fantasy alternative to the difficult challenge of becoming a man. When he gave in to the identity of Candi, he relinquished his manhood.

Religion's power to heal homosexuality comes from its ability to ground one's authentic identity in a paradoxical way—that is, in a source *outside* the self. That source is the transcendent reality of Christ, which shatters the fundamental illusion that one can reinvent oneself as gay. That was an infantile belief, a means to avoid the challenge of growing into complete gender identity as a man—a fantasy option.

The experience of the living Christ dwelling within us is, if nothing else, humbling; the perfect cure for narcissism and self-deception. Christianity shatters the illusion of gay. In John's case, Christ and Candi could not coexist within the same soul. When Christ came in, Candi went out. It had to be, simple as that.

But how can psychology explain this shift in core self-identity? It does not yet have the intellectual tools to dissect such an awesome phenomenon. I do know this phenomenon is real because I see it every day in my clinical practice. It is a slow process, but it happens—through insight, effort, prayer, and healing relationships. People do change.

The principles of reparative therapy are quite compatible with Christian theology and spirituality. The vocabulary is different, but they explain the same phenomenon: healing.

Those countless events in the course of healing, what believers call "little miracles," psychologists can only call "insights." But mere insight does not cure; only years of sublime and seemingly random occurrences, filled with truth and offered at receptive moments, can cure.

In this regard, John's story approaches the truth of the matter. His healing, with the help of friends and faith, was the result of an accumulation of little miracles . . . I mean, *insights*. But the amazing thing about John Paulk is not only that he overcame his homosexuality, but that he had the courage to tell us about it. And this is why we need more testimonies of ex-gay men and women, so that we can learn from them, and thus teach others.

JOSEPH NICOLOSI, PH.D.
Author, Reparative Therapy of Male Homosexuality

ONE

A S THE DOOR to the K swung open, the music's near-deafening bass as-
saulted me like a huge, muscular hand. I must have hesitated for an
instant, because I felt Richard's knuckle nudge my backbone, and I edged
forward into the K's huge mass of sound, light, and smoke. I'd never been to
a gay bar before. I had known since my early teens that I was sexually attracted to men, and I had thought often about being held in their arms. But
even my two best friends, Richard and Sarah, who'd brought me here for my
eighteenth birthday, knew nothing about those feelings and fantasies. And I
had never really attached the label of *gay* to what I'd felt about men.

Still, I wasn't surprised that Richard and Sarah were taking me to a gay
bar. Richard had told me he was gay. Sarah said she wasn't gay, but she loved
to dance. Back then, in 1981, kids at our school thought it was cool to have
gay friends, and Sarah said there was no greater place to dance than a gay bar.
She'd been to the Kismet (nicknamed the K) with Richard dozens of times.

Suddenly I felt overwhelmed, plunged into what might as well have been
a giant, surrealistic pinball machine: gleaming, refracted disco lights with fren-
zied bursts of every color imaginable . . . ultraviolet lights, fluorescent tubes
and neon shapes twisted like flying phantoms . . . mirrored balls spun out
spattering starbursts . . . beer and alcohol fumes, tobacco, and other smoke
mixed in a pinkish haze.

But most thrilling of all, muscular male bodies—more than I had ever
imagined seeing in one place at one time. Men leaned against walls, each one
more striking than the next, holding cigarettes and drinks, walking smoothly
as on ball joints, their proportions dramatically enhanced to maximize other
men's admiration. Tight-fitting clothes, like form-sculpted T-shirts, were the
norm. Some men had stripped off their T-shirts; others wore button-down or

15

dress shirts open nearly to the waist. Below the waist, pants were various colors and fabrics, but all of them were tight as a second skin. Footwear varied from cowboy boots to tennis shoes. *How well do I fit in here?* I wondered.

Two weeks ago I had bought off-white Yves St. Laurent pants and a matching shirt with purple piping, plus a pair of ivory, suede Frye cowboy boots—all of which I was wearing for the first time on this special occasion. I had guessed at how to dress, and I had guessed right: I *fit*.

Sarah and Richard gently guided me deeper into the K's inner sanctum. I passed men playing pinball machines while other men clustered around as spectators. I passed still more men, leaning against a long ledge, their belt-buckle-thumbed hands framing their groins, as they flexed sweat-slick, sinew-defined forearms. As my hungry eyes drank in the scene, my mind drifted back to Sarah's warning on the drive downtown to the K.

"Prepare yourself," she'd said, as the three of us sipped Asti Spumonte from champagne glasses she'd snuck from home. "You'll see fabulous-looking men everywhere, the most gorgeous men you've ever seen in your life." She giggled. "I wonder where they hide them all. You never see men like these walking the streets; they only seem to appear at the K. I know they don't care about me, but I sure have fun flirting with them!"

She was right. Just moments ago, in the corridor by the front door, a heavily muscled, shirtless guy had been sitting on a stool in a blacked-out window. Thick black hair glistened on his broad chest as his dark eyes scanned my body from head to toe. He tried to lock his gaze on mine, but I looked away. When I glanced back at him, he winked. Then he reached out, stamped my hand, and pressed a little voucher into my sweating palm. "That gets you a courtesy drink on the house," he grinned. I could feel his eyes follow me as we moved past him.

A pang of anxiety clutched at my chest, and I reached out awkwardly for Richard's arm. "Don't walk so fast," I called, looking over my shoulder for Sarah. To my relief, she was close behind and I drew her beside me. Nearly every man I passed looked at me like the man at the door: Alert, curious eyes fondled me up and down, trying to rivet my eyes to theirs. Richard and Sarah steered me to the right, and we came to a small nook marked CHECK ROOM. Behind a dutch door sat a shirtless, sweat-riveted man. He was looking right at me.

"Check your coat?" he boomed. I tried to open my mouth; it was bone dry. I tried to say, "I'm not wearing a coat," but no sound came out.

A little smile curled his lips. "Check your shirt, maybe?"

"Thanks anyway," I giggled. "I think I'll keep it on."

He laughed and I pushed Richard in front of me. "Where's the bar?" I asked. "I need a drink!" We maneuvered through ever-tighter clumps of men. Everywhere, eyes slipped from others' to find mine. As arms and backs touched mine, I breathed rainbow welters of exotic colognes mingled with liquor scents and a variety of tangy body odors.

We reached the bar. "What'll it be?" a light tenor voice asked. I was eighteen that very day, April 13, 1981. I knew I looked it and so did the bartender. I ordered two 3.2 beers, knowing that was all he would sell me here in Columbus, Ohio. A beer mug in each hand, I turned my back to the bar and swiftly spilled cold, wet fizz down my dry throat. Richard, toting a beer of his own, turned to me and yelled, "How're you doing, John?"

"Great, cool!" I didn't want Richard to know yet just how excited I was to be here. Mixed with the earlier champagne I'd had, I hoped the swift second beer would help me relax. If I felt looser, maybe I could start gazing at men more intently, catch more glances and hold them longer. I loved the looks I was attracting, and I knew I would love looking back—once I could muster the courage. Even now, though I couldn't yet fully let myself go, I was savoring a brand-new, delicious feeling of contentment. I felt special here, like I *belonged*. I never wanted to leave.

At that moment, a smooth, circular movement snared my eye. In a nearby dark corner, a man stood slowly massaging the shoulders of another man who was seated on a stool. The sitting man wore pale yellow shorts and a white tank top that scooped well below his underarms. The other man, who looked about my age, wore cutoff blue jeans with bleached-out holes in front. He turned slightly, and I noticed he also had holes in the back of his cutoffs, providing glimpses of pale flesh.

Suddenly, the man sitting on the stool grabbed the other man's shorts by the belt loops and pulled him onto his lap. As their hips pressed tightly together, the standing man bent down and pressed his lips to the sitting man's, mingling their thick mustaches.

I stared transfixed. I knew this was a gay bar, and in my fantasies I'd imagined men kissing forcefully. But I'd never actually seen them do it. Utterly fascinated, I stared at them for several long seconds.

A jostling elbow to my back broke my trance. "Oops, sorry!" It was Sarah; someone had apparently pushed her into me. "Let's move on, John." As we walked away I drained my other beer. But I couldn't help sneaking looks behind me at those two guys, still locked in each other's arms. We passed several pool tables, and I was surprised to see two heavy-set men playing at one, men who weren't beautiful like the others here at the K. I looked closer, then it hit me: These weren't men at all; they were *women*—but unlike any I'd ever seen before. Masculine; overweight; dressed alike in faded blue jeans, matching sweatshirts, and scuffed work boots; with short-cropped hair and longer "sideburns" curling over their ears.

Sarah saw me staring at them. "Bull dykes," she said with a grin. I left my empty beer mug on a ledge and nodded as if I'd known about lesbians all the time.

So not just gay men come to these bars, I thought. *Hmm . . .* We walked down a short hallway and Sarah pointed ahead. Before us loomed a room enormous as a warehouse: Iron gridwork strung with purple, blue, and yellow lights spanned the length of its ceiling. The room's entire space throbbed with laser beams, spiny stars, sirens, strobes, spotlights—the whole ensemble rhythmically timed to thunderous music.

One wall, mirrored from end to end, roiled with heads, hair, and limbs, all with little space between them. A strange thrill ran through me. For the first time I was seeing men dance together, and what dancing it was! Nothing like TV news flashes I'd seen of straight singles bars. No "socially acceptable" body posturing here. Pelvises unabashedly writhed together with a sensuousness bordering on violence.

I turned to Richard and Sarah. Their eyes gleamed in eager anticipation. Sarah's tight blue jeans and flowered blouse turned circles within circles as her ponytail bounced across her cheeks. Lanky, blond Richard looked ready to burst his preppy gear and shed his upper-crust family image like a snake shedding dry skin. Sarah yanked my arm. "Come on, John—let's dance!" Richard raced for the floor, but I felt myself draw back.

"Go on!" I yelled. "I'll just stand here at this pole and watch for now."

"OK, kid!" She whirled away and quickly disappeared into the wild welter of bodies just a few steps from me. I leaned against the pole, content to soak up the hyperkinetic, sexual energy around me. My eyes danced along with the hundreds of writhing male bodies on the dance floor. The tantalizing sight was everything Sarah had boasted—and more. Had she and Richard somehow known what I'd never shared with a soul, that I longed for other men?

I turned from the floor and let the music carry me into the short hall that led back to the bar. The bartender let his fingers touch mine and linger as he handed me a frothing mug. I smiled and turned coyly away, only to find myself gazing directly into a pair of piercing dark eyes. He stood only a few feet away. Light-hued khakis and a white T-shirt accentuated his slim swimmer's build. Brown, wavy hair flowed above a handsome face with high cheekbones and a coarse black mustache.

I felt my throat tighten. Nervously, I lifted my mug for a sip of beer. I glanced down the hall toward the dance floor. At this moment, I was both glad and terrified that I had gone off on my own. Then, forgetting Sarah and Richard, I focused all my attention on the man my eyes were enjoying. We exchanged smiles, and he stepped close to me. I stood as still as a deer trapped in a car's headlights.

"What's your name?" he asked.

I swallowed hard. "I'm John. And you're? . . ."

"Andy."

There, that wasn't so hard, was it? I asked myself. With the ice broken, I felt a little calmer.

"You look like this is your first time here." Andy's eyes seemed kind, gentle, and genuinely curious.

"You're right. I'm kind of new at this." He bought me another beer as we sat on two stools facing each other. I tried to keep composed as words poured out of me in answer to his questions. I was a high-school senior, attending Columbus's exclusive Fort Hayes Career Center for the Performing Arts. Since enrollment was by audition only, I was especially proud to be there. Hayes had high-tech lighting and audio boards, real television and recording studios, soundproof practice rooms, the ultimate in theater arts, dance, vocal, instrumental music, equipment, and training. My mom, my sister Vicky, and I had recently moved into Fort Hayes's school district. My high-school vocal teacher told me about Fort Hayes and encouraged me to audition.

Most exciting, I had just landed the romantic male lead role in the senior musical, Cole Porter's *Anything Goes,* quite an achievement for a new boy on the block. I was also slated to win the state scholastic award of achievement and head for Ohio State to study voice and train to become an operatic tenor. At Fort Hayes I felt accepted and popular for the first time in my life. Recently I'd become increasingly aware of students whom people said were gay. In fact, one guy named Roger had tried to hit on me in the bathroom. But the thought of what he was proposing nauseated me. I'd had one quick, drunken, sex-play tumble at age fifteen with a friend, who wasn't particularly attractive. But I still thought I was going to be a heterosexual person when I grew up.

In fact, I treasured dreams about my future. Someday I would be married, have a family, and tend a house with a white picket fence. Monogamy was my secret ideal. No important male in my life seemed faithful for very long to anyone, including me. It always seemed as though someone or other was walking out of my life. I lost track of time as I went on to tell Andy about my life, my family, my upbringing, my growing attraction to men, my two friends who'd brought me here (and the lies I had to tell my mom about where I was going), and how much I was enjoying my first time in a gay bar.

Later, I thought to ask Andy about himself. He was on spring break from the University of Indiana. He told me about his interests, his classes, a little about his family, about his coming out as a gay man, and about what it meant to be gay in a straight world. I felt mesmerized by his warm, dark eyes. Suddenly I became aware that Andy was leaning close to me. A moment later, I felt his legs brush mine, then clamp around them. Suddenly I felt light-headed. Andy's intoxicating cologne was enfolding me like the hands of a seductive genie.

Suddenly Andy stood up and slowly leaned forward. His strong arms encircled my waist and drew me close to him. Then his lips lowered to mine, and my whole body began to tingle. I felt dizzy but not the least bit frightened. With no hesitation I leaned my body against Andy's and pressed my lips into his. Over and over, his rough mustache scraped my upper lip, leaving a tingling sensation whenever our lips parted.

I felt immersed in his embrace, totally one with the lush music pouring through the K's speakers. I didn't care who might be watching; I had never felt so desired. Andy opened his arms and cupped my face in his hands. "You know, John, you are really cute."

"D-do you really think so?" I was enraptured. What could I say in return that wouldn't sound utterly stupid? What spilled from my mouth was, "Well, y-you're cute, too."

"John," he purred, "I'd love to get to know you better. I'm staying in an apartment with some friends downtown. There's lots of room if you'd like to go there with me."

I stammered voicelessly for a moment, overwhelmed by this gorgeous man's invitation. *I must go with him!* I thought. Finally I said, "I'd love to, Andy." He smiled eagerly and reached out to take my hand.

Just then a sharp tap on my right shoulder distracted me. I turned; the hand tapping me was Richard's. "What are you doing? Going somewhere?"

I gulped. "Oh, hi!"

"So you were just curious about seeing what a gay bar was like? There's a lot you haven't been telling me." Richard's voice held more than a hint of sarcasm.

"Don't rub it in." I lowered my voice. "You know I've never done anything like this before. I couldn't help myself. You of all people should know what this place can do to someone. And can't you see? Andy likes me!" I leaned closer and stage whispered, "Isn't he cute?"

"He is hot, I must admit."

Thrilled that Richard agreed with my taste, I added, "Can you believe it? Andy asked me to go home with him!"

Suddenly, as if from nowhere, Sarah thrust her face into mine and grabbed my arm. "I can't believe it. Oh, no you don't!" Her brows were pinched. Had she heard everything? "John, you're not going home with this guy!" she insisted. "Listen, you just met! You don't know who he is. Besides, what would your mother say if you didn't come home?" I hadn't thought about my mother and what I'd tell her. *I can tell her tomorrow morning that I spent the night with Richard. She knows we're friends.*

"Don't forget you're our ride home!" Richard added.

"But you can take my car."

Sarah's glare remained strictly no-nonsense. "John, you are not going home with this guy!" But my mind was spinning. How could I give up a night with this terrific man? Would he think I didn't care about him? I couldn't understand the hostile looks in Richard and Sarah's eyes. Did they really think this gentle man might be dangerous? Were they going to tell my mother or other kids at school what I'd done? I didn't think so, but I couldn't chance defying them, and I knew there was no way they'd let me leave with Andy.

"I'd love to go with you," I told him, "but I just can't do it tonight. I'm driving my friends home. And my mom is expecting me back." Andy's smile faded. "Could I have your address and phone number?" I asked.

He reached for a bar napkin and asked the bartender for a pen, then scribbled quickly. "Here's my number and where I live at Indiana U. You can call me." I folded the napkin carefully and tucked it in my pocket.

Andy leaned over and kissed me. "Goodbye, John. It's been fun getting to know you." He turned and disappeared into a cluster of men. Immediately a huge emptiness seemed to engulf the pit of my stomach. How could I have just let him walk away? I might never find a guy like him again. Well, at least I had his phone number. I would call him, and we would surely find some way to be together again soon.

Richard broke into my thoughts. "Ready to go? It's about two in the morning." I was shocked; I had no idea so much time had passed.

I sighed. "Sure. Why stay any longer?"

Slowly we made our way past the front of the bar. As we rounded the corner, the coat-check man was still sitting on his stool. He looked at me with a smirk. "Looks like you had fun, cowboy."

I felt my face flush. "Why do you say that?"

"Your hair's all messed up, and your face looks like raw meat!"

I laughed nervously. "Is it that obvious?"

"Hey, it's cool." He winked. "It's what this place is all about. See ya next time, kid." As we walked outside, the cool night air engulfed me, and I realized my body was drenched in sweat. The freshness felt good—but my yearning for Andy clung to me like the faint scent of his cologne on my face.

Moonlit darkness swallowed us as we walked across the street to the parking lot. I glanced back. Who could guess from the outside that this stark, cinder-block building held such magical inner spaces? *I'll bet not many who work in this industrial area of Columbus have any idea of the fabulous place that's inside that dingy building.*

As we drove out of the parking lot and headed up the street toward the freeway, Richard looked over at me. "So what did you think of your first night at the K, as if I didn't know?"

I laughed. "Need you ask? I don't think I'll ever forgive you and Sarah for not letting me go home with Andy. Maybe you were right to make me leave with you, but he sure was cute. It felt so natural with him, and now I might never see him again." I glanced into the rearview mirror. Sarah was slumped in the back seat, probably already asleep.

"Don't worry, you'll see him again," Richard reassured me. "You got his phone number, right?"

Thirty minutes later, I dropped Richard off, then drove to Sarah's house. She threw her arms around me, mumbled "G'naht" and planted a big kiss on my forehead before wobbling to her front door.

Within another five minutes I was home. I tiptoed up the stairs and into my bedroom and flicked on the end-table light by my bed. I reached into my shirt pocket for the bar napkin and carefully unfolded it. I ran my finger over Andy's name several times, memorizing his address and phone number. Then I folded the napkin carefully and hid it in the top drawer of my dresser under some socks.

As I put on a fresh T-shirt and shorts, moonlight streamed through the window. All I could see in my mind's eye was Andy. I already missed him. Would I ever see him again? A few steps later, I eased onto my bed. With a pleasant, longing ache still hollowing my stomach, the moon trickling softly between the curtains and across my bedspread, I let myself glide slowly down what seemed like a long spiral stairway to sleep.

TWO

M Y DIGITAL CLOCK read 11:42. Familiar bird choruses chirped outside my window but were soon drowned by my vivid memories of the previous night's sights, sounds, and scents. Rushing like high surf over all were thoughts of Andy. My mind slowly crested and troughed through every detail of his appearance. . . . Thick, wavy hair. Calm, dark eyes. Scratchy mustache and full-lipped smile. His tanned body and slim, muscular build—and everything the night could have become if I'd accepted his invitation.

I treasured one thought: Hundreds of men had come to the K last night, and of them all, Andy had desired and chosen me! I scolded myself for failing to get his address and phone number where he was staying in Columbus. We could have gotten together before he went back to Indiana. Would he come back to the K tonight? I couldn't ask Richard and Sarah to go there again so soon. And I was too frightened to go alone. Now I'd have to wait two whole days to hear Andy's voice. Well, I'd just savor the waiting. For the first time in my life, I was in love—and with another man. And it had happened in a gay bar. What could it all mean?

Andy was gay. Did my feelings for him make me gay? I'd had some romantic thoughts about women, but never sexual thoughts about them. My only sexual thoughts had been about men. Well, if I was gay, so what? I had no negative feelings about homosexuality. I couldn't remember my parents or any other adults in our social set ever saying anything uncomplimentary about gay people.

During the next couple of days my brain spun only with thoughts of Andy Spangler. I found myself returning over and over to the top drawer of my dresser, gently unfolding the bar napkin on which Andy had written his name, address, and phone number.

On Monday I walked through my classes at school in a daze. Even Richard noticed. "John, you seem light-years away." I just laughed quietly. After school I ran most of the way home, then went straight to my room and opened the top drawer of my dresser. My hands trembled as I slowly unfolded the napkin. I picked up my phone and cradled the receiver against my shoulder, holding the napkin by an edge with my other hand. My palms were sweating as I carefully dialed.

There were three rings, then I heard a man clearing his throat. "A-Andy?" My voice sounded like water forcing its way through a well-rusted drainpipe.

The voice sounded tired. "Sorry, Andy's not here, he's studying."

"Oh. Do you know when he'll be back?"

"No." Silence.

"Uh-h . . . can I leave a message?"

"I guess so."

"Tell him John from Columbus called." I promised to phone back later if he didn't call me first. The tired voice muttered something and hung up. I felt numb, almost relieved. I'd been so eager yet nervous. Then a peculiar panic seized me. *Who was that guy? Andy's roommate? Boyfriend? No, it can't be! Why am I thinking such a thing? I'm certain Andy told me the truth. He wants me. Now just wait and keep calm.* I lay on my bed staring at the ceiling for a couple of hours. Then I dialed Andy's number again. Ring. *Be there, Andy, please!* Ring.

Click. "Yeah." It was a different man's voice.

"I'd like to speak to Andy Spangler, please. Tell him it's John, from Columbus."

"Hmm . . ." There was a pause. "Hold on a minute." I heard muffled voices, like someone's hand was covering the phone. *What in the world? . . .* More fuzzy sounds, for at least a minute. I felt my neck sweating. Then the voice again: "Can I ask who's calling?"

"This is John. We met in Columbus last week."

"Uh . . ." More covered mumbling. "I don't know where you got this number, but Andy doesn't live here."

"Are you sure? Can you give me the number where he lives? I want Andy Spangler, at the University of Indiana!"

"Look, I'm sorry, I've never heard of Andy Spangler. You must have the wrong number." Click. Dial tone.

The receiver seemed to fall from my ear in slow motion until it drooped at arm's length by my side. Soon the dial tone turned to angry beeps, and I hung up the phone. I couldn't believe what had just happened. When I called the same number not long before, hadn't the guy known Andy but said he was out studying? What was that muddy conversation when I called again? Could Andy be there but not want to talk to me? No, he wouldn't. Not the Andy who'd been so caring, so open and interested in me. *There must be some reason . . . I don't understand what happened. I know Andy would want to talk to me!*

For the next few days I tried again and again to call. Each time I got the same answer from various voices that sounded more annoyed each time I called. I wrote to Andy at the address he'd given me, asking him to please contact me. Indiana was only a state away. I was sure I'd hear from him in a few days.

But I didn't. "Any messages for me?" I'd ask my mother every day after school. I lay at home on my bed every night, staring absently at my TV, thinking of Andy and waiting for him to call. But he never did. I stayed home all Saturday hoping for the call. By that night I was pitch-black depressed. Andy must have had second thoughts about me. What had he found wrong with me? Why had he rejected me? Had I been just a quick thrill on a night when he couldn't find anyone better?

But then, why should I be surprised if Andy didn't want me after all? My whole life, no one had ever seemed to want or like me for long. *Why has it been that way?* I asked myself. *Why haven't people wanted me?* Why did it seem that my whole life, as I recalled it, had brought virtually nothing but an endless series of rejections? Simply because I was *different?*

Different. That word again. Hadn't Andy said gay people were fundamentally different from heterosexuals?

Andy. I was deeply hurt by his failure to contact me. Maybe his lack of response to my letters and calls had been some kind of unfortunate mix-up. Maybe a jealous roommate or someone else was "protecting" him. But, during the next few hours, I came to a resolution: If I couldn't have Andy, neither would I let his rejection destroy me. Even if I couldn't have him, why shouldn't there be some other wonderful man—someone just for me?

I had another thought as the clock downstairs chimed midnight. *If I can find that man, and he can find me, maybe all the pain I've been through in my life will have been worthwhile.* Despite losing Andy, maybe I could still hope to find a fulfilling gay relationship.

Heterosexual relationships certainly held no promise. My mother's friends had shown me the basic nature of heterosexual females: unstable, brittle, self-absorbed. And heterosexual men, try as they might to love, seemed cold, uncaring, and distant. Heterosexuals got trapped in miserable marriages, rife with infidelity and child neglect.

Then this startling thought struck me: *Could it be that my parents and other straight people have been the sole cause of my pain because they don't fully understand who I am as a gay person?* Could it be that they hurt me simply because they didn't know how to deal with a child who's gay? If this was true, no wonder they always seemed confused and uncomfortable around me. No wonder straight kids picked on me. No wonder I'd never felt normal—like I fit in. No wonder I'd always felt different from other boys! I *was* different!

Now, thanks to the glitzy K and a scintillating Saturday night, at last I'd found a place and a people who made me feel comfortable and wanted. Might Andy still want me? It was possible. Maybe he'd come back to Columbus, and things would be the same as they'd been the night we met. But whether they were or not, I certainly wanted everything being gay might have to offer. I knew I had the talent and the quality to be somebody very special. And I knew that, somehow or other, from here on I would find my way in life as a gay person. And as I found my way, I would find someone to love me.

I spent the next ten nights at home, telling myself I was watching television. But, as April turned to May, I was able to forget Andy as I plunged into rehearsals for the musical at school. Basking in the sudden glow of becoming Billy Crocker, I relished the show's classic tunes like "Friendship," "It's De-Lovely," and "All through the Night." I found my warm fantasies of Andy cooling to a dull ache that, after a while, I could scarcely feel.

Gradually my self-esteem soared again as I got into my role. And what sheer irony! This was me, John Paulk, Mr. No-Good, Mr. Fag, homo, queer, sissy, strutting in the spotlight as the romantic lead. Me, the object of every woman's affections? In real life just a few weeks ago, I'd thoroughly enjoyed kissing a man for the first time. I'd fallen in love on the spot and realized I was gay. Yet here I was, playing every woman's dream man!

Weekdays I played the part of clean-cut, smooth-mannered, funny, bright-and-budding, lusty young heterosexual singer John Paulk. But on weekends, I went back with Richard and Sarah to the K, where I gleefully tried out the role of gay, intoxicating, seductive John Paulk, who would now stop at nothing (short of close dancing) to attract the attention of other men. I wasn't ready to have gay sex yet, or even to let anyone get as close to me as Andy had. But the humiliation of being the last kid picked for the baseball team seemed far behind me.

No longer was I the brash kid, lonely and frightened underneath, who had to act obnoxious just to seem significant to anyone. Of course I didn't really share Billy Crocker's knack for charming all the women, but I was getting a feel now for my impact on men. And I was growing confident that by the final curtain of *Anything Goes,* I would charm every member of the audience—male or female.

The play's opening night was a triumph. Mom and Grandma Charlotte sent flowers to my dressing room and came to cheer me on. Dad and his wife sent best wishes from Phoenix. As I sat down at the makeup table, I felt like I was in another dimension. I put the finishing touches on my eyes, then slipped into my opening-scene costume before checking myself in the full-length mirror.

No doubt about it: I looked great. I was twenty pounds slimmer (director's orders), my hair clipped to a '40s front wave with cropped sideburns. Supremely confident in the wings, I heard my cue, hit my first mark on the money, and the night turned magic. For the next two-and-a-half hours, I sang and danced my heart out, not missing a beat, muffing a line, cracking a note, or scuffing a dance step. Afterward, my heart swelled as the draperies lifted for the first curtain call. The audience rose en masse to their feet amid tumultuous applause. I smiled and glanced from eye to eye along the front rows.

Suddenly I saw him. He stood in the second row—tall, blond, rugged, studying me intently with blazing blue eyes. I tried repeatedly to tear my eyes away, only to be drawn back to find his eyes locked on mine. When the curtain came down for good, it broke this man's gaze. *John, you can't have every tantalizing man you see!* I thought with a sigh.

I walked back to the dressing room, where Richard, Sarah, and other cast members met me with congratulations. I wiped off my makeup, changed from my costume into civvies, and together we all headed into the hallway. Our next destination was the cast party at a pizza parlor across town.

Laughing, I looked down the hall—and almost paused in midstride. Casually strolling in our direction was none other than Mr. Blue Eyes from the second row. He stopped momentarily for a drink from the water fountain, and I grabbed Richard by the arm. "Who's that guy?"

"I think his name's Parker," Richard whispered. "I've seen him around. He hangs out with Roger."

Sarah, who overheard me, piped in, "He goes to the K, John. He's gay, y'know."

"You're kidding," I purred. "I think he is so handsome. But you say he sees that slime Roger—that scum who's been hitting on me?"

"The same." As we neared Parker, he straightened up from the water fountain and his eyes meshed with mine. "Don't even think about it," Richard mumbled, "he's taken." My pulse quickened as Blue Eyes stepped right into my path.

"Hi, my name's Parker Rayburn." He smiled warmly. "And you're John Paulk, according to the program."

"That's right. Glad to meet you." I held out my hand.

Parker took it gently. "I really liked your performance tonight. You were terrific."

"Thanks a lot." I felt my heart pounding as my face flushed. Suddenly I had an idea. "Hey, we're on our way to the cast party. Wanna join us?"

"Sure, thanks." His eyes brightened. "Actually, I was heading there myself. I know some people in the cast."

"Really—who?" We started heading down the hall, making polite conversation. Our eyes locked together as we walked. Within a few steps we'd communicated much more than mere words. Outside, Parker pointed to his car in a distant corner of the parking lot.

"See you at Mother's Pizza," I called as he headed off. After a few seconds, I turned to Richard. "So he's taken, eh?" He shrugged wistfully. We piled into my car, and twenty minutes later loud claps and cheers greeted our entrance to the party. Immediately I scanned the crowd but didn't see Parker. More cast members came in right behind us, dispensing backslaps, guffaws, and hugs.

"Debbie, you were great tonight," I yelled at one cast member, "except you almost made me sneeze when you threw that feather boa 'round my neck!" Everyone howled and other voices swelled around me. But I felt detached; I just wanted to see Parker—if he ever arrived. I had just found an empty chair when Julie Robbins waddled over. She threw her arms around me and smeared a fat, juicy, orange-lipstick kiss all over my cheeks. Suddenly she looked over my shoulder and cried, "Parker! Parker!"

Oh, that's right. She's one of the cast members who knows him. Scheming witch!

Parker looked over at me sheepishly as Julie smeared him with gloopy affection. I jumped into the first lull in her affectionate massacre. "So, Julie, how do you know Parker?"

"We went to school together before I transferred to Fort Hayes. How do you know him?" she smirked.

"He's our guest." I pointed to Richard and Sarah. "We invited him."

She raised one eyebrow quizzically and looked from Parker to me. Mercifully, just then Debbie called her down to the other end of the table. As soon as she was out of earshot, Parker turned to me with a grimace. "Yuck! She's such a rich, fat snob. Hangs all over me like white on rice."

I snickered and tried not to look at him too goo-goo eyed. I glanced down at Debbie and satisfied myself that Julie was well preoccupied. Then I asked Parker to tell me more about himself. Soon we discovered that both of us would be going to Ohio State in the fall, Parker for his second year. I could scarcely believe my ears when he asked me if I'd like to room with him. Would I? Only an hour ago, he had been a blue-eyed stranger in the second row. Now I would be sleeping in the same room with this cute guy? My quick "I'd love to!" couldn't have concealed my excitement from anyone.

After the party, Parker shook my hand. "Could I call you some time?" He penetrated my eyes once more.

"Sure." I gave him my phone number.

"Can I call you tomorrow night? I get off work at ten." I quickly nodded, and he reached out to squeeze my hand. I felt my whole arm tingle in his strong yet gentle grip. "I'll call you," he said. I mumbled something, then watched him disappear through the pizza parlor door into the darkness.

Later I lay awake in bed. Life was suddenly becoming pretty exciting. I had just starred in a fabulous musical. I was on my way to college to study to be an opera singer. I'd been offered a summer job singing at an amusement park. And now I was falling in love with a great-looking man who would soon become my college roommate.

THREE

T HE FOLLOWING NIGHT, I sat by the phone, feeling my pulse begin to race as ten o'clock approached. Exactly at 10:00 I jumped at the phone's first ring. Taking a deep breath, I let it ring once more before I picked it up.

"Hey, kid, how are you?" Parker's voice was warm and friendly. The minutes flew by as we talked like old friends. He told me he lived in Reynoldsburg, an east side suburb of Columbus. "Can you believe it? I've lived with the same two parents in the same house since I was a baby. They've been married for over thirty years."

I was impressed. "That's incredible. Both my parents have been divorced, my mom twice." Before long I realized I had never felt so comfortable sharing with another guy—even Richard. We talked about college, and Parker promised to call the registrar's office and make the arrangements for us to be roommates. I couldn't have been more thrilled. I wanted Parker to know I was attracted to him, but I didn't know how to say it. I didn't even know for sure if he was gay.

A few minutes later, Parker solved the problem with a leading question: "What do you like to do on weekends?"

"Oh, hang out. I usually do stuff with Richard and Sarah. You know them, right?"

"Sure."

"How?"

"Uh, I'll tell you later." He paused. "You haven't really told me what you like to do weekends."

We were both being evasive. Was he trying to figure out whether I was gay? I plunged ahead. "Richard, Sarah, and I go out dancing sometimes."

"Yeah?" he responded. "Me, too."

"Where do you like to dance?"

"Where do *you* like to dance?"

"I asked you first," I said merrily. We both started giggling.

Finally he admitted, "My favorite place is a bar called the K."

"Oh? What's the K?" I asked with mock innocence, amazed that I'd never seen him there. Then I started laughing so hard I had to put the phone down for a few seconds.

"What's going on?" he chuckled when I picked up again.

"I'm sorry." I stifled another giggle. "I can't help laughing, because I think we're really talking about the same thing."

"What do you mean?" Now he was playing dumb.

"I go to the K, too. I'm gay."

"That's nice, John—I'm gay, too." We both laughed with relief that our mutual secret was out at last. With sudden boldness, I asked Parker if he'd like to go to the K with me sometime.

"You bet!" he answered quickly. "Would you dance with me if we go?"

"Uh-h . . ." I was tongue-tied; no one since Andy had asked me such a direct question. But I quickly recovered. "Sure, I'd love it!"

"Slow or fast?" He was coming on stronger now, and I found myself loving every minute of it.

Maybe it's my turn to be coy, I thought. "Parker, I've never slow-danced with a guy before."

"You haven't? We'll have to get together soon so you can try it!"

I could tell he was as excited as I was with the prospect, but we let the subject shift to our mutual acquaintances at Fort Hayes. Roger's name came up, and I told him that Roger had tried to hit on me several times.

"Oh really?" Parker sounded irate. "He'd better not try it again." His voice sounded strong and protective, making my pulse quicken.

I wanted to hear more. "What if he does?"

"I'll beat the crap out of him!"

"Oh, I'd like to see that." I felt so affirmed by Parker's response. He was willing to protect me, even fight for me. Knowing that touched something deep inside, and already I felt myself drawing close to him emotionally. I felt more than just attracted to his good looks and the fact that he seemed to want me, too. Parker had character qualities that I found irresistible.

But our conversation also opened my eyes to another side of gay relationships. After some direct questioning on my part, Parker admitted to being part of an off-and-on sexual relationship with Roger. I was horrified. Slimy Roger having sex with impeccably groomed Parker? "Let me get this straight," I said. "You've had a relationship with Roger all year. That's impossible—Richard told me he's been involved with Roger, too!"

"John, if you find those two things unbelievable, then you'll really have a hard time grasping what I'm about to tell you." Parker sounded sheepish. "I've been having sex with Richard at the same time I've been seeing Roger."

Parker was right, this news was hard to handle. I had a sinking feeling inside, like something deep within me had been violated. Were all gay relationships superficial? Were these guys just out to get as much sex as they could? I pressed on. "So you aren't committed to either Roger or Richard, right?"

"To be perfectly honest, I didn't love Roger for long. He seemed sweet and caring at first. He only showed his true colors later on. But the sex was great with him. I felt addicted to it. And his personality was so strong, like he controlled me."

"So where do you two stand now?"

"We split several months ago," Parker said eagerly. "Don't worry about Roger. He's completely out of my life."

"What about Richard?"

"I've never had any kind of relationship with him. He used to come over sometimes during his lunch hours at Fort Hayes. We'd have sex in the shower, then he'd go back to school."

My mind flashed back to Richard's comment when we'd seen Parker in the hallway after the last show: "He's taken." No wonder Richard had known: He knew about Roger, and he himself had been having sex with Parker! I was far from understanding it all. But so what? *Whatever happened, Parker's through with them, and now he wants me. So be it.* I'd make sure the same thing didn't happen with Parker and *me*. I took a deep breath. "Richard knows I'm attracted to you. I hope I don't shock you by saying that. But I think you're awfully cute."

"John, I really want to get to know you, too. We're both out of school this summer. Why don't we spend the next three months together, then be roommates this fall?"

Parker and I stayed on the phone for more than three hours. We talked about everything: our childhoods, schools, relationships, families, and future dreams. Before hanging up after 1:00 A.M., we arranged to meet the next night at the K.

Around eleven-thirty the next evening, I pushed my way through the K's throbbing atmosphere to the bar. "Chuck, I need a beer to take the edge off," I hollered over the din. The bartender handed me a beer, and I strolled over to lean against the black wrought-iron railing next to the dance floor. I didn't see Parker but spotted some familiar bodies gyrating to the music. Suddenly a hand squeezed my shoulder. Parker's blue eyes crinkled at me as I turned around. "What a relief to see your face in this sea of strangers!" I told him. "I was wondering if you'd show up."

"I wouldn't have missed it. I had such a good time with you on the phone last night." We eased over to two stools at the back bar and picked up last night's conversation right where we left off. As time drifted on, Parker leaned closer to me until I could feel his breath on my face. He closed his eyes, gently reached a hand around my back and pulled me close until our lips touched. Surges of excitement coursed through me as we held each other. After a long time, Parker drew back and looked at me intently. "John, please come home with me tonight."

I glanced around; we were sitting in nearly the same place I had talked with Andy. *What should I do now?* Parker must have seen the confusion in my eyes. "I want to, I really do," I told him. "But I can't. My mom is expecting me home. If I'm not there in the morning, she'll be worried."

Parker pleaded with me. I wanted him more than anything, but even as I said no, I knew the problem was more than my mother: Deep inside I was utterly panic-stricken. All my prior fantasizing was worthless now. How could I tell Parker I'd never had sex with a grown man? I was ignorant and naive, afraid I wouldn't be adequate or know what to do.

At last he reached out and took my hand. "Don't feel bad—it's all right. Why don't you come over and spend the night with me next Saturday? My parents are used to me bringing friends home."

My heart leaped higher than my fears. "OK, I'll come. Is it all right if we meet here first—about the same time?" Parker nodded. We hugged and parted quickly. I wanted to leave fast, before I changed my mind. On the drive home, I felt clouds of anxiety drifting through my brain. Why was I so afraid to go home with him? What was wrong with me? Scores of men at the K seemed to have no inhibitions about crawling all over each other. They took their shirts off, glowed under the spotlights, grated their pelvises against each other in front of the whole universe. Why couldn't I?

Sex was so free flowing at the K, and part of me wanted that. But another part kept insisting that sex and love were meant to be linked. How could I ever really enjoy sex unless it was with someone I loved and trusted? I sensed Parker *could* be that kind of man, someone to meet my deep, lifelong desires. I had no doubt that he cared for me. Life could be satisfying and truly happy with him.

At least, that's what I made myself believe until the following Saturday, when I walked into the K, went straight to the bar, and quickly drained three beers. Once the alcohol kicked in, I told myself I was going to be completely different. I'd take my place on the dark side of the cruising rack with everyone else, watching all the guys walking slowly past, meeting my gaze. But I determined I'd only give myself to Parker. A while later I saw him walking toward me, smiling awkwardly, holding an almost empty beer glass. We greeted each other with an affectionate hug, then stood holding hands. He seemed hesitant. After a few minutes of light conversation, Parker looked at me nervously. "Are you ready to go?"

"Whoa, hold on!" Why was he so eager to get home? "Let's have a couple more beers." Parker waited patiently until two more beers boosted my courage, then we left. Half an hour later we pulled into his driveway.

He shut off the ignition and turned to me. "We'll have to be quiet. My folks are probably asleep. They have no idea I'm gay."

My eyes widened. "Why on earth did you bring me here?"

"Don't worry, they know my friends spend the night. I've done it since high school." He put his finger to his lips and opened the front door. We stepped into a formal, powder-blue living room; soft light came down the hallway. Parker led me to the kitchen. He got orange juice from the refrigerator and offered me a glass, with some cookies for a snack. I could only sip and nibble as butterflies erupted in my stomach. Then Parker put the dishes in the sink and headed for the doorway, motioning me to follow. I felt my armpits getting moist. *This is it, John. You're scared to death, but you do want this, don't you?* Parker stopped at the foot of the stairs. "Take your shoes off," he whispered. "We have to pass my parents' room."

I tucked my shoes under my arm, then followed Parker up the stairs and down the dark hallway to his bedroom. Once we were both inside, Parker gently closed the door, locked it, and flicked on an overhead light. "Let's get ready for bed," he whispered.

He walked across the room and turned off the overhead light. Then I watched him, lit only by the soft pink glow of the stereo dial, as he took off his clothes and slipped into bed. He waited as I fumbled off my outer clothing. Still in my underwear, I lay down trembling beside him under the covers. I knew I couldn't wait any longer to tell him the truth.

"Parker," I whispered, "I-I'm sorry, but I've never had sex before. I'm a virgin—and I'm scared."

"Why didn't you tell me?" he whispered tenderly. "It's OK, we don't have to rush into this. Let's just hold each other for a while." Parker couldn't have said anything more comforting and reassuring to me at that moment. I breathed a huge sigh, relieved that he respected me enough to wait.

"Thank you," I whispered. "I know I'll work through this. Just give me time to get to know you better."

"Take all the time you need." His breath whisked my ear like a warm feather. "After all, cuddling can be lots of fun, can't it?" I rolled over, secure with his arms around me, and soon drifted into a deep sleep.

During the next two weeks I slept at Parker's house several times. Each time I felt more comfortable with him. He always let me know he'd love to have sex with me. But he also never failed to tell me he was willing to wait until I was completely ready. Then, three weeks after our first night, as I was driving to Parker's house I found myself aroused at the mere thought of him. Suddenly I knew I had to have him that night, and now I would know just what to do.

When I arrived, Parker told me his parents were gone for the evening. We spent the next few hours watching TV and cuddling. I gladly surrendered to his caresses as we became sexually intimate. Afterward, we lay together in a close embrace.

"That was incredible, feeling so close to you," I whispered.

"It was for me, too."

Inside I felt deeply satisfied, even exhilarated. *You've met the challenge of your fears, John. You've shattered your insecurities.* I felt a sense of warm confidence welling up inside. And I realized that, for the first time in my life, I finally felt like a man.

FOUR

GRADUATION AND SUMMER flew quickly by once Parker and I broke the ice with each other. My proposed amusement park singing job didn't pan out, and I needed to find a job until fall. I ended up working as a busboy in a Marriott hotel restaurant. Parker, meanwhile, kept his evening job as a short-order cook.

We met numerous times at one another's homes; I got to know his folks, and he got to know my mom. We all seemed pleased with one another. To our knowledge no one suspected Parker and I were gay, and our relationship developed beautifully—at first.

As we talked more deeply, we discovered that both our lives had contained similar painful undercurrents. Parker told me his father had been distant and his mother emotionally controlling, similar to mine. He also casually mentioned that he'd had girlfriends in high school and many girls had crushes on him. He laughed. "Guess I'm just a guy both sexes are equally attracted to." I could well understand his attractiveness to both genders. But thinking of women vying for his affections filled me with anxiety, even more than the idea of competing with other men.

In any event, we were definitely a young couple in love, "steady boyfriends," as we called ourselves. I took that description with the utmost seriousness. In fact, I became extremely possessive. I wanted to know precisely where he was and what he was doing every waking—and sleeping—moment. Parker, on the other hand, didn't seem a bit jealous of me. He was the aloof half of our relationship; I was the attached one, and I wanted him attached very securely.

But I soon learned that shadowy figures would continually threaten our relationship. Sleazy Roger, for instance, kept popping up. To my annoyance he called Parker from time to time, even after we were intimately involved.

Roger wanted sex with Parker and didn't care how I felt. He'd heard by now that Parker and I were together. But for Roger, our exclusivity represented a challenge to get anything he wanted. Roger's calloused stubbornness drove me crazy; I knew I was powerless to change his predatory nature.

Another guy from Parker's past also reappeared. Earl lived a straight life, was engaged to be married—but still had sex with guys now and then. One night I called Parker at our usual time, and he wasn't home. I had a hunch he was seeing Earl, so I called his number. Earl answered on the second ring.

"Hi. Is Parker there, by any chance?"

"Just a second." Pause. Click. The phone went dead. So Parker *was* there, all right. I was furious.

The more Parker strayed, the tighter I tried to twist my grip. Hoping to hold him closer, I pursued several strategies, like going to the K with him more often, since both of us enjoyed it so much. But, to my surprise, I began finding myself relishing our jaunts to the K for more reasons than the health of our relationship. The truth was, I couldn't help basking in the stares that cruised my face and body every time we stepped in the door. It was a real gloat to walk into the K with a boyfriend. I'd sway along with Parker as my trophy, broadcasting loud look-at-us-we're-committed vibes. But at the same time I felt unexpected things happening to me. Like David.

He was six-four, the vision of an archetypal lifeguard—blond, lean, with beautiful golden curls on his tanned chest. He wore no shirt but had red suspenders over white "painter's pants." For weeks David flirted with me ceaselessly every time Parker strolled out of sight. Sometimes I'd deliberately walk out of Parker's view so I could find David. Then I'd flirt like crazy, and he'd beg me to go home or slip out to his car. I enjoyed tormenting him. "I can't— you know I've got Parker with me."

Later I'd find Parker, and we'd resume our couple routine. But if I had thought monogamy was my trip, I had also begun to admit to myself that it might have some disadvantages. Sometimes I felt severely tempted to find out what sex with David was like. Of course, I'd never do it because I was Parker's. But I was learning that being gay might mean being open to numerous options. My friendship with Richard began waning since all my energy was aimed at Parker. Sarah completely faded out of my life.

That fall, Parker and I moved together into a dorm at Ohio State. However, being roommates never became the paradise I'd envisioned. Parker and I weren't alone; we were assigned to live with two other guys whose demeanor was arrow-straight and who didn't seem likely to be the least bit tolerant of our gayness. We slept in bunkbeds, me on top and Parker on the bottom. Our passionate times together were fewer than when we'd been living in two separate houses across town.

If our roommates eventually figured out we were gay, they never talked about it. Parker and I developed surreptitious ways of communicating our affection. At night, when the lights were out, I'd reach my hand down from the top bunk; he'd take it, and we'd hold hands for a while before we went to sleep. I'd tap on the wall, once for "I love you" and twice for "good night." When we could no longer stand not having sex, we'd go out to my car, which I parked across the river from the dorm in a rather secluded place. It wasn't too satisfying, but it was better than nothing.

I was thrilled to be away from home and excited to be part of the bustle of a sixty-thousand-student maze. In a gutsy move for a first-year voice student, I decided to audition for Ohio State's prestigious ensemble, The Scarlet and Grey Show, one of the best collegiate song-and-dance variety groups in the nation. Dozens auditioned that year, but only twelve women and twelve men were selected, and I ended up being chosen.

Not long after rehearsals began, I discovered that I was far from the only homosexual in the group. Nine of the twelve guys in the group were gay. We practiced intensely for two hours a day, learning songs and dance routines, and several of us gay guys developed a sense of camaraderie. Sometimes we got more than a little campy. And I got the distinct feeling that our shenanigans were not impressing our director, who was known to be a straight-laced Roman Catholic.

Thanksgiving weekend came along, and Parker and I went home separately to be with our families. One night that weekend, I got an unexpected call from Julie Robbins, the round, redheaded flirt who'd bugged Parker and me at the *Anything Goes* cast party.

I could tell long before her "How are you dear" routine was over that Julie was bursting with some strain of evil gossip, so I cut her endearments short. "I know you didn't call to inquire about my general well-being. What's up?"

"Well, John-John, you know I'm always grief-stricken to play Chicken Little. But I feel it's my duty to tell you that your sky may be falling."

"By which you mean?"

"I'm afraid your dearly beloved has flown the nest and landed in a pig-sty—and one of the nastiest—"

"Julie, don't play mind games with me. Either get to your point or get off my phone."

"Testy, testy!" She faked a few crocodile snuffles. "Especially to a true friend who has only your best interests at heart."

"Julie!"

"If you must know, I'll tell you. Your precious Parker is spending this weekend in a cozy trough with none other than Roger the Dodger." She sniffed again in mock sorrow.

"You're lying—"

"Am I? Ask around, dear. Everybody knows. And never say I don't love you bunches and bunches."

"Thanks loads," I sneered and slammed down the phone. I wanted to throw a thing or two at the wall, but I held myself back and stood clenching my fists until my temperature subsided. After I had calmed down a bit, I began investigating Julie's allegation. Several K friends told me the rumor was true. I decided to let the matter keep until Parker and I returned to school.

I was alone in our dorm room when Parker returned. The moment he opened the door, I let him have it with all my verbal artillery. For hours I drove him relentlessly to admit his guilt. He flatly denied my charges, though I knew he was lying through his teeth. At last he begged me to forgive him for whatever he might have done to enrage me. But I refused, not just because of what he had really done, but because he was too cowardly to admit it. At last one of our other roommates showed up, and I was forced to quit.

Our relationship slowly collapsed. I gave him no peace and laid guilt on thick as cement at every opportunity. Though he pleaded his love for me whenever he could, I was adamant. Torn up inside, he began developing a peptic ulcer.

On weekends we'd still go to the K as a couple, but things weren't the same. We'd drink heavily, get into vicious fights, and make scenes over my jealousy. Parker's family invited me to spend part of Christmas vacation with them, but things remained tense between us. As the time neared for us to go back to school, Parker couldn't stand my incessant pressure anymore. At last he admitted that he'd spent that weekend with Roger. Then he dropped the bomb: He wasn't going to room with me anymore. I was too shocked to know how to respond. I pleaded all night with him, but nothing would change his mind. His ulcer hurt him so badly, he said, that staying away from me seemed almost a life-or-death matter.

Angry as I'd been, I couldn't handle the thought of being without him. I cried for a solid week after Parker broke up with me. My mother had no idea what was wrong. For weeks I tried every possible tactic to resurrect our relationship, but to no avail. Even more excruciating was the emotional pain over my inability to find a man who would love me unconditionally and forever. Andy hadn't found me desirable enough to even start a relationship. Now I had driven Parker away. I loved being gay—that felt right and natural. But what would it take to make me ready for a strong and lasting relationship?

I just couldn't face going back to school without Parker. I made some excuse to my mother that Parker and I couldn't get along with our roommates and couldn't change our room assignments, so I'd decided to commute to school from home. I eventually dropped out.

Though not officially enrolled at Ohio State, I did continue taking private voice lessons. And, with the director's permission, I was allowed to stay with the Scarlet and Grey Show through the quarter. We soon set out on a whirlwind tour, with scads of performances, and probably only the tour's intensity kept me from going nuts with grief over losing Parker. In desperation I carried on outrageously, especially with one other gay member of the tour, at every opportunity.

By the start of spring quarter I felt sane enough to enroll again at Ohio State, though I'd decided to continue living at home. Scarlet and Grey's performance tour continued until midway through the quarter, then gradually wound down. The show had been exciting but exhausting, and I was more than ready for it to end. Almost immediately the director scheduled auditions for next year's cast.

Audition day for returning cast members arrived several weeks later. "A mere formality," past members said. "You just sing one song for Gallagher. If you finish on key, you're back in."

When my turn came, I was nervous. But I imagined an invisible audience in front of me, tore into the lyrics, and tossed them way to the back row. Mr. Gallagher looked pleased when I was done. "Thanks, John. The acceptance list will be posted on the rehearsal door around four tomorrow." I felt completely confident the rest of that day and the next. I'd never sung a song better. Scarlet and Grey vanished from my mind until close to four o'clock the following day, when I made my way over to Weigal Hall.

I could barely see the white acceptance sheet thumbtacked to the rehearsal hall door; several dozen heads were trying to peer at it. I said nothing to anyone as I worked my way through the mob and at last got close enough to begin reading: Tina, yes. Tom, of course. Judy, Molly, Cecelia. Ron, Theo, Lee, Grace—twenty-four in all, but none of whom was me.

All of a sudden, a cold embarrassed chill ran through me. I felt naked, standing in front of this crowd of excited people. A few consoling voices tried to catch my attention as I turned quickly and forced my way through the crowd, down the hall, and out into the spring air.

I couldn't believe it. *Why wasn't my name on the list?* Then it hit me: Only one other eligible returning cast member's name was also missing. Gary was the only other returning auditioner besides me who was flamboyantly gay and had camped it up with me through the whole tour. I knew Gallagher hadn't turned us down for lack of talent. It could only have been our outrageous camping. For a moment I felt ashamed of my behavior, then dismissed the thought. *Homophobia, thank you very much,* I thought bitterly. My eyes got bleary as I stumbled down the sidewalk.

"Hey, you OK?" A female voice sharp as a baroque trumpet came from close behind me. I turned around and looked down to see a small, pretty black face smiling up at me from no more than four feet above the concrete walk. "You OK, baby?" she repeated.

"Yeah—no, not really. I'm a bit shook up. I auditioned yesterday for a second year in Scarlet and Grey and just found out I didn't make it."

"Hey, no sweat! All they ever sing is white music anyhow." She stuck out a small hand that sprouted long, hot-red fingernails. "Name's Jackie Cole. You're John Paulk, right?"

"Yeah. But how do you know me?"

"I see you on Hughes second floor almost every day. Heard you sing a time or two. You're pretty good. You take from Eileen Davis, right?"

"Right again—and you?"

"Paul Hickman."

After a few minutes of conversation, she invited me to go for a drink, and I readily agreed. For the next couple of hours we chatted and chuckled about our lives. Jackie had ended up at Ohio State studying voice because she could sing like a tornado. She was also fully subsidized by Uncle Sam because of her disability.

"What disability?"

"Scoliosis." She took a swig of beer. "Extreme case. Dramatically curved spine, colostomy in front—all that jazz. That's why I'm so short and gimpy."

"I hadn't noticed—"

"The devil you hadn't. Listen, man, no pity, hear? I got a red carpet ride in life." Jackie was feminine, yet rough around the edges and outrageous enough to make me like her right off.

I also felt comfortable enough to tell her why I'd failed the audition. "I'm gay. Just came out about a year ago. I've had a rough year, broke up with my first lover a couple of months ago. I was trying to make myself feel better, and I guess I camped it up too much in rehearsals and on tour."

It turned out that Jackie often sang at Trends, a gay piano bar in town. I teased her a bit about that. "Isn't that where all of Columbus's aging queens hang out?"

"Hey, if Trends is too tame for you, the Garage is right out the back door." I'd never been to either place, but I'd heard the Garage was a pretty tough joint. Jackie was plenty tough, too, in her own right. After we parted company that day, I asked around about her. Seems the upper echelons of the music department frowned on her because she was such an independent loud-mouth.

More than anyone else, Jackie was responsible for introducing me to gay life. Though Parker and I had frequented the K, he was never interested in making other gay friends. He had no taste for camp or gay wit of any kind. Although Jackie was straight, she seemed to get a great howl from the gay life, and she was pleased to hear I loved it, too. Soon after we met, she took me to Trends. She was obviously well known there; soon the patrons had her up on the piano bar, belting out tunes to great acclaim.

As I'd heard at the K, most Trends men looked over thirty—too old for my taste. But from watching Jackie perform, I learned that men didn't mind feminine cavorting if it was done in the right spirit. And if Jackie and several drag queens I got to know were any indication, a person could attract a lot of attention by acting female in a gay bar.

Jackie and I spent increasing amounts of time together. Her apartment was in a rundown section of Columbus, but I often slept over on our nights out. I'd stretch out on a mattress on the living room floor, and Jackie would go to the bedroom. I brought Jackie over to see Mom from time to time. My mother didn't like Chittenden Street, where Jackie was living, but she did grow to like Jackie. So Mom didn't put up too much of a fuss when I told her Jackie was lonely, I was sick of living at home, Jackie and I were just friends, and I wanted to move in with her. I trucked my stuff over to Jackie's place in a few car trips and slowly began straightening up her apartment.

Now and then at school I saw Jackie talking to another music student named Tom Goodrich. I was fascinated by his silky, shoulder-length brown hair and the way he'd bat his lush, dark eyelashes every time he took a breath between blows on his sax. When I mentioned his name to Jackie, she told me he was gay.

One night Jackie was in the kitchen opening a bottle of wine when I heard a knock at the door. My eyes widened when I discovered Tom Goodrich himself standing there holding another bottle of wine.

Jackie, you sly witch, you probably set this up, but I'm not about to complain, I thought as I invited him in. I soon learned that Tom wasn't like most gay men I'd met; he didn't go into the usual stare and cruise routine. But it also became apparent before long that he found me attractive. It just took him some time to loosen up.

As I got to know him, I discovered Tom's real problem was ambivalence about his sexual orientation. One day he'd flirt with me, the next he'd be cold and aloof. He couldn't communicate well, and I found his inconsistency un-nerving. I was hoping to replicate the open, caring relationship I'd had with Parker. Tom was none of those things. But he was so physically attractive I couldn't resist pursuing him. One night when my mother was out of town, I invited Jackie and Tom to spend the night with me at Mom's apartment. Eventually Tom and I ended up in bed together upstairs.

It didn't go well; I felt nervous and insecure, not to mention uncomfort-able because I didn't really know Tom. He asked me what was wrong. "I'm very attracted to you," I told him. "But we hardly know each other."

My discouraging experience with Tom hurt me more than I cared to admit. Beautiful as he was, it was also obvious that he wasn't relationship material. But we did eventually have sex a couple of times. Still, Tom was too confused about being gay for my liking, and I was not about to waste time with someone who was unsure about his sexual identity. I felt quite secure in mine. By now, aside from my family, nearly everyone knew I was gay.

After I decided not to see Tom anymore, I did begin feeling bad about how I'd treated Parker. And I sensed a longing, not so much for Parker him-self, but for that first feeling of safety and security I'd known during our early days together. And of course, I remembered fondly the great sex that feeling had inspired.

From my conversations with other gay men, I discovered that my entry into gay sex with Parker was quite unusual. Few gay men seem to begin having sex in the context of a love relationship like the one I'd had with Parker. For many, anonymous sex long preceded the development of any love involvement. I wondered if I had fallen into a first relationship of love by chance. Even more important, would I be able to recapture that kind of love with someone else?

By the end of spring quarter, I had gone to more bars, picked up gay lingo, and flirted a lot. As Jackie and I got to know each other better, however, I sensed something changing in our relationship. She seemed to wrap her personality around me like a coil, which felt suffocating. I caught her looking at me differently sometimes, almost as if she'd become attracted to me. She no longer seemed able to tolerate my wanting to run my own life. If I wanted to visit a bar without her, she acted angry and hurt. When we were out together, she refused to let me mingle by myself. *She knows I'm gay,* I thought. *What's her problem?*

One night I managed to escape and shared my dilemma with a gay friend. Mark listened, then broke out laughing. "Don't you know Jackie is a notorious fag-hag?"

"She is?" The thought had never occurred to me. She was so hip and cool.

"Look at her, John. She's crippled and four feet tall with a colostomy. What man would want her? But you've been kind. You've hung around with her, even cleaned her place up and brought some order to her life. She's fallen in love with you. Can't you see that?"

"But I'm *gay,* for heaven's sake. Why would she fall in love when she can't have me?"

Mark laughed again. "You're so naive—that's one reason I love you so much. Think about it. You're safe. Nonthreatening. You treat her like a lady and don't demand sex in return. You're what every woman wants!"

"Well, the thought of sex with a woman—any woman—disgusts me. I love Jackie, but I can't stand the thought of her acting like we're married or something."

Mark urged me to get away from Jackie as soon as possible and, from that night on, I starting plotting some means of escape. Then Jackie got news that her mother, a severe diabetic, had taken seriously ill. She died several days later. I decided to stay with Jackie while she grieved her mother's death. With her only sister in prison, Jackie had no shoulder but mine to cry on.

Then some people from her mother's church started showing up regularly at our door and pressuring Jackie to return to her former faith as a Jehovah's Witness. Soon she began talking seriously about rejoining the church, and I took the opportunity to tell her I was looking for another place to live. She looked devastated, but I insisted our lives were taking very different directions.

"You're headed back to church," I added, "and that's the last thing I want any part of." When she broke down in tears, I promised that no matter what happened we'd always stay friends. Secretly, however, I didn't like the vibes that seemed to have taken over her, and I couldn't wait to get away.

Then I heard about a gay guy named George who was looking for a roommate. He lived in a nicer section of Columbus, not far from campus, and I went to check it out. George was about five-five, dark brown hair, dark skin, and beady eyes—not my type, which was just fine. Our nonconnection was more likely to make us good roommates. He asked me to pay less than half the rent, and I agreed to move in.

I never gave Jackie advance notice of my departure. My friend Mark brought his lemon-yellow Cadillac convertible over to help me move. But it took us a little longer than we'd figured, and Jackie came walking up the block just as we were loading the last box. She stopped with a stricken look. "John, you're really leaving?"

I put my hands on her shoulders. "Jackie, you've been a great friend. You know I'll always love you, but it's time for both of us to get on with our own lives." She didn't say a word as tears ran down her face. Quickly I reached over, kissed her on the cheek, and gave her a brief hug.

Little straight thing, I thought, *I'll always be grateful to you for helping me find my way into gay life.* She looked at me a moment, rubbed the tears out of her eyes, then turned and walked up the stairs into her building without looking back.

George and I kept vastly different schedules, which suited me just fine. I went to school all day and worked at a retail food store from late afternoons into the evenings. He slept all day and went to work from 6 P.M. until 2 A.M. Then he came home and smoked pot with his friends in the living room before going to bed. Our paths seldom crossed.

My living situation gave me more freedom than I'd ever known. With increasing frequency, my nights out at gay bars ended in sexual encounters.

But sex with a series of strangers, although physically exciting, left me wanting something more. In fact, one day when I was feeling desperately lonely, I called Parker on the phone, "just wondering" what he was doing. I apologized for my past insensitivity and invited him over for a beer. After several drinks, we ended up in bed together.

It was the first of several sexual occasions with him. I enjoyed the comfortable feeling of having sex with someone familiar. It was completely effortless; we knew so well what pleased each other. But gone was the safe, secure feeling that had been part of our early love. I think both of us were actually relieved; neither expected a commitment. Yet, with that pressure gone, I found that there were still things I liked about Parker. For all I knew, our true destiny might turn out to be a lasting friendship.

That summer, however, I found myself getting involved sexually with some men without even worrying about the element of friendship. One morning I was soaking up some rays on The Oval, a five-acre grassy area on campus where students met to relax, toss Frisbees, and socialize between classes. It was also the area where gay students cruised. A few hundred feet away, I noticed a tall, handsome, shirtless guy with shiny blond hair and a deep, burnished tan.

He sat nearby each day I returned, then began cruising me when I'd look in his direction. He'd look directly at me, then subtly run his hand across his chest. I sent signals of my own, but neither of us made any definite moves until one day a woman opened a cardboard box nearby and announced she had some kittens to give away. The blond guy and I used her presence as an opportunity to meet.

As we played with the kittens, I learned his name was Harry and his major was electrical engineering. I decided to take home a female kitten, an orange calico. "What are you going to name her?" Harry asked.

"Amanda. I've seen this drag queen with that name. He's about six-five and his hair is the same color as this kitten. Amanda just seems to fit." Harry laughed, picked up Amanda, and scratched behind her ears, eliciting a loud purr.

A few days later he asked me if I'd like to go see a movie with him. Afterward, Harry drove me around Columbus. Chatting pleasantly, he told me he was a virgin. Though I didn't believe him, I announced it was my "duty" to introduce him to gay sex. So we pulled into the parking lot behind Harry's apartment and started having sex in the back seat of his car.

But the whole episode seemed to drag on forever. *Please hurry up and get this over with,* I thought. *I want out of here.* Finally I looked up. "Harry, I've had enough. Could you take me home?"

"Huh?" He looked surprised as I began putting on my clothes.

"What's the matter?" he said. "Wasn't it good for you?"

"To be honest, no, not really."

"No sweat. Guess I'm just having an off night." After Harry drove me back to my apartment, I didn't invite him in. Not bothering to turn on any lights, I slowly undressed by the faint glow of an outside streetlight. Then I walked into the bathroom and started the shower.

As the hot water pelted my chest, I sensed a weird realization dawning on me, something that had been growing in me over the past few months. Suddenly I realized that I'd become numb to my need for love to accompany sex. Why should I have to love someone like Harry to enjoy sex with him? If I were ever to fall in love with a man again, that would be fine. But sex and love wouldn't have to go together anymore.

I lay awake, thinking about it some more. Lately, I'd been feeling an increase in sexual appetite that demanded more physical satisfaction—love or no love. So I would learn how to enjoy having sex, whether I cared for someone or not. Sure, I had felt used by Harry. But hadn't I been using Parker and all the other men I'd slept with? There might be many Harrys and Parkers in my future. I couldn't let it matter anymore. Some kind of change had taken place in me. Now, somehow, that fabulous first night at the K with Andy seemed as dim as the shadows from a distant streetlight on my bedroom wall.

It was awhile before I managed to fall asleep, and the dull feeling was still there the next day. In fact, it seemed to saturate my being during the final six weeks of that summer quarter. I found the gay crowd at the bars becoming my main social outlet and source of new friendships. More and more I found myself going home with people I had just met at the bars. My new pattern was becoming fixed: I'd see some guy cruising me near the bar's entrance. I'd go in and get plastered. Just before the bartender hollered "Last call!" I'd join the scramble to find someone to pick up. Usually it would be the guy who had cruised me as I came in, if he wasn't already taken.

Almost imperceptibly during these weeks, I became part of the last-minute herd. What I really still wanted was love, but I didn't care to go home alone. So, if I had to, I'd settle for sex. And why not? It was easily available in the gay life. And people had been cruising me for so long. Why not just give in and go with the flow?

FIVE

A BOVE THE SIXTH FLOOR of Ohio State's marble-columned library were scarcely lit, maze-like corridors of gray, metal bookshelves known as *the stacks*. When I studied at OSU, not many dared to venture to the stacks but the most dedicated grad students—and gay cruisers. Four old wooden desks cluttered a barren corner of the eighth floor near one lone bathroom. Guys brought gay porno and scattered it under the desks to see who might "bite" on it.

Men paced the stacks, cruised one another, paired off, disappeared into the bathroom, locked the door, and reappeared minutes later, walking around nonchalantly as if all along they'd only been looking for books. Once I discovered what was going on, I found myself making plenty of trips to the stacks to explore its nameless joys.

Then there was Derrick. *This guy can't be gay, he's too straight looking,* I thought when I first spotted him, the parking-booth attendant outside Hughes Hall. He was leaning against a concrete pillar, hands shoved into his back pockets. He had thick, medium-brown hair with a strong side part. His powerful Kirk Douglas jawline complemented his pillar-massive legs and knotted forearms. I scanned him head to toe, just longing to be wrapped up in those huge arms.

Amazingly, the next week I met him at the Garage. After some friendly conversation, I moved in slowly for some physical affection. To my delight, he responded in kind. "Wow! You're the first guy I've ever kissed," he told me, and I believed him.

Derrick took me back to his frat house near campus. After we locked the door to his bedroom at the end of the hall, we launched into hours of fabulous sex. *What a privilege to usher this hunk into gay sex,* I thought, *just like*

Parker led me. But as the night wore on, I wondered where it would lead. Derrick was just too different from me, acting much too straight, which made me feel inferior. And he was too withdrawn, too uncomfortable being gay. It was déjà vu—Tom Goodrich all over again. He said he was in love with me, but I didn't feel the same way.

Later I introduced him to my roommate, George, who craved him even more than I had. I was glad to let him go. There were plenty more men where Derrick came from.

That fall I enrolled in voice, music history and theory, symphonic choir, obligatory astronomy, and even Italian—"to help the voice." Early that quarter I heard a rich, lyric soprano bouncing off the walls of a nearby practice room in the music building. When the voice's owner came out at the end of the hour, I introduced myself and complimented her. Susan Atkinson was a freshman and had gotten stuck for voice with the infamous McHenry Boatwright.

I told Susan why she should drop MHB and gave her some tips on how to work the department in order to get a better teacher. She took my advice, was grateful to get a new teacher, and thus we began a warm friendship. Shortly afterward, I told Susan I was gay; she had no problem with that. Soon we were hanging around campus as buddies and bar crawling together at the K and the Garage.

As my social circles expanded, I developed a yen to find a place of my own. Then I heard about a small attic apartment that was open back in my old Chittenden Avenue neighborhood, and soon I moved in. I got in touch with Parker again, and we met now and then just to talk rather than for sex. We settled into a comfortable friendship, almost like we'd never been lovers at all. I felt good that we were no longer using each other sexually.

As summer approached, Susan made plans to return home to Cleveland. I hoped to keep on with my job at Pepperidge Farm and cruise my way freely through the hot months ahead. Then, in early June, I was laid off from my job. In order to keep my apartment (and avoid moving back in with my mother), I had to find a way to make some money—fast.

I began scanning through the want ads of the *Columbus Dispatch*. Advertising sales? Nah. Aerobics instructor? I could just see it: Me in tight spandex shorts, tank top with headband, jiggling along with fifty flabby women to Olivia Newton-John's "Let's Get Physical." Probably five bucks an hour, part time. Puhleeze . . .

Then, further down in bold print, I saw a bold headline: ESCORT SERVICES. I had just finished reading a gay porno novel. Tory, the hero, earned a stimulating living as a sophisticated New York male prostitute. He lived in a penthouse apartment; his exploits generated such fame that men paid big bucks just to look at him and hundreds of dollars an hour to have sex with him.

Maybe I could find a similar destiny—plush, white, wall-to-wall carpeting; a four-poster overlooking the river; Jaguar in the garage. *No harm calling to see what it's all about.* There were several escort ads, but the one for an outfit called Dulcet looked the most interesting: "For those who can afford the very best. Male and female escorts wanted. . . ."

I dialed the number and talked to a guy named Wayne. In response to his questions, I gave him my background: No escort experience, but young, very outgoing, good-looking, a hard worker, and willing to learn. "Boyish?" Wayne asked. "We're looking for that type. When can you come in?"

We set up an interview for 3:00 the next afternoon. I got out my best suit, a light blue starched shirt, and periwinkle silk tie splotched with little tan belt buckles. It rained the next morning, so I added a stylish umbrella to the ensemble. Dulcet's office was in an isolated building on Columbus's far east side. I entered the front door and announced myself to a bored-looking receptionist with a pile of platinum blond hair.

I thumbed through a dog-eared copy of *People* for several minutes while Ms. Platinum Up-Do disappeared, then came back with a middle-aged guy wearing frameless glasses. He offered his hand, and I recognized his bass voice. "I'm Wayne. Nice to meet you, John."

Wayne's office was more plushly furnished than Ms. Up-Do's environs. Still, I wondered what Kiwanis, Lions Club, and Better Business Bureau plaques were doing on the wall. Wayne was nice looking, though his polyester slacks, plain shirt, and cheap-looking tie reminded me of a hard-boiled detective's outfit from some B-grade movie. Pictures of his wife and kids leaned on his desk. *This doesn't look much like "Tory" country,* I thought.

Wayne took down some more information about me, then explained that Dulcet had been in business about six months, had fifteen female escorts, and now needed a man for "other types of male clientele." I also found out that Wayne had indeed been a private detective, tracking stray husbands and solving other small crimes. Dulcet evolved when AAA Investigative Services discovered that escorting was an easy way to make a lot of money.

Then Wayne went straight to the point. "We're a high-class service for Columbus, one of the best. We offer three things: nude modeling, nude conversation, and nude massage."

"Nude?"

"It's all completely legal. There's no sexual contact, of course. We charge our clients eighty dollars an hour—you keep half of that. One of our drivers picks you up at your place, takes you to your destination, walks you to the door, collects the money, then picks you up one hour later."

"Seems easy enough," I said, wondering if it really would be.

Wayne glanced at the photos on his desk. "We're looking for a discreet individual with the maturity and commitment to stick with us. We work mostly evenings, with occasional daytime appointments." I nodded, and Wayne stood up. "If you'll wait right here for a moment, I'd like to talk to my associate in the other office."

He walked out, and I heard a light tap on another door, then muffled conversation. I slipped over to the wall and put one ear against it. ". . . send him over and I'll check him out," was all I caught. I ducked back into my seat before Wayne returned. He smiled and motioned for me to follow him. I followed him into another office, where a slim, gray-haired man greeted me with a weak handshake.

"This is Doyle, my associate," Wayne said. Then he walked out, saying over his shoulder, "I'll leave you two to get better acquainted."

Doyle gazed at me, stony eyed. "Please close the door." Suddenly my stomach tightened.

Could these two guys be cops using this setup as a lure to catch prostitutes?

Doyle slowly lowered his hands from the desk to his lap. "Wayne tells me you've never been an escort before."

"That's right, but I'm really interested in the job." It was hard to sound enthusiastic; it felt like a walnut had lodged in my throat.

Doyle's eyes began to wander all over my body. "I'd like to take you through the second part of the interview process now," he said at last. "Since clients will be paying eighty dollars an hour for your nude company, I'd like to see what they'll be getting."

"What was that?"

"Would you please disrobe? I'd like to watch you."

I hesitated, then remembered Tory, my novel's hero. He had to "audition" for his job, too. Slowly I began removing my clothes, struggling to maintain some dignity. I didn't want to show any fear or unease. *Make him think you're totally confident and self-possessed.*

I placed each article of clothing on the chair beside me, stopping when I'd gotten down to my underwear and black dress socks. As I stood stock-still, frigid blasts from the air conditioner gave me goose-bumps all over. "A-all right?" I stuttered.

Still expressionless, Doyle snickered softly. "I don't think you're quite finished, kid."

Seconds later I stood completely naked under the cold fluorescent light, trying not to shiver. Doyle got up and walked around me, scrutinizing my body as dispassionately as a couch at a department store. Apparently satisfied with what he saw, Doyle looked at me with just a trace of smile curving his lips.

"You've completely passed phase two of the interview," he said. When I didn't immediately answer, he added, "That means you're hired."

I managed to stifle a sigh of relief and mutter, "Thank you." This creep was giving me major freezes, even aside from the air conditioning.

"You can get dressed now," Doyle said. As I reached for my underwear, he added, "By the way, you've got a cute butt." He winked and walked out; I never saw the man again.

After putting on my clothes, I walked quickly back over to Wayne's office. He met me at the door and said, with hearty false enthusiasm, "Congratulations, John! When can you start?"

"Uh, right now. What do I do?"

Wayne let out a hearty laugh. "That's the spirit! Actually, we start business about seven o'clock at night and go till seven in the morning, if there's enough business. Go home, rest up, and wait for us to call."

I shook Wayne's hand (at least his was warm), turned tail, and made my way quickly back to my car. I put the key in the ignition, then paused before turning it. *Forget how Doyle treated you. Get excited—you've got a job!*

Of course, I wasn't about to tell anyone the details of my new employer. I phoned my mother and told her I'd been hired as the phone switchboard operator at a private-eye outfit called AAA Investigative Services.

Around seven that night I laid out my tweed blazer and slacks, a shirt and tie, and silk underwear, then waited for the phone to ring. Hours went by. Every now and then I rang the office and asked Karen, the night operator, if there'd been any requests for my services. "No, but don't worry," she said. "It takes awhile for word to get around. You'll get an appointment sooner or later." After four nights of watching prime-time TV and late movies, the phone rang around 11 P.M. I'd gotten my first call.

"I can be ready in five minutes. When do you need me?"

"The car will be there in half an hour," Karen said, then gave a description of the vehicle. "And John," she added, "if anything funny happens during your appointment, try to reach a phone and call me pronto."

I threw on my outfit and checked my hair, then went downstairs and waited outside. Soon a light gray sedan drove slowly down the street. Its passenger-side window opened. "Are you John?" a friendly voice asked.

I nodded and got in. Paul, the driver, introduced himself. As we drove away, he picked up a CB mike. "Mobile one calling base, over."

Karen's voice crackled back. "This is base, mobile one, over."

"Package picked up for east side drop-off, over."

"Ten-four, mobile one, roger and out." I was impressed. And the car was nice. Maybe this was a pretty sophisticated operation after all.

"Your first appointment, right?" Paul's jovial tone surprised me.

"Yeah."

"You're the first male to work with us." His smile revealed a big gap between his front teeth. His accent was hick, southern Ohio. "I'm taking you to the East Side Red Roof Inn. Client's name is Steve. You'll be there for one hour, sharp. When time's up, I'll meet you in the lobby and take you home, or back to the office if you like. Or maybe to your next stop, if something pops up while you're with Steve."

Paul drove to the inn and then walked with me to a back door. "I bring girls here all the time. It's best we keep things on the sly." He winked. On the elevator to the sixth floor, I thought about Tory, my callboy superhero. Would I be able to stay as cool, confident, and professional as he'd been? *Why are you so nervous? Lots of other people do this for a living.*

The tweed sleeves of my blazer itched my wrists. I discretely dried my wet palms on the seat of my pants. The elevator doors opened and we walked down to room 622. A TV blared from inside. "Ready?" Paul grinned.

"As I'll ever be," I said. Paul rapped three times on the door. Inside, the TV volume banked down and bedsprings creaked. A moment later the door swung open. Steve was dressed in jeans and a blue golf shirt. He looked about thirty-five, medium build, and very heterosexual.

"Hi, my name's Paul, and this is John. We're from Dulcet."

Steve said nothing as he shifted his feet. "I'm John's driver," Paul added. "I'm here to drop him off for the next hour and then pick him up. And to collect the fee—in advance."

Steve fumbled in his pants pocket and came out with a wad of bills. "Eighty bucks, right?" Steve sounded shy, and he looked even more nervous than me.

"Right." Paul nodded, and Steve peeled off four twenties. Paul took the cash, then turned to me and checked his watch. "Five minutes after twelve. I'll be back to pick you up downstairs in exactly one hour." I nodded, and Paul looked at Steve. "Have a good evening, sir," he said, and I watched him disappear around a corner.

I swallowed hard, then followed Steve into the room. Steve cleared his throat but said nothing. I knew he must be expecting me to initiate things, so I walked toward the king-size bed and sat down. Outwardly I tried to remain calm and cool as I explained the services we offered and asked Steve which he would like.

"Let's try a massage," he said quietly. He turned out all the lights but left the television on low, then lay facedown on the bed. He looked reasonably attractive, I thought.

I tried to sound friendly. "Don't you think you'd better take your shirt off?"

"Oh, I forgot." He looked embarrassed as he stripped to the waist and lay back on the bed. "There's some hand lotion on the nightstand. I guess you can rub me down with that." I spread some lotion between my palms and began massaging Steve's shoulders, wondering what on earth the next hour would bring. *I'm sure this guy didn't pay all that money just to get his back rubbed.* I poured more lotion on my hands and glanced at the red glow of an electric alarm clock. Soon, fifteen minutes had gone by. Whew! Only forty-five more to go. But would this man accept no more than a rubdown for that whole time? I desperately hoped so.

After trying a few more minutes of small talk, I kneaded his back in silence. Then I felt a bit bolder and quietly asked, "Would you like me to take my clothes off?"

"Sure, if you want to," Steve barely whispered.

This guy's a case study in passivity. I might be able to control this situation after all. I stood up and slowly undressed to my underwear. Steve turned his head slightly to watch me. Then I continued the rubdown. More long minutes passed. Steve breathed gently, but never said a word. I looked over at the clock—thirty minutes had passed. Though the air conditioning was running high, I felt a rivulet of sweat run from my forehead to my chin.

What'll I do if he asks for more action? I felt I had to break the tension somehow, so I laughed lightly. "By the time I'm through with you, you'll be slippery as a greased pig. And you'll have the smoothest skin this side of the Mississippi River." Steve said nothing, so I added, "You know, Doris Day used to coat her hands with Vaseline and then wear white gloves to bed."

At last Steve spoke. "Really? Why did she do that?"

"To keep her hands smooth and free of age spots," I said merrily. "I read it in her autobiography." I felt my face flush in the semidarkness. How stupid! What did this straight-image guy care about what Doris Day put on her hands? All he probably wanted was sex, but he was too shy to ask. Suddenly he reached his left hand back and rested it lightly on my calf. I jumped a little; I hadn't been expecting him to move. The clock told me only fifteen minutes remained. With five to get dressed, that really meant ten. *If he's finally making a pass, he's making it too late,* I thought with relief.

As those last minutes buzzed by, Steve's hand crept up my leg. I was grateful there wasn't time left to do anything. With five minutes left, I stopped. "We're just about out of time." I stood up. "I'll have to get dressed now."

"That sure went by fast," he said without moving. "It seems like you just got here." He lay completely still as I rushed back into my clothes. Once I was dressed I felt at ease.

"It was nice meeting you, Steve."

"You too. Can you find your way out?"

"Sure. Have a good evening." He didn't answer. I walked out the door, then almost ran to the elevator.

Downstairs I nearly dashed past the lounge before I caught sight of Paul sitting at the bar. He was supposed to be in the lobby, but I was about two minutes early. I sat down on the empty stool next to him and ordered a double Scotch on the rocks. "How'd it go?" he asked.

"Just great." I broke into a huge smile. I guzzled my drink as Paul told me how he much loved jazz; he was eager to attend a festival opening in Columbus that week. He didn't ask a thing about my client or what we might have done. As he talked, I felt myself sitting about three inches taller than usual. I had just made forty bucks, merely for giving someone a quick massage while almost nude. "This is such easy work," I said aloud, "I can hardly believe it."

"You ain't seen nothin' yet," he chuckled over his drink. I hoped he meant something good by that.

SIX

ONCE I'D BROKEN IN as an escort, Dulcet started getting frequent calls for my services. Soon I was spending more nights at the AAA office than I was at home. Usually a half-dozen women would be there when I arrived. At night Karen replaced the usual harsh fluorescent lighting with soft lamps to create a cozy atmosphere in which coffee and chatter flowed freely.

Karen, of course, handled the switchboard; the female escorts ran the gamut from tacky (but never trashy) to chic sophisticated. Early on, Karen explained to me how Dulcet's system worked. I was their sole male escort, but they didn't want clients to know that. So when Karen got a call for male services, she'd offer some options, such as "Chris" (nineteen years old; 5'10"; 145 pounds; shoulder-length, sandy-blond hair; dark brown eyes and tan); "Stuart" (twenty-one, almost six feet tall, slim, golden skin, blond hair); or "Mike" (twenty-two, 135 pounds, thick brown hair, six feet tall, and a beautiful smile). But no matter who the clients ordered, they got me.

I got to know all the Dulcet female escorts, but one in particular appealed to me. Joanne, in her early thirties, always dressed and made up tastefully, showed definite signs of "good breeding." In fact, she had grown up in an environment quite similar to mine. Now she lived in a sumptuous house in high-toned Upper Arlington and had two children under ten, each by a different father. Joanne told me she worked for Dulcet because the money was good and she'd built up a large clientele over the years. At one time, she'd been mistress to a Mafia chief, lavished with fine clothes and jewels. She'd also been a well-known, high-class, New York City call girl for a while, before running her own operation. Eventually she moved back to Columbus to give her children a "healthier" upbringing.

Soon Joanne and I found ourselves hanging around together days as well as nights. Sometimes we'd go swimming late mornings, then out to lunch and maybe drive the kids to the ice cream parlor. Later, while a sitter minded the children, we'd pleasantly pass the hours at Dulcet between appointments.

The first client with whom I had sex was a guy who welcomed me to his hotel room with a tumbler of Chivas Regal. He asked me if I'd ever done any coke and I told him the truth: "No, I never have." Would I like to? "Sure, I'm game." So he set up lines of coke, and I snorted for the first time and loved it. He was straight, he said, in town on business, and he liked to "do" boys now and then when he was on the road. As the Chivas and coke warmed my brain, I didn't care whether or not I made any more money. I wasn't really attracted to the guy, but giving him sex seemed like fair payback for the good stuff he was giving me.

One night I went to the home of a very nice, straight-seeming man, who told me all about his wife and two children. She was off to Hollywood with the kids, who acted in TV commercials, he said. He even popped in a couple of videos of spots his children had done. I complimented him on his kids' attractiveness, and he showed me pictures of his wife all around the house. I was puzzled; in fact, I asked, "Why am I here?"

He explained that he'd had an intense relationship with a male lover back in college. Then his lover died in a car accident. He'd never gotten over the man's death and had never pursued another such relationship. Eventually he'd gotten married. "But I'm gay," he said. "I've kept it a secret all this time. I don't want to get deeply involved with any other man. My college lover was the only person I ever really cared for or ever will."

Often my clients were married men, deep in the closet, away from home on business, and using the opportunity to express a gayness only some professional like me might ever know about. One was a noted political figure who'd recently thrown an inaugural ball for the governor. He had me for four hours in the most palatial mansion I'd ever seen, swimming in spotlit Grecian fountains with multicolored cherubs.

Another was a doctoral student from India. For some reason he wanted to take me to the state fair; he even paid me for the time we spent there. That afternoon, I jumped into a fifty-cent recording booth and burst into "My Heart Belongs to Me." They piped me through the fair's whole loudspeaker system while a crowd gathered around to listen. He became one of my regulars outside of Dulcet.

Client followed client, night after night. I never got to choose the clients—unless they were off Dulcet's books. Most of the time I went where I was told, whoever called, whoever paid. The longer I was an escort, the more sex I had with clients. I heard many sob stories, which might have been ploys to gain my sympathy so I would ask for less money. Usually it was easier for me to say yes than to fight them off. My best experiences were with men who'd never had sex with another man; I really felt in control of those situations. In my eyes, these were straight men. And there was nothing better than emasculating a straight man. Somehow it put us on the same footing and made me feel like I was breaking down part of that barrier I'd felt between myself and the straight world since childhood.

After a couple of months of this dusk-until-dawn existence, I thought, *You're turning into a vampire. At sunup, you crawl back into your coffin; at sundown, you creep out into the night.* The irony of being constantly sexed but never loved was getting to me. So were some of my clients. A few were young and good-looking, but many were older, ugly, and thoroughly disgusting.

Some were downright scary. One night Paul dropped me off at a Best Western. A fat man about fifty with thick white hair and mustache opened his door in response to my knock. If he'd worn a beard below his rimless glasses, he would have made an ideal Santa Claus. "Come in, come in!" he cried in a jolly, grandfatherly voice. How was I going to hold this guy off for the next hour? I sat down in a chair near the bed and started my usual small-talk routine. "Grandpa" didn't let it go very far. With a big smile, he interrupted me. "I didn't exactly pay eighty dollars to tell you my life story."

Strike-out, I thought. *Five minutes and he's already cutting to the quick.*

"Let me be right up front," Grandpa said. "I didn't hire you for sex, either."

I stared at him. "You didn't?"

"No," he laughed. "I want to be strangled."

"Pardon?"

"Well, not strangled to death. There's this little game I like to play, see—"

"Sir, I don't know if I feel comfortable with this. What exactly do you mean?"

"What I'd like you to do," he said, "is climb up and sit on my stomach. Then wrap your hands around my throat and squeeze as hard as you can."

"Uh, sir," I held up my hands in mock surrender, "I don't think I can do that. I mean it sounds awfully painful." *What kind of freak is this guy?*

"Don't worry. It's perfectly safe. I've done this with plenty of other escorts. Here, let me show you." He took me by the arm and guided me to a "seat" on his stomach, just above his red-and-white striped boxer shorts. After I had my balance, he took my hands and wrapped them around his throat. "Now, just start to squeeze. Take your weight and press down on my windpipe."

"I can try it," I said dubiously, "but I'm really not comfortable with this."

"It's safe, believe me. Before anything dangerous happens, I'll tap on your arm. That's your signal to ease off."

"This just doesn't sound kosher."

"Son, this is my eighty dollars. I don't want sex from you, but this is what I *do* want."

I took a quick look at the clock on the nightstand. I'd been there thirty-five minutes. *Twenty more and I'm outa' here.*

"Humor me," he grinned.

"If you say so." I leaned over and began squeezing his windpipe as I pressed down with most of my weight. I watched his face turn red and then darker shades of purple. Then his face turned blue and his eyes began bulging. *When are you going to tap my arm, Grandpa? I can't take much more of this.* Just as he began to turn a dark shade of blue, I felt his tap on my arm and let go. Almost instantly his face turned pink and he started to breathe.

"See, that wasn't too bad, was it?" he whispered hoarsely.

"I-I just can't believe you want me to do that to you. Doesn't it hurt?"

"No, I really enjoy it. Would you like to try it again? This time, raise your entire body off mine. I want all your weight on my windpipe."

"That's a lot. I weigh 145 pounds."

"Trust me, it's OK." I began the ugly process again. As the purple again suffused his face, he clenched his hands into fists and started to lightly pound on my chest. Suddenly he screeched in a high, tight voice, "No, Daddy, no! Daddy don't—that hurts. I'll be good, I promise I'll be good!" Spit flew from his mouth and pelted me in the face. Suddenly Grandpa tapped me on the arm, and I let go immediately. I reached for a tissue and wiped my face as I glanced at the clock. Four minutes left—thank goodness!

"It looks like it's time for me to go."

"You were really great," Grandpa said exultantly, "the best I've ever had!"

"I'm glad I've made you happy. But I must admit to you, sir. This is the most unusual encounter I've ever had."

He pulled a fifty-dollar bill from his wallet. "Here, let me give you a little something extra for your fine work." I thanked him, jammed the money down the front of my shorts and began getting dressed. I looked over at Grandpa, still lying relaxed on the bed. "Thanks a lot," he said, rubbing his neck. "Catch you later—maybe next time I'm in town."

"You know where you can find me," I said, hoping desperately that he never would. I almost ran out the door.

I got back to my apartment well after dawn, but felt too restless to sleep. I pulled on some jogging shorts and ran the length of Chittenden Street, crossed Fifth, jogged along the next block, and headed for North High Street. On a whim, I stopped at a cute apartment building and asked the manager if there were any vacancies. Maybe a change from rundown Chittenden Street would do me good. One place was just opening up and another was coming vacant in a month. She told me to come back later to see the vacancy. I walked back to my place and had a cool bath. As I got out of the tub and started drying off, suddenly an overwhelming sense of loneliness swept over me.

In recent months I'd had countless sexual encounters; I felt like a hunk of meat being tossed from one hungry animal to another. I was dropped off at hotel rooms, houses, or double-wide trailers, never knowing who or what waited for me on the other side of a door. Suddenly it all nauseated me. Sex had turned into a mercenary cat-and-mouse game, fighting off men so I could delay that tooth-grinding moment when they'd have their way with me. How many months had it been since I'd chosen a date? How long since I'd been with someone I found attractive, someone to really love and have them love me in return? To my customers, I was merely a naked body without a face or feelings, without hurts or wounds. These hungry, horny men I called "my clients" didn't care about my hopes and dreams; they just wanted my body for their selfish pleasure.

But how could I complain? In some ways I didn't care anymore. I felt like an empty shell. And where were my real friends? Susan had been gone all summer, and I rarely phoned her anymore. Parker was wrapped up in his relationship with Don. Mama-escort Joanne was the only friend I had left.

I flung myself down on my bed, grabbed my pillow, and hugged it close. How I wished some man who cared for me was lying by my side, loving and protecting me, telling me I was OK. All I wanted was someone to love me.

The nightmare of old Grandpa turning black-purple molested my mind, and tears flooded my eyes. What in the world could have happened to that desperate man? What had his father done to him when he was a child? What compelled him to repeat that horrible episode, over and over? I began sobbing uncontrollably into my pillow. From somewhere deep inside came a wrenching cry. I knew I needed help, but I had no idea where to find it. I wept until exhaustion overtook me. I reached for a T-shirt on the floor by the bed and wiped my eyes and face with it, tossed it aside, turned up the dry side of my pillow, and immediately fell into a deep sleep.

My alarm jarred me awake at 3:00 P.M. I washed my face, put on some clean clothes, and walked back over to High Street, stopping on the way to grab a cheeseburger and fries. As I neared the steps leading to the apartment complex I wanted to visit, I noticed a man wearing an emerald green bathing suit lying on a lawn chair, sunning himself in the courtyard. With his arms outstretched to tan his underarms and his dark-eyelashed lids closed, he looked utterly vulnerable.

I knocked on the manager's door. After Jane greeted me, she showed me a delightful apartment with lots of dark hardwood, a staircase to a second-floor landing, French doors with crystal knobs, a bedroom with an antique-style gas fireplace, and a porch with hanging wind chimes. From the porch I saw the man below, still sunning himself but now lying on his stomach.

Jane showed me another large room, suitable for dining, a study, or another bedroom ". . . if you get a roommate," she said. My mind was still on the lawn below. *Straight men don't wear green bikini bathing suits,* I thought as we walked from room to room. I loved the apartment, and though the rent was more than double what I was paying on Chittenden, I was making good money with Dulcet and decided I could manage it. I told Jane I'd get back to her shortly; as we walked outside, I noticed the man sitting up, misting his slim, tanned body with a water bottle. I caught his eye and held it for a long second. *He's gay, all right!*

After a few parting remarks I started down the sidewalk, then turned and glanced back at the man. He was watching my every move. I was too shy to say goodbye, but I raised my eyebrows, and he answered with a toss of his head.

As I walked back to Chittenden, I began to dread going back to work. My day had been emotionally draining; after three months, six nights a week, I craved a night of my own to go out and find some fun. Later I called Karen and asked her if I could take the night off. She agreed, much to my relief. I decided to grab a bus downtown and visit Imaginations in a couple of hours. It had been months since I'd been to a gay bar. Would anyone even remember me?

Imaginations was a cut above all the other gay bars in town. It sported tuxedoed doormen, Chippendale-quality bartenders, and rich decor. That night the place was absolutely jammed with handsome men. It felt good to be properly cruised again by gorgeous guys, instead of being chased around a motel room by another horny old geezer! I decided to take my time and let the ambiance soak into me. I meandered into the quiet piano bar, ordered a beer, leaned back, and basked as relaxing melodies tinkled from the grand piano.

After four leisurely beers, I was ready to try something unusual. I made my way to the disco and ventured onto the floor without a partner. David Bowie's "Let's Dance" was the lure. As I danced, someone passed me a dark brown vial of amyl nitrate. I sniffed greedily, lavishing the familiar rush. It was great to be back.

I passed new faces who asked if I was new. "Hardly," I told them, "I've just been busy working?" At what? "I work nights—don't ask."

I flirted my way through the euphoria until another beer seemed in order. I walked to one of the front bars, got a brew—and backed into Bob, who I'd seen suntanning outside the apartment building. We struck up a conversation about ourselves, my music and his Ohio State studies in landscape architecture. Bob had just gotten his master's degree and was planning a move soon to Pittsburgh to accept a position with a fine architectural firm. I told him I was working as a radio dispatcher at AAA Investigative Services. Before long we moved to a plush, purple velvet sofa. He talked and acted so straight and looked so masculine that I could hardly contain myself.

Bob didn't try to contain himself. He moved aggressively but smoothly and soon persuaded me to head for his place on High Street. Only one light glowed in Bob's apartment: an old Frank Lloyd Wright-style lamp sitting on a marble table. I couldn't believe I was actually "home" with someone of my own choice again. That night I decided Bob was everything I had been missing for so long. I felt so safe and secure in his arms. Best of all, we took all night. I had no desire whatsoever to watch the clock and leave when our first hour together was up.

As our relationship deepened during the next two weeks, I grew less and less inclined to go to work. I gave Karen every excuse I could think of: I was sick, I had too many things to do, I was getting ready to move—any dodge to keep from returning to the awful grind. I could stand working for Dulcet as long as there was no one in my life. But now the thought of having sex with any man other than Bob was intolerable.

When my dwindling resources forced me back to work, I found that Dulcet had hired Lonnie, another male escort, to pick up the slack from my absence. So I made a deal with Karen to give me three nights off during the week. Gradually some of my regular clients switched to Lonnie. *Probably want new meat,* I told myself. Lonnie and I did a couple of three-ways together, but the dazzle of "Toryland" had long since faded, and I didn't even much care about the money anymore.

I kept up the investigative services facade with Bob, and he never questioned it. All my free nights I spent at his apartment. We'd lay on the couch together and watch TV, or sit on his front porch swing and get high together. Bob was so affectionate with me, called me "kid," "little buddy," "puppy," or other endearments I enjoyed. It was so difficult to bear the thought that in a couple of weeks he'd be moving to Pittsburgh. *Somehow, something will happen to change his mind about moving,* I told myself. *Maybe the Pittsburgh job will fall through.*

After he helped me move my things from Chittenden to my new place, eventually the time came for Bob to leave. For several days I helped him pack, growing sadder as his things disappeared into boxes. I happily agreed when Bob asked me if I'd drive with him to Pittsburgh. The next morning I helped him pack the U-Haul trailer, then we left. The three-hour drive seemed both like an eternity and an eyeblink. "Bob, I just can't stand the fact that you're moving," I said about halfway there. "What am I going to do without you?"

He began caressing the back of my neck with his free hand. "Puppy, you have your whole life ahead of you. You're going to be a famous singer some day. And we'll always be friends. Pittsburgh's only a three-hour drive from Columbus." As we drove I deliberately allowed the grief and loneliness to overtake me. If I let myself feel some of the pain now, maybe the full brunt of it would hurt less later. We found Bob's beautiful apartment building in Pittsburgh's Shadyside suburb and unloaded his things. After a last night together, Bob drove me to the Greyhound bus station downtown. Before I stepped onto the bus, we hugged each other goodbye.

"Keep in touch, Puppy," Bob whispered.

I held him tightly, ignoring a few passing people's stares. Struggling to keep my emotions under control, I said, "I love you, Bob" with only the slightest sob.

"Hey, cut it out, kid! No tears—get yourself on that bus!" He gave me a parting swat on the backside. I climbed on and sat on a front seat. The driver released the hand brake and ground the stick shift into first gear. As the bus pulled away I stared out the window. Bob stood in the station lot, both hands in his pockets, watching me wave goodbye. The farther the bus traveled from Pittsburgh, the less I understood what had just happened. If Bob truly loved me, how could he just leave me like that? How could he just say goodbye and act as if everything would be OK?

Why doesn't he want me to move and live with him in Pittsburgh? Why hasn't he even asked me if I'd like to? Wasn't I good enough for him? Had I just been just a plaything for his few weeks in Columbus? No, I couldn't have been. I knew Bob loved me and cared for me. But why did our relationship have to end so soon? *Why does everything good have to end for me? Why do the people who love me always end up leaving me?* No answers came to my questions as I closed my eyes, pressed my cheek against the cold window, and listened to the sound of the tires whirling down the long road back to Columbus.

SEVEN

I'D NEVER FELT SO LONELY in my life. I had to grit my teeth and force myself to return to Dulcet after Bob moved away, and I was too depressed to register for another school quarter. My spirits rose somewhat when Susan called to announce she was soon due back in Columbus. A few days later, I spied her familiar blue Nova turning the corner at the end of the apartment building and sprang from the front porch to meet her.

We hugged and kissed. The rest of the afternoon passed quickly as I helped Susan move into her new place, just three doors down from mine. Our reunion was great—until she asked about my school plans.

"I'm not signed up for fall quarter."

She stopped dead, almost dropping her armful of clothes. "What do you mean?"

I suggested a break so we could talk about it. Susan stirred up some instant iced tea, and we sat down in her new kitchen. "Susan, remember I told you I was working for Triple-A Investigative Services? Well, I wasn't exactly being honest." I squirmed inside as she waited. "The company I work for *does* investigative services—but that's not all."

"Go on," she urged, so I told her the whole story about how I got involved with Dulcet and watched her face squint in frank disgust. "You mean you're a slut—a *hooker*."

"Hey, it's not like that at all." I tried to keep from sounding defensive. "I give a service to people who pay eighty bucks an hour for massages."

"I find that very hard to believe." Her glare said volumes I didn't want to read.

"Actually, I massage them in the nude—it's perfectly legal."

Susan let out a snort. "John, I can't believe you'd do that. What on earth has happened to your morals?"

"Look, it's no big deal, and I make a lot of money. How do you think I got out of that rat-trap on Chittenden and moved here?"

"But how do you know who you're getting involved with? You could be raped or even killed."

"Nothing like that has ever happened." I knew I'd already told Susan more than enough. I'd never admit how right she was: I'd had more and more sex during my time at Dulcet. And escorting was dangerous. Vice cops, drug over-doses, and venereal diseases were only some of the risks I faced every night.

She broke into my thoughts. "John, I'm not sure I even know who you are anymore." She got up from the table, rinsed her glass in the sink and turned to me. "Does your mom know anything about this?"

"Of course not." I laughed. "What a silly question—she doesn't even know I'm gay."

"So you're still working for this outfit?"

"Yeah. I need an income, right?" This conversation was making me up-tight. "Please don't judge me. I'm still the same person I've always been."

She walked into the nearby bathroom, riffled through an open cardboard box, and found a small bottle. "I think I'm getting a migraine—the two-Midrin kind."

"One's enough. You know how potent they are." She shrugged and gulped one down with water. I changed the subject, and she didn't mention Dulcet again. But I sensed her attitude toward me had already changed. Was she secretly in love with me, and now I'd betrayed her? I couldn't ever tell her what really went on during my nights at Dulcet or how awful I felt about it. Or how many times I'd cried myself to sleep in despair. I had told her about my relationship with Bob. Although she tried to sound happy, I could tell she hated hearing about my gay affairs.

After we finished unloading Susan's things, I stepped back into the refuge of my beautifully furnished apartment. I'd rented a queen-sized bed with a solid brass headboard and a three-paneled glass screen etched with a moun-tain scene that made shadows on the ceiling at night when a floor lamp shone through it. Unfortunately, my maxed-out credit cards were putting me way over my head financially—especially since I kept avoiding work at Dulcet. *Somehow I'll keep making things work,* I told myself.

Parker still lived on Chittenden with Don, but I could tell their relationship was falling apart. Don would go off on business trips, then come back and beat up Parker. After each beating he'd talk Parker into having sex again, "to kiss and make up." It was a classic pattern of spousal abuse. Since Parker and I got together now and then to talk, I invited him to come over and see my new apartment. He already knew from gossiping gay friends what I'd been doing all summer. We both agreed that, for better or worse, we'd come a long way from our innocent days only two years ago.

Parker was visibly impressed with my apartment. "This is a beautiful place, almost big enough for two."

"Big enough for me and a husband," I joked.

"Hey, I've got one," Parker jibed, "and look how happy we are. Perfect wedded bliss." He rolled his eyes. "At least I've got someone waiting when I get home from work at night."

Dusk was deepening as we strolled back toward Chittenden. About halfway to Parker's, I slowed down. I was dying to tell someone how I felt inside. "Parker, one more thing before we say good night."

"What's that?"

"I think I need some help."

"How do you mean?"

"I don't know, I just—my life seems to be falling apart. I know things look good on the outside. I always 'smile though my heart is breaking', but . . ."

"Come on, John, you're the tough one. You've got the strongest personality I know. You can weather any storm."

"Sure, like Gibraltar—but listen. My relationship with my dad is almost nonexistent. I can't seem to keep a lover, and I can't figure out why. Do you know anyone I could talk to?"

"You mean, like a shrink?"

"I guess so."

He suggested that I contact the Gay Alliance at Ohio State. I thought it sounded like a good idea and called them the next day. They referred me to Dr. Howard Bryant, a well-known gay clinical psychologist who specialized in gay men. I called his office and set up an appointment.

Less than a week later, I walked into Dr. Bryant's office. A man dressed casually in tan corduroy pants and a maroon pullover emerged from a back room and introduced himself. I was a bit puzzled as I followed him into his office. He didn't look anything like a shrink, and he looked anything but gay. He appeared about 35, and his stocky build made him almost cuddly, like a big teddy bear. In fact, I realized that he resembled a rounder, older version of Parker!

The doctor motioned me to one of two matching sofas. His office was more like a den, with cozy, soft lamplight. One wall featured a huge tank with hosts of brightly colored tropical fish. He grabbed a clipboard and started eliciting some information from me. Soon I felt quite comfortable with Howard; he was very open and a great listener, and we talked for the next hour about my life.

I had few concrete memories before the age of seven, I explained. But I vividly remembered a fall day when my father took my sister, Vicky, and me to a park in Columbus. We played on the big swings and my father bought us snacks. Near the end of the afternoon, Dad knelt in front of us and tears began streaming from his eyes. "Kids, there's something I have to tell you that's very hard for me. I'm not going to be living with you anymore. Your mother and I are getting a divorce."

When Howard asked me, I couldn't remember my immediate reaction to this announcement. But later, when Dad left us at our apartment, although I tried to be brave, I began sobbing uncontrollably.

Sometime during the next several weeks, I looked in my mother's closet and found some man's clothes I didn't recognize. *What are these doing here?* I wondered. Then her friend named Garry came over for dinner. Later, my mother sent Vicky and me upstairs to our bedroom. As I tried to sleep, I heard strange sounds coming from downstairs: male grunts and my mother moaning. Frightened, I started downstairs to see what was going on. Suddenly Garry rose from behind the couch wearing nothing but a loose robe. "Go back upstairs—right now!" he yelled.

I was terrified. Why was he hurting my mother? I started crying hysterically. "Mommy, Mommy! What's wrong?" I couldn't see her, and she didn't call out to tell me things were all right. With this menacing man standing between us, I had no choice but to run back to my room, trembling in fear. I don't remember anything more, except that I decided to hate that man for as long as he stayed in my mother's life. Garry moved in with us before the divorce was final and then married my mother a few months later. After that, Vicky and I saw Dad on weekends. He'd come and pick us up on Saturdays, and we'd go see a movie, visit the park, or drive to a taco place.

"My memories of those times with Dad are mostly pleasant," I explained to Howard. "The hard times seemed to come at my mother's." I didn't trust Garry and didn't want him in my house. He attempted to befriend me, but I wanted no part of him. On the other hand, I adored my mother. Though she had a volatile temper, she seemed like a goddess—the epitome of glamour, style, and sophistication. She wore the most exquisite clothes, acted with impeccable manners, and turned heads wherever she appeared. I deeply admired her and wanted to be exactly like her.

Mom told me all the time that she loved me. Yet, strangely, I never really felt sure of her love. She could be amazingly petty about the smallest expenditures. One day she discovered that I had thrown away some unused facial tissues. She was very upset. "Why did you do that, John?" she cried. "I paid for those tissues, you know!" I felt guilty for days.

Meanwhile, I felt unacceptable to Dad. I was physically clumsy and talked too much. Whenever I tried to tell him about something I had done that I thought he might like, I felt alienated by his emotional distance. He rarely said he was proud of me; I never felt good enough for him.

A few years after my father and mother divorced, my dad remarried. He stayed with his new wife, Nancy, until I grew to adulthood. I liked Nancy very much; her even temper represented security to me. One day I put on my best clothes when Dad took me out to a restaurant. I screwed up all my courage and asked if I could live with him and Nancy. Quickly he told me, "No, I don't think that would be a good idea."

He doesn't want me, I thought. *It must be my fault.*

I also told Howard about my problems at school. By age ten, I couldn't sit still; I disrupted classes and mouthed off at my teacher in class. Always wildly extroverted, the clown in every class, I couldn't concentrate on schoolwork and wouldn't let anyone else concentrate, either. My teacher sent me to the school psychologist. He was tall, dark haired, spoke with a slight foreign accent, and dressed immaculately. He fascinated me.

I was devastated when, after only two visits, I never saw him again. I missed him terribly. "Please don't leave me," I wanted to beg him. Actually, I was also dying to ask him, "Will you take me home and be my dad?" But instead, I was referred to therapists at Children's Hospital. They gave me more tests and diagnosed me as dyslexic and hyperactive, then gave me Dexedrine to calm me down.

I had other troubles at school that the medication couldn't fix. I was afraid of hanging around with other boys; they were too rough-and-tumble for me, and I didn't want to get hurt. I felt comfortable and safe with the girls, playing foursquare, hopscotch, and Chinese jump rope.

One kid at school named Bruce was very effeminate. Other kids teased him incessantly. They did the same to me. "Sissy, fag!" they shouted at Bruce. I didn't know what they meant, but I knew I must be a sissy, too, because I was just like Bruce.

When I was fifteen, my dad and stepmother decided to move from Columbus to Phoenix. Although Dad never knew it, I was devastated when he told me the news. *You've spent so little time with me,* I thought. *How can you move away and leave me altogether?* I tried to convince myself that it didn't matter. *He doesn't care anyway.* Alcohol and marijuana were a big help to dull the pain.

The next summer, Vicky and I stayed with Dad and Nancy in Phoenix. While we were there, the first *Superman* movie hit the theaters, and I became infatuated with Christopher Reeve, the lead actor. My dad must have seen the adoring look on my face. Later he made a remark about gay men, and I wondered if he was implicating me. Did he suspect something that I was trying so hard to hide?

That summer, my mother wrote constantly, telling Vicky and me how much she missed us. All too soon the summer ended, and it was back to Columbus. There, my cycles of rage, love, guilt, and resentment against my mother—and my continuing hatred of Garry—picked up where they had left off. I could tell that their marriage was getting rocky. My mother withdrew from the growing conflict by purchasing a Steinway grand piano and practicing for up to eight hours a day. She engaged a well-known local piano professor for private lessons and said she wanted to start performing again. *Well,* I thought, *at least you never drink while you're playing.*

With piano music playing continually through the house, I sometimes vocalized along with it from a distance. I discovered that, since my voice had changed, I could sing some pretty good high notes. On a whim, I auditioned for my high school's madrigal group and was accepted on a fluke: Only two males auditioned, and the other guy dropped out. With the group's acceptance, I finally found a small subculture where I fit. It was here that I met Richard, who soon became my best friend.

Before my senior year in high school began, Mom and Garry filed for divorce. The minute they separated, I took charge and found an apartment for us in the Hayes school district. I was proud that I had immediately become "the real man of the family." Soon after we moved into the new apartment, I auditioned into Hayes and enrolled for the fall.

Then, to my disgust, almost immediately my mother found another man, someone barely above a homeless bum. Her alcoholism had increased dramatically by this point. She was living off an inheritance but seemed to be swiftly degenerating. She stopped playing the piano and began dressing in T-shirts and jeans. She quit doing all household chores and essentially stopped being a mother altogether. She and her boyfriend went on booze benders, where she'd disappear for days without letting us know where she was. Vicky began suffering severe migraines, and I had to learn how to shop, cook, and run the household.

Eventually I called my dad and let him know what was going on, and Vicky went to live with him. Mom and her boyfriend split up, and she turned the situation into a living hell by blaming me for everything that had happened. One night when she was drunk, I confronted her, "I'll bet you think every problem you've ever had is my fault."

"That'sh right, I do," she slurred.

That felt like the ultimate betrayal, I explained to Howard. "And that comment came after all I'd done to help Mom and Vicky!" Soon Howard knew all about my coming out, my open gay life, and my desire to find one man who would always love me.

Then, as I talked about Bob and his recent move to Pittsburgh, I was overcome with grief. I dropped my face in my hands, and my soft crying escalated to open sobbing. Howard put his hand on my shoulder. "What is it—why are you crying?" His fatherly touch was very comforting.

"I'm just so lonely. I hate myself. Nobody stays with me. All my life people have left me. What's wrong with me?"

"Did you ever think that maybe it wasn't you? That maybe it was them?"

"I tried—but it doesn't seem to solve the puzzle." I sniffed and wiped my eyes with a tissue. "I'm sorry, Howard. I guess this just needed to come out. It's been bottled up for so long."

I had told Howard almost everything about my life. I even told him about my problem with getting sexually aroused on meeting new guys, and about my sexual inhibitions unless I got drunk enough to feel relaxed and self-assured. But I couldn't tell him about Dulcet—I didn't want him to think badly of me. Howard assured me that my dreams could be fulfilled. He'd been in a relationship with a man for five years. I told him how wonderful that sounded to me. "It can happen to you, too," he said soothingly.

All too soon our time was up. We agreed on weekly sessions for just twenty-five dollars an hour rather than his usual fee of seventy-five dollars. I wasn't sure how much benefit I'd receive, but it felt great to have someone listen to me.

One night several weeks later, Dulcet gave me a client out in Darbydale, a small town about ninety minutes from Columbus. We'd never booked a job so far away, but the client had asked for two hours, and I sure needed the extra money. My driver dropped me off at a ramshackle place that gave me a major attack of the creeps; it looked like something from the Alfred Hitchock movie *Psycho*. I wasn't the least reassured when I saw my client. He looked at least seventy years old, bent over with a hump on his back. He wore baggy polyester pants and a dirty T-shirt.

"You'll be back in two hours, right?" I hollered to my driver before the old man slammed the door shut. I stood inside the front door while the gnarly geezer stared at me with a tight, crooked scowl. "Sit down," he said in a high-pitched voice, then turned and disappeared into another room. I glanced around; the room was strewn with old clothes, newspapers, and dirty dishes. A lamp with a dim bulb supplied the only light.

I sat fidgeting until the old man walked back into the room a couple of minutes later. "I've paid for you, and you're mine," he snapped. "Why are your clothes still on?"

"Let's not be so hasty." I tried to keep my voice warm. "We don't want to jump right into this, do we? Let's relax—after all, we do have a whole two hours together."

He was in a no-nonsense mood. "I paid for sex," he snapped, "and sex is what I want. Now get undressed." How was I going to keep this guy away from me for 120 minutes?

"Do you mind if I use your bathroom first?"

He looked at me suspiciously. "Sure, if that'll speed things up. Down the hallway, past the dining room, on the right." I walked around an old mahogany dining table, slipped into the bathroom, and quickly latched the door. My mind was racing. *Something's really wrong here. Get out—right now!*

Quietly I opened the bathroom door, poked my head out, and looked both ways. No one was in sight. I crept down the hallway toward the dining room and spied an old black phone sitting on a buffet. I picked the receiver up, dialed my driver's beeper number, and whispered a message to come back and get me as soon as possible. Then I gently replaced the phone in its cradle and walked back to the empty living room.

Suddenly the old man hobbled in from the kitchen. Both his hands were behind his back. "Thought you were going to take your clothes off," his shrill voice whipped.

"Why don't we have a drink first?"

"I want you to take your clothes off!" he shouted. "I paid for you, so let's get to it!" At that moment the phone rang shrilly. Startled, the old man flinched and pivoted to his left. I saw a quick, faint flash of light leap from behind his back. A huge butcher knife waved between his knotted hands.

Icy chills ran through me as the hairs on my neck prickled inside my shirt collar. Without thinking, I bolted for the front door, hurled it open, and plunged down the dark road toward the distant lights of town, the old man shrieking behind me. I found a phone booth on the town's main street and left another message for my driver. I was still catching my breath and trying to slow the pounding of my heart as he drove up a few minutes later.

That was my last night at Dulcet. After I got home, I locked the door, drew a hot bath, and scrubbed myself over and over, sobbing the whole time. I felt like the filth from the last three months was clinging to me, and I couldn't rub hard enough to get rid of it.

At last I lay in my bed, totally exhausted. Surely there had to be more to the gay life than what I'd been experiencing. Somewhere, somehow, there had to be some man out there who would want to really know and love me. Someone who wouldn't just find sexual pleasure with my body, but who would want to enter my soul. But it seemed so unattainable. I cried myself to sleep yet again as the sun rose that morning.

EIGHT

W HEN I AWOKE the next day, I called Wayne and told him I was through;
he promised to put a final paycheck for me in the mail. Then Joanne
called to invite me out for coffee to discuss a proposition. She wouldn't tell
me what she had in mind, but I quickly agreed to meet and hear her plan.

"John, why don't we start our own escort service?" she said, munching a
Danish. "It's easy—I've done it before. We just get a phone system installed in
my house and your place. Then we run an ad in the paper and get a few girls
to work for us.

"I've got some friends who'll go into it with us, and I can do a call myself
now and then to help us get started. We'll get most of the money, and you can
run the phones. You won't have to face a steady stream of sex-hungry johns,
the girls and I can handle that part of the business." It sounded great, especially since I was wondering how I was going to pay my pile of bills. Joanne's
beautiful home would be a perfect cover. We decided to call our service
"Aaron's" so we would get listed early in the classified's alphabetized listings. I
was excited to think of all the money we'd soon be making.

Joanne and I did get an escort operation up and running, although we
never earned much money. But we did work well together and in the process
became even closer friends. But the more I learned about Joanne's life, the
sadder I felt. I had figured by her looks that she was in her late forties; I
learned she was only thirty-two. Her careers as madam and Mafia mistress
had been tough on her. She told me how much she missed her New York
Sicilian boyfriend. He'd lavished all the best on her, and he'd promised to
bring her back to New York some day.

Her parents didn't know—and would never know—how she really lived. They owned her house in Columbus, and her father sent her a monthly check to help with expenses.

Before long, we began to suspect that we were wasting our lives in the escort line. I was getting tired of the flaky girls in our employ, and the slow rate of business. "Still," I told Joanne, "there's something about this business that's exciting, something alluring the rest of the world doesn't know anything about."

"I know what you mean," she nodded. "Maybe that's why, no matter what else I do, I always run back to it."

Meanwhile, Howard and I began the process of trying to put together the jigsaw puzzle pieces that made up my background. In our early sessions, Howard mainly listened as certain details of my life began returning to my memory. He helped me see that I had not only worshiped my mother, but resembled her more than any other person on earth. She probably never knew how deeply I cared about what she thought about me. But I ached above all for her approval, though I was never certain I could completely earn it.

At the same time, I loved my mother more than I loved any other human being. But I felt that somehow, in subtle ways, she was controlling—even devouring—me. "Whenever I was emotionally distraught," I told Howard, "especially if I'd been picked on at school, I would come to her for consolation. She'd put her arms around me and say, 'John, I don't know why the kids are saying bad things to you. Maybe they're jealous because you're different. You know, lots of the world's greatest people were different. And I know how you feel, because sometimes I feel different and unhappy, too.'"

Invariably my mother's focus would turn to herself, her childhood, her own troubles and feelings. She was trying to show me that she understood. But whenever she responded like this, I felt as if my problems were not important. I seemed to be my mother's confidante and emotional caretaker. I was flattered by her intimacy with me, but I always left these conversations feeling drained, somehow robbed of my identity. I felt like an extension of her; I couldn't see where she left off and my personhood began.

Howard helped me realize that Mom wielded a kind of "golden lasso" that she pulled tightly around me. She never physically abused me, but she was verbally cutting and domineering. I resented her unconscious efforts to control me, while craving her love and attention.

I told Howard about a conversation with my dad when I was about twelve. He had glanced over at me and coldly said, "You're becoming more like your mother every day." *Then you must really hate me,* I thought. And I told myself, *You'd better watch everything you say and do around Dad.* When I was at my mother's, I acted like her; when I was around Dad, I changed since I knew he couldn't stand her anymore. But I could tell deep inside that I wasn't succeeding, and I was sure he despised me just as much as he despised my mother.

"Howard, I can see now that my parents tried to love me, but they just didn't know how. My dad kept an emotional wall between himself and me. And my mom absorbed me into her gaping pit of emotional need. Either way, I disappeared."

Howard also explored with me my childhood feelings about being a boy. I told him that I'd always felt more like a girl. "For me, watching other boys was like looking through a windowpane. I could see them on the other side, but I felt separated from them by some invisible barrier. I was fascinated by other boys, but I just didn't understand the way they thought or the things they did."

I told him about the day, at age fourteen, when I was looking for something in our house and discovered some hard-core porno films my stepfather had hidden. From then on, I'd get out his projector when no one else was home and watch some of these movies. For some reason, the private parts of the men fascinated me far more than the women.

Howard and I also talked about my first sexual encounter at age fifteen. It was a Saturday night, and I was alone at my house with Jim, my best friend. Both of us were drunk. We started talking about masturbation, then fell into mutual sex play—more to see what it felt like than anything else. But even that night, I sensed that our exploration was far more interesting to me than Jim. But we never talked about sex again.

Meanwhile, apart from my therapy sessions, Joanne and I struggled to keep our escort service alive. One night when the phones were slow, we decided to leave the answering machines on and head down to Imaginations.

We were out on the dance floor sniffing poppers when a woman in the corner caught my eye. She was extremely tall, but it was her face, not her height, that seized my attention. With a sudden shock I realized "she" was Larry Simms, a fellow student with me back at Hayes. I hadn't even known he was gay, much less a drag queen. I looked closer. Larry wasn't exactly what I'd call beautiful. But if you hadn't known him, you might have found him pretty convincing as a woman, with jet-black hair, bright red hoop earrings, dark blue eye shadow, vibrant red lipstick, tight black miniskirt, and a big over-sized white blouse. I crossed the dance floor. "Larry," I blurted, "is that really you? I can't believe it!"

With an icy glare Larry was quick to correct me. "Please get it right, girlfriend. The name is Lauren, and I'm so pleased to meet you, daahling."

"Lauren" extended a bent-wristed hand in my direction, with the obvious expectation that I would adoringly kiss it. I couldn't help myself—I doubled over and laughed until my sides ached. Lauren didn't move a muscle until I finally recovered myself, gently took her hand, and kissed it. "Delighted to meet you, too, dahling," I smiled. "Do you remember me? I'm John Paulk—from Hayes Performing Arts. Gosh, you look great!"

"Thank you soooo much, and how well I know it, dear. But tell me—who is that cute thing I saw you dancing with?" I brought Joanne over and introduced her with appropriate flourishes. Joanne was delighted with Lauren; she'd known plenty of drag queens in her time. After a few moments of light conversation, Joanne said, "Come on, girls. Let's get a drink."

"Yes, dahling, let's," Lauren piped, and we walked off the dance floor, past the elegant cocktail tables and plush sofas to the piano bar.

"Let's sit outside on the patio," Joanne suggested. "I'm hot, and my feet are killing me."

Lauren giggled. "Your feet—what about me? I'm four inches off the floor on stilettos." She flashed her spiky high heels. *How in the world does he walk on those things?* I wondered.

We sat down, and Lauren looked at me with a smile. "What have you been doing with yourself for the past two years? Still at Ohio State?"

Lauren shook her head in wonderment when I told her about our escort service. Then Joanne piped up, "You know what, Lauren? I'll bet you, me, and John could make piles of money together."

"Oh, do tell, dahling."

"We could send you out as a cross-dressing call girl."

Lauren giggled with delight. "What a naughty idea! You know, I'm not really doing much these nights. Maybe working with you could earn me enough money to do a better job of dressing me." After a bit more discussion we agreed to meet at Joanne's house the following night.

Joanne and I had some doubts that Lauren would actually show up, but she did. Together we clued her into the more intimate secrets of escorting. We started sending Lauren out, with only mild success. But a raucous camaraderie developed between the three of us, steeped increasingly in alcohol, amyl nitrate, and top Colombian marijuana.

A few weeks later, Lauren and I were hanging around Joanne's house waiting for the phone to ring. Joanne was out on a trick, and Lauren hadn't painted herself up yet. But she did have her drag bag of makeup, wigs, and other paraphernalia. As we chatted I noticed Lauren kept cocking her head and scrutinizing me intensely. "John, you have perfect features for a drag queen. Beautiful, almond-shaped eyes; a gentle brow-line; and a tiny, narrow nose. Not even an Adam's apple to mar the neckline. You'd be utterly flawless in drag."

"Lauren, you're nuts! Me, in drag? I don't want to be a woman!" I'd never even considered drag nor been attracted to people in the drag life. Lauren was the only drag queen I'd ever talked with at length. And the only makeup I'd ever put on—or dreamed of putting on—was for stage performances.

"Come on, it'll be fun. Let me try it once—just to see what you'd look like. Nobody but you and me ever needs to know."

Lauren was obsessed with the notion and begged me for the next hour. Finally I gave in, and she reached for her bag. She turned it upside down on the kitchen table, spilling out stuff I'd never seen my mother use. She arranged everything in a neat semicircle around her, then said eagerly, "Now let's get to work."

She took two bottles of different-colored heavy foundation and shook them thoroughly, then dabbed liquid from both bottles all over my face, meticulously smoothing color into my skin. After applying this thick layer of dark pancake, she took a giant powder puff and molded the foundation into place. "John, your face makes such a perfect, blank palette. On it, I'm going to create a transcendent new face."

"Hand me that mirror. Let me see what you're doing."

"No—not one peek until the transformation is complete!"

Then Lauren began correcting my one flaw. "Those eyebrows have got to go," she explained. "They're bushy as wooly worms. Ugh!" She camouflaged my "hideous" brows with a glue stick, then took an eyebrow pencil and drew thin brows. "Just the right feminine touch," she gloated.

Next she attacked me with several shades of dark blue eye shadow, then seemed intent on trying to poke my eyes out. "Sit still," she scolded when I blinked. "It's only eyeliner, you big baby!"

I squirmed as she scraped my eyelids, and my eyes started watering. "Let me wash this abominable stuff off," I pleaded.

"And ruin my ultimate masterpiece?" Lauren screeched. "Don't you dare. Sit still, you booby, and let me finish!" Curiosity was killing me by this time, but Lauren was far from finished. She reached for what looked like little spider webs, then applied a thin line of glue to one and blew gently on it, then repeated the process with the other. When the glue was dry enough, she caressed these false eyelashes onto the upper lids of both my eyes and told me to keep them both shut. "Don't move a muscle," she growled. "Wait for the glue to dry."

"Whatever do I need these for?"

"John, you amaze me. No drag queen would dare be seen without proper eyelashes."

"I'm not a drag queen, and I'm not being seen anywhere."

"Just shut up or they won't stick right."

When the glue at last dried I was horrified to find I couldn't open my eyes. "Lauren, you idiot, you've blinded me!" I hollered.

"No, I haven't, you fool. Be quiet, or I'll leave you sightless just for spite." She began to pry under my new lashes with a toothpick until finally I could open my eyes again. Lauren's face glowed as she reviewed her handiwork. "Perfect," she cooed. "You look the image of Marilyn Monroe."

"Always one of my idols, I assure you."

"Now for the true magic," said Lauren triumphantly. She used three different shades of blush to make my cheeks radiate the ideal highlights. "A darker shade for underneath the high part of the cheekbone," she explained, "and then contrasting light and dark shades: light, to make things stand out; dark, to make things sink in. Your cheekbones need to stand out, so it's dark contour blush underneath to make you look positively cavernous." She studied my face a moment. "I do think your nose needs thinning."

"I thought you said it was wonderfully slim already."

Lauren was not to be denied. "Listen to your drag mother, child. We must use a dark medium blush and contour the sides of your nose to give it just the cutest little upturn on the end." I glanced at the kitchen clock; over an hour had gone by. Who was I going to look like when this ordeal was over, Marilyn Monroe or a circus clown?

"Lipstick is next, dear." Lauren drew a fine line around the outline of my lips with a red pencil. "Full lips are in this year, you know. They make a woman look sexy and seductive." Next came a glossy red lipstick. When Lauren finished, I begged for a gaze in the mirror. "Nothing doing. What glamorous woman would be seen without a glorious hairdo?"

She took more than a dozen bobby pins and used them to stab my hair into a knot atop my head. Then she raced out of the room and came back with a mop of black curls, which she plopped over my head and pulled snugly around my ears. The wig's soft locks tickled my shoulders as they fell. Then she grabbed still more bobby pins, combs, and hair spray to rearrange the wig. Finally she put down her instruments of torture, sat back, and looked at me critically.

After a long moment of silence I was fit to burst. "Don't move!" Lauren burst out. "One more finishing touch before you look in the mirror—earrings!" They were the ultimate insult, excruciating pinches by large red buttons clamped on my ears.

"Now we're ready," she said, glowing. "Close your eyes." She guided me out of the kitchen to a large mirror in the living room. "Now, open your eyes!"

I did—and went into profound shock. There, staring at me from the large mirror was a gorgeous, fiery, Italian woman! For a long minute, I stared at myself in wonder from every possible angle. The illusion was flawless. "Unbelievable!" was the only word my lips could form.

Lauren's voice behind me was filled with awe. "You really are beautiful, John. I thought I might be able to do some good work on you, but I had no idea. There isn't a queen anywhere you couldn't put to shame."

Suddenly the front door swung open and Joanne walked in. "I'm through for the night—" she began, then stopped. "Where's John?" In the mirror I saw Lauren nod, smiling, in my direction.

"John, is that you?" she gasped. "My gosh, you are totally beautiful!"

Lauren laughed with delight. "Let's get John upstairs and finish the job with some clothes!" Joanne quickly agreed, and the two of them practically dragged me up to Joanne's bedroom. From her closet they picked out a long blue sweatshirt dress and a huge red belt. Joanne hitched a bra on me and stuffed it with socks. Lauren used three pairs of nylons to hide my hairy legs. They jammed my feet into a pair of size-ten, lollipop-red high heels, put on the dress and belt—then planted me in front of the full-length mirror.

I turned every which way, marveling at the dress's sway and my wig's fluid toss. "I-I can't get over it," I said. "You know, this is the ultimate disguise.

Absolutely the perfect way I can totally forget myself—and fool the whole world if I want to."

The femininity of the result excited me, but the sheer audacity of the illusion tantalized me even more. I'd never in my life been involved in such an elaborate performance. I gazed into Lauren and Joanne's admiring faces, and an outrageous thought entered my mind. "Let's go to Imaginations—just as we are! I'd like to see just how many people I can really fool!"

NINE

SOON DISCOVERED that fooling anyone in my new disguise was much more easily said than done. I couldn't even walk across Joanne's bedroom in her three-inch, sling-back shoes. Lauren politely informed me that I possessed all the grace of a Brahma bull charging through Tiffany's in New York. Both Joanne and Lauren begged me to forgo my first public appearance until I'd had a few lessons in posture and poise, but I was too fascinated with my transformed image to delay this second "coming out" for another moment. So Lauren took my driver's license and some money from my pants pockets, slapped them into an old white wicker purse, and we headed for Imaginations.

Will anyone know me? I wondered on the way. I was a popular figure at the bar. How would this change affect people's regard for me? I hadn't thought all that through a few minutes ago—but it was too late to turn back now. We stepped out of the car into the parking lot. I made my movements as graceful as possible for one so new to the female gender.

Suddenly my heart almost stopped. Several of my best friends were walking by. Amazingly, they greeted Lauren and Joanne but showed no sign of recognizing me! A rush of adrenaline throbbed through me; it was almost like being a first-timer to a gay bar again. Once we were inside the door, I hobbled to the bar and ordered two double Scotches on the rocks. Surely the bartender would recognize me—I made no attempt to disguise my baritone voice. But Morris said nothing. Drag queens were common here, and he didn't look twice at me.

I knocked my drinks back and tried to stumble around the bar. Morris glanced my way but must have figured I'd come in drunk and looked quickly aside. "Do not leave my side," I hissed to Lauren and Joanne, who followed hard on my heels. "I'll never get through this without you." I was horribly nervous—but also exhilarated. Not one soul showed any sign of recognition. I felt something like Eliza Doolittle at the embassy ball, but only a lot more awkward.

"Here comes the acid test," Lauren whispered, as several of her drag friends approached us. Never batting an eyelash, she crowed, "Hi, dahlings! I'd like to introduce my new friend. Isn't she beautiful?"

Brandy Lamont, one of Columbus's premier queens, who was out of drag tonight, slithered all around me, perusing every inch. "My, my, Lauren. I thought you were through slumming in the straight world. What are you doing with this gorgeous creature?" Brandy was short, early forties, with a heavily wrinkled face and a huge nose. *This guy could never look good as a woman,* I gloated to myself.

As the evening progressed, numerous men and women, gay and straight, friends and strangers, commented on my beauty and glamour. There were awed whispers all evening. Even straight men who had brought their dates to this chic hangout stole glances at me, and I was thrilled to let them catch my eye. I could tell some of them wished I was the woman on their arm. And everyone did seem to assume I was a woman—as long as I didn't open my mouth. When I spoke, no one knew I was John Paulk unless I told them. Even then, they had a hard time believing it. I felt the thrill of a magic anonymity again and again. I could escape—right out in the open! Once I had this act down pat, nobody would ever need to know John Paulk lurked underneath the mask.

By the end of our evening my feet were killing me; I could hardly limp back to the car. My scalp itched like a massive flea infestation, and my wig felt like it was about to crawl off my skull. My waist, sliced with multiple elastic pantyhose bindings, felt like some malicious magician had almost cut me in half. My face felt as if it had been encased in four inches of dry mud, like I would need a whole package of Brillo pads to scrape it completely clean.

But despite this excruciating discomfort, I had never felt so energized or affirmed. In drag I could even forget who I was on the inside. I could create a whole new identity and be as intense with my new self as I wanted—someone totally new. That first night gave me a taste of drag, and I was hooked.

In the following weeks, I begged Lauren to put me in drag again. She agreed, as long as I let it be known that she was my one and only drag mother—the one who had given birth to my drag personality. Lauren had another drag daughter named "Jennifer Heart" (after Stephanie Powers of TV's *Hart to*

Hart). Jennifer and I would go over to Lauren's every weekend. Under Lauren's watchful eye, Jennifer would put herself in drag, Lauren would put me in, and we'd all go out together.

During the next month, I went out in drag about six times. Slowly I began to feel more comfortable in my drag role, and other queens in the bars began to recognize me. Though drag queens tend to congregate together in gay society, they carry on admire/hate relationships with one another and compete savagely for attention and preeminence. Being a legendary drag queen can mean a measure of notoriety—and even money, since bars award cash prizes for drag shows, beauty contests, and other social events.

About this time my financial plight turned severe. My gas and electricity had been turned off. I had once again enrolled in school but had no money to pay tuition. It was clear that Joanne's and my escort service was failing. My mother, now in regular therapy, decided to stop any financial support until I demonstrated "more stable decisions about my own future." And now I had a new habit—drag—that I was going to need money to support.

So I got a job at a copy center on campus, gradually lost touch with Joanne, and almost immediately began to feel somewhat better about myself and my prospects. I was honestly glad to be out of the escort business, and I didn't care what anyone thought about my drag predilection. I was willing to take major risks to achieve drag's illusion of perfection and to have my life changed into this fascinating new personality I was discovering.

One night Lauren took me to the Ruby Slipper, a drag bar where she worked on the east side of town. I had never been to a bar exclusively devoted to drag, and I was eager to see how regular queens would react to me.

The Ruby Slipper featured an enormous, red-sequined bar in the shape of a woman's pump. Drag queens lounged all over the place, some beautiful, some grotesque. I quickly established myself as one of the best-looking queens there.

One Sunday night, amateur queens were featured in a lip-synch contest. Lady Sonya Ross, a renowned drag queen who had competed in national contests, directed these shows and scheduled the queens who performed.

"You really ought to get up and perform tonight," Lauren said to me when the contest was announced. "All you have to do is lip-synch."

"I think you're right. I've been singing half my life."

"Let me introduce you to Sonya. The winner gets twenty-five dollars, you know."

"Sounds like a heckuva lot easier money than we made as escorts." Despite my bravado, I was jittery. Lauren introduced me to Lady Sonya, who promptly asked my name. I was going to say "John" when Lauren leaped in. "Sonya, she's so newborn I haven't even thought about her name yet. You're so clever. Why don't you give her one?"

Sonya cocked her head from side to side, then her eyes brightened. "How about Randi? R-A-N-D-I." She giggled. "In England it means horny."

"Perfect," I agreed, then selected Barbra Streisand's "Come In from the Rain" from Sonya's extensive backup track collection and awaited my turn. When they announced my new drag name, I made my way onto the stage. I was blinded by the amber spotlight as the first bars of my song poured through the speakers.

"It's a long road when you're on your own . . ." My lips moved precisely in time with Barbra's words. I lifted my left hand gently, letting my bent wrist trail until my hand was above my head. Then I waved my palm skyward and synched, "And it looks like sunny skies . . ."

Sweep that hand, girl, sweep that hand, I thought. I knew drag queens always made expansive gestures, the more dramatic the better. As the song swept on, I spread my fingers apart, closed them into a fist, then exploded them toward the sky, pretending they were bursts of sunshine. Then I began gently fluttering my fingers back and forth, miming rain pouring down. Then a thought struck me: *Get going, start moving around!* At stage right a few men leaned over the railing, waving dollar bills at me. I walked as gracefully as I could toward them.

Yells reached out from the audience: "Go get 'em, Miss Thing!" "Go on, girlfriend!" I acted charmingly tipsy as I leaned toward one of the men teasingly waving a dollar at me. I reached out to take it, and he grabbed me behind the shoulders, pulled my face into his, and kissed me full on the lips. My knees started to shake, and I almost lost my balance. But somehow I kept my feet—and my place in Barbra's song. I found the presence of mind to fan myself and exaggerate my stagger, as if the man's kiss had totally disoriented me.

I backed up a few steps, threw my right hand out, palm upward, and with one finger began to beckon him seductively. He whistled and hollered joyous approval. "Whoa, whoa! You're hot, girl, you're hot!"

"Go, Randi, go!" screamed another voice from stage left. "Shake those hips, girl!" I flipped my head, swinging my dark hair across my shoulders. I was full into it now, walking to the edge of the stage to collect bills from the hands of my adoring new fans. As the last chorus wound down, both my hands were spread fingers-wide with crumpled-up bills, and I backed toward center stage for my finale. Precisely as the song ended I scattered the money like rain around me, dropped my head to my breast, with my arms and hands completely still at my sides.

The final note faded, and the applause and foot stomping thundered from all corners of the bar. As the spot sank to blackout, I reached down to scoop up all the money I could and then fled backstage. Lauren ran up and hugged me. "Great job, Randi! I knew you could do it, girl!"

"Was I really OK, Lauren? I was such a nervous wreck." I felt like a newly popped bottle of champagne; my first drag number had been a huge hit.

Just then, Brandy Lamont strolled up. "Missy, a little more practice and you'll have it down pat." Lauren winked approvingly at me. What a compliment, coming from a legend in her own right! From that moment on I knew I could make it in the drag world. I'd rise above the rest of them; I had something unique inside of me. I wasn't polished or notorious yet. *But just wait,* I thought. *I'm already on a fast track to the top!*

From then on, I couldn't wait for Friday night. Even my normal desire to attract sexual partners was overshadowed by my all-consuming desire to make up as a woman. I decided my life was too busy for school that quarter. Once Susan started attending classes, we saw less and less of each other. Now all my Friday nights were dedicated to drag and hanging out with Lauren and Jennifer.

Week after week I'd watch Lauren perform at the Ruby Slipper. She inspired my awe no matter what clothing she chose: glamorous gowns or quirky costumes, black tights or oversized white cotton shirt with black hat and jet stiletto heels. I tried to copy everything she did. Still, while I admired Lauren as a performer, I knew inside that I was prettier. Lauren's look was "hard," like a Joan Crawford type: thick eyebrows and angular features, not soft and round like my look. She also had a bulbous Adam's apple, while I had none. Yet despite her flaws, Lauren was the best drag performer I'd ever seen.

My own royal progress to queenhood proceeded more slowly than I would have liked. My walk was my greatest flaw. Lauren and Jennifer worked with me for hours, back and forth across Lauren's kitchen floor, into the hallway, toward the living room, back to the kitchen.

"You have to get your hips into it," Lauren scolded.

"What on earth do you mean, you witch? My hips *are* in it!"

"Haven't you ever paid any attention to how women walk?"

"No. I'm gay, remember?"

"You're also hopeless. Now listen: You have to shift your weight back and forth from one side to the other, like this. See? Like doing figure eights with your hips."

Jennifer walked up behind me, put her hands on my hips and tried to move me in the right little circles. "Randi," she said disparagingly, "if anything gives you away as a boy, it's your walk. You've got to look as if you were born in pumps."

"Be patient, I'll get it eventually! And quit leering at my body, you depraved thing." After my best efforts failed ludicrously, Lauren, Jennifer, and I collapsed in laughter on the couch, a frantic jumble of arms, legs, blue jeans, men's T-shirts and ladies' pumps.

I did get better as time went on. And I enjoyed getting to know the other regular drag queens—bigger-than-life personalities who lit up the Ruby Slipper. But there was another kind of gay bar that unexpectedly provided the site of a major turning point in my drag career. On a cold Wednesday night in January 1984, Lauren phoned and asked me if I'd go with her down to Trade Winds for Quarter Beer Night.

"Trade Winds?" I screamed. "Are you kidding? Nobody goes to that smelly old leather bar. I was in there once with Parker a couple of years ago, and it was scary. They don't let drag queens in there, Lauren!"

She sighed impatiently. "Where have you been, girlfriend? Everybody goes there on Wednesdays now. It's a midweek ritual for all Columbus drag queens—the one night we get to go out as boys. Y'know, just for fun? We wear hiking boots, cutoff shorts, and baseball hats."

"OK, if you say so." We walked into the stark bar at the Trade Winds and onto its unfinished cement floor. Blown-up, black-and-white photos of tough-looking men on Harley-Davidsons sprawled across the walls. Explicit sexual drawings also adorned the surroundings. As we ambulated through the bar I thought I heard some familiar voices, but I didn't recognize anyone. Lauren told me plenty of queens I knew were there, but none of them had come in drag. As she pointed out a couple, it seemed so weird to see them unshaven with policeman's caps on—and with long, manicured fingernails.

All of them had one other thing in common: heavily plucked, highly arched eyebrows—which I hadn't yet let Lauren talk me into. I didn't want the feminine look those kinds of eyebrows gave a queen when she was out of drag. By keeping my nondrag face masculine, I could attract more men.

About an hour into our Trade Winds caper, I was flabbergasted to find that I was talking to Damara DeGenaro, the usually glamorous, wild-haired Black Queen of the Night. Without her sparkling eye shadow and spectacular costumes, Damara was a short, skinny man with a close-cropped Afro and a pock-marked face—a very ugly man beneath his customary mask of femininity.

For the first time I met Louie, much better known by her drag name, Gretchen Foster. I loved her instantly. Immediately entranced by each other's company, Gretchen and I chatted at the bar while Lauren and Jennifer flitted around. As we talked, Gretchen did express one reservation: "I simply can't understand why you chose Randi for a drag name. Something that boyish doesn't suit you at all."

"Actually I didn't choose it," I explained. "Sonya Ross pinned it on me the first time I performed on Amateur Night at the Ruby Slipper."

"Hmmm. I don't think she did well by you. Randi is too androgynous for someone so pretty. Have you ever considered changing it?"

"No . . .I don't know—what would you suggest?"

Gretchen gazed at the far wall for a few long seconds. "How about Candi? C-A-N-D-I Randi is dandy, but Candi is sweeter!" As I laughed, Gretchen added, "At least there's no mistaking which gender Candi is, right?" I agreed, then asked her how long she'd been doing drag.

"Forever," she said with a wry smile. "My whole life."

"How do you mean?"

"When I was eight I stole my sister's navy-blue-and-white-checkered school uniform, put it on, and rode my bike down the street."

"Did anyone give you trouble?"

"No, even then it was obvious to my family and everybody in the neighborhood that I had problems." Gretchen went on to tell me about her troubled life; there was no mistaking the soft undertones of resignation. "What I really want," she added, her voice brightening, "is *the change*. And what I need right now is a rich boyfriend who'll pay for the surgery." I had never before met anyone who truly desired sex-reassignment surgery. Lauren, Jennifer, and I did drag for fun, and we were happy being gay; Gretchen was a real, live "pre-op" transsexual. Getting to know her was really intriguing and even more fun than meeting other drag queens. Gretchen leaned forward and perused me carefully. "I've seen you a couple of times in drag at the Garage and the K. Can I be honest with you?"

"I guess so."

She ordered more beers for us and then continued. "I'm gonna be real frank with you. When I first saw you, I thought, *Oh, she's kind of pretty, but she looks too much like Lauren's younger sister.*"

"How's that?"

"When Lauren puts that nappy black wig on you and all that dark blue eye shadow and blood-red lipstick, she makes you look like a Mexican whore just off a banana boat."

I felt my face flush. "That's nasty, Gretchen. Aren't you being a little harsh?"

"Hey, I'm not telling you this to hurt your feelings. Listen. You shouldn't be a brunette at all, you should be a blond."

"A blond?"

"Absolutely! With your lovely skin tone, you'd definitely look much better." Then came her tantalizing offer: "Come to my house Saturday night, and I'll transform you from a Mexican tamale cook into a blond Hollywood ingenue who can climb over any casting couch."

I was sold, and we clanged beer mugs on the deal.

Of course, I never told Lauren about my plans. That weekend, Gretchen made me far more beautiful than I'd ever imagined was possible. Instead of harsh blue eye shadow, she applied soft browns, mauves, and pinks, completely softening my look. Then she gave me a soft, golden-blond wig, mostly straight but slightly curled on the end. She helped me put on all the hose and underwear I needed. Then she let me look in the mirror. I was amazed—Gretchen's work far exceeded Lauren's skills.

My eyes were radiant, their almond shapes accentuated with just the right amount of black eyeliner. Instead of bright red lipstick she had used a soft, frosted maroon. "Candi," she said, "you are absolutely gorgeous. But don't let it go to your head."

"I won't," I lied, while prancing around, doing my best hip-figure-eights in honor of the new me. Gretchen got herself ready, then we headed out the door. We stopped to pick up Velveeta before we headed downtown.

Velveeta—real name Kevin—was about five-five, slightly chunky, with striking slanted eyes and fair skin. I didn't find him particularly attractive, which was just as well. Lauren had told me about the unwritten code of drag queens: They don't get sexually involved with one another.

As we entered Imaginations, it became apparent that things had dramatically changed for me. People gave a lot of attention to the brand new and ravishing persona known as Candi.

It wasn't long before Lauren heard about my new look, and she was spitting mad. She couldn't believe that, behind her back, I had changed my name and adopted Gretchen as my new drag mother. For a long time, she refused to acknowledge that I existed. Jennifer ran back and forth between us, trying to patch things up. But nothing seemed to repair what Lauren considered the ultimate betrayal. Our friendship was over.

With my new look, I began noticing that most of the other drag queens weren't nearly as impressive as they had seemed at first. In fact, they looked very much like men on stage dressed as women. *Why is anyone paying these guys to look like that?* I wondered. Fat, hairy clowns with oversized eyelashes and clothes that never fit. One queen even had a huge wart on the end of his nose. Why did some people think they were so fantastic, hollering and waving their too-muscular arms hysterically about them?

I'll never become that kind of caricature, I vowed. Instead I determined to be the most skilled, beautiful, glamorous, elegant drag queen that Columbus had ever seen.

Nothing, absolutely nothing, would stand in my way.

TEN

ONE FRIDAY NIGHT at the Garage, Gretchen pointed out a poster in the lobby. In a week the bar was holding a Miss Ingenue contest. "I think you're ready for it, Candi," she said. "They're competing in sportswear and evening gowns, and I have all kinds of ideas. . . ." As she babbled excitedly, I decided she was right: I was ready. My walk was smooth and flowing, my look ravishing. I'd even developed a convincing impersonation of a woman's voice. So we filled out an entry blank and gave it to the bartender.

"What do I do now?" I wondered aloud.

"Don't worry about a thing, sweetie," Gretchen said. "Leave everything to me."

On Monday she called me. "Time to get busy on your wardrobe for the pageant. I know the perfect outfit. Velvecta has a hot, zebra-striped jumper that will be gorgeous. It's looow cut, has lots of gathers, and drapes on each side of the waist. We can tease your hair out savagely and put on bright red lipstick. You'll be a supervixen!"

"Hold it, Gretchen, I'm a conservative queen. Doesn't that getup sound awfully wild?"

"Get over yourself, Missy. Don't I know who you are? Let's go out and find you an evening gown. I know exactly where."

The next night, Gretchen and I walked into her favorite store and combed through racks of long evening dresses. Suddenly she nearly screamed with excitement. "Candi, get over here right away!"

"Calm down," I hissed.

"Look! Lemon yellow, maure taffeta with spaghetti straps—it's perfect! Size twelve, and only thirty-two dollars."

"Gretchen, you know I don't have that kind of money. And I can't wear spaghetti straps. I'm not shaving my underarms—for you or anybody else!"

"Would you stop? I'll buy the dress—and I have ways to hide your bony shoulders and stinky pits." That week Gretchen gathered the rest of my outfit: rhinestone earrings, necklace and bracelet, white satin pumps (to complement the yellow evening gown), and black pumps to go with the zebra-striped pantsuit (for the sportswear competition).

The big night finally arrived. I sat patiently as Gretchen painstakingly applied my makeup and teased my wig to a perfection of soft, golden-blond curls that encircled my shoulders. "I'm purposely designing your hair so a tiara can sit on it," she told me.

"Sure, like I'm really gonna win my first pageant."

"Candi, you will win. You're a gorgeous drag queen, so get over yourself."

"You're making me nervous. Let's get out of here and down to the bar."

When Gretchen, Velveeta, and I arrived at the Garage, we discovered that more than thirty drag queens had signed up to compete. Some I knew: Damara DeGenaro, Lana Davis, Anita Peters, and Erica Daniels. And Lauren, of course, who still wasn't speaking to me. We laid our gear out in the dressing room area.

As Gretchen and Velveeta got me ready, the pageant coordinator came in and quickly bellowed the rules to everyone: "You girls will each parade past the four judges, first in your sportswear outfits and then your evening gowns. Oh, and you'll also have to answer a question," she added. "Be witty—and good luck, girls!"

I was nervous as a shrew. As I zipped up Velveeta's pantsuit, I asked her to run and get me two double Scotches on the rocks. I gulped them down as soon as she brought them. By the time it was my turn, a roaring buzz was careening through my head. I had trouble keeping my knees together as I walked past the judges' table, but I wasn't too woozy, and I got a lot of applause.

Then Velveeta got me two more Scotches as I changed into the snug, buttercup-yellow evening gown. In addition to my large rhinestone earrings, bracelet, and necklace, I wore a huge cocktail ring on my right hand. Gretchen fixed me up with a short, white taffeta bolero evening jacket to cover my shoulders and hairy underarms. Tiny rhinestones encrusted the jacket, so when the spotlight hit it I would sparkle and shine like a shower of stars.

By the time I lined up for the gown competition I was starting to see stars—blurry ones. I heard loud, dizzy applause as I paraded by the judges.

You've drunk much more than you need to take the edge off, I thought as I struggled to walk straight.

I stood at the far end of the floor with the rest of the girls until they announced five finalists. The emcee called out one at a time, each to rabid hoots and cheers: "Finalist number one, Denita Daroe! Number two, Damara DeGenaro! Number three, Jonda St. John! Number four, Lauren Stevens! And number five . . . Candi!" My heart pounded as the applause soared, and I walked forward. I had done it—I was a finalist in my first pageant! As I glanced aside, I smiled smugly at the nonfinalists walking off the floor, smarting disgusted glares. *Eat your heart out, witch,* I thought as I gloated a big, fake smile at Lauren. "Hi, Mish Shtevens," I slurred, "don'tshou look lovely tonight!"

"You too, Candi. Who'd you steal the gown from?"

"Jealoush?"

"Of that K-Mart special?"

"You should look sho good in your wildesht dreamsh, witsch!"

The mistress of ceremonies walked up with a hand mike and announced, "Now, ladies and gentlemen, I'll ask each of our finalists a question to judge their poise. We'll begin at the far end with Damara!" By the time she got to me, I vaguely remembered that she'd asked all the girls the same query, but I couldn't remember what it was or what they'd said, and I didn't have any prepared answer of my own.

"Tell us, Candi," the emcee said, "if you're crowned Miss Ingenue 1984, how will you serve the gay community of Columbus?"

I flipped up my left wrist and slurped out, "Well, Mish Thing, can we talk, can we talk?" I was trying to be catty-witty, but I was barely articulate, and no one laughed. I heard myself giggle and hiccup as I took a woozy step back, "Oh, Mish Thing, I'll sherve Columbush by shpreading love and joy around to all my friendzh and loved onezh!"

Boy, was that lame, I thought. I tried to cover my lack of savoir-faire, but nearly fell on my face. The emcee helped me back to my feet while people laughed and applauded. Stewed as I was, I knew I had embarrassed myself. *But so what? It doesn't really matter what I said. I'm beautiful, and my sheer beauty will win it for me.*

The judges had us parade once more so they could calculate audience applause. I exaggerated my figure eights in a ludicrous attempt to conceal the fact that I was nearly staggering. Nonetheless, it quickly became clear from the applause that the winner was to be either Lauren or me. Soon enough, the emcee announced the decision: "The First runner-up is . . . Candi!"

I stepped forward, trying to keep my balance and feeling more than a little humiliated. "And the winner, and Miss Ingenue 1984, is . . . Lauren Stevens!"

Lauren deserved to win. She'd been doing drag a lot longer. She'd stayed sober, kept her composure, and evidently given a bright answer to the big question. Still, I hadn't shown badly for a first-time contestant—and a drunk one at that. And even though I'd lost, I had enjoyed the audience's applause and the attention I was attracting as Columbus's fastest-rising drag queen star. So I applauded fervently as the emcee placed the rhinestone tiara on Lauren's head, threw a satin sash over her shoulders, and handed her a bouquet of long-stemmed roses. I stumbled up to her; gave her a big, wet kiss on the lips; and slurred her fond nickname at her. "Congratulationzh, Latrine, you dezherve it, honey."

"Thanks, Candi," she said. "Why don't you show up sober next time?" She laughed and kissed me back in a way that told me, "Maybe we should let bygones be bygones, girl. We can still be friends if you like." As I weaved off the dance floor, Lauren took off her tiara, put down the roses, and burst into a torrid song-and-dance rendition of "Let's Hear It for the Boy" amid a loud ovation.

Next morning, as I reflected on the events of the night before, I reached an important decision: I was not going to compete in any more beauty pageants. It seemed obvious that if I hadn't been drunk out of my gourd, I would have won last night's pageant hands down. But maybe it was better that I hadn't won. If I had reached the top on my very first try, there would be nowhere to go but down. I knew I could be really great at these competitions, but were they worth the effort? The whole business was just too frenetic and stressful.

Instead, I decided to do something utterly unprecedented: I would become a unique drag queen, different from all the others. I would demonstrate unquestionably that I had no competition—by avoiding competition altogether! After all, every other queen in Columbus was cut from the same mold: They all did drag shows, entered pageants, and fought over titles and tiaras. They all felt they had to wear crowns and possess the trappings of majesty to prove they were "real" queens.

Well, I was obviously the queen without any of those trappings. I didn't need them. To my knowledge, I was already the only drag queen in central

Ohio who went solely by a stand-alone first name. I didn't even need a drag surname. So I would be more than a mere entertainer; I would be the eternal bar queen, the personality every gay person in Columbus knew, loved, laughed with, and admired. I would be the final gay-bar party favor and more. Why shouldn't I, when no one else possibly could?

Meanwhile I continued my therapy sessions with Howard. As we went deeper into my psyche, I began realizing that, despite my growing weekend popularity as an infamous drag queen, my life still suffered from a perplexing duality. On the outside I seemed happy and content enough; my nights were filled with friends and thrills. But on the inside I sometimes sensed that I, John, was slowly disintegrating. Candi was beginning to replace my real identity as John. The woman in me seemed to be devouring my masculinity.

I began eagerly awaiting each session with Howard; they seemed to be the only times when I could be something like my true self and tell someone who I really was. Still, I was afraid to tell Howard the whole truth about myself: my compulsion to dress in drag, my increasing tendency to drink, and especially my summer of wild escort escapades.

I was working full time at the copy shop during the day, but my personal finances continued to worsen. Used to a rather free-spending lifestyle from escort earnings, now I worked for little more than minimum wage, yet I refused to cut back on expenses. I started to write bad checks, and soon the gas company turned me off again. So, in the middle of winter, I had no hot water or heat for my apartment.

In my sad plight, Susan pitied me, and I took every advantage of her trust. I knew where she kept her bank card, and I knew her security code. On my way out to the bars, I'd borrow her bank card and siphon money from her checking account. The next morning I'd slip the card back into her wallet. I also snuck into her apartment from time to time and filched dresses so I'd have new things to wear to my latest drag appearances. Susan must have been wounded by my treachery, but she never reproached me for it. Whenever I got really down, she'd let me cry on her shoulder. Then she'd feed me dinner and let me sleep on her couch, since it was freezing in my apartment.

On rare occasions I'd go to the bars as John, just to assure myself that I could still attract men. But most of the time, I went out socially as Candi. As a drag queen I kept a very strict ethical code: I always enjoyed myself socially, but I never looked for sexual partners.

As Candi I wanted to be gregarious and admired, always the center of attention, but not desired sexually. In fact, I considered abnormal any gay man drawn to me sexually while I was in drag. Deep down, though I felt light and free as Candi, her popularity didn't satisfy my inner longing to be loved for who I really was. What I wanted, most and always, was for a man to love and desire me for what I looked like and who I was as a man.

So this was my constant conflict. On the weekends as Candi, I was glamorous, funny, and sophisticated, with laughing "groupies" following me everywhere. Yet I felt unloved for myself. During the week I was John, increasingly empty and unwanted, realizing that even Candi couldn't meet my desperate longing for love from a man.

So my sessions with Howard seemed my only solace. They alone provided me with temporary escape from both my insufficient identities. These conflicting aspects of my personality puzzled me to no end, but I had no idea how to explain them to Howard without telling him more about myself than I wanted him to know.

Gretchen, Velveeta, and I graduated to dropping acid nearly every Friday and Saturday night. I thought LSD was the most wonderful drug of all. Not only did it give me a euphoria I'd never known, it didn't seem to have any irritating side effects. It didn't bring me down, give me the "munchies," put me out of touch with reality (too much), or slur my speech. My world looked a lot brighter when I did acid. Best of all, on acid, Candi felt like a genuine woman.

Once, on acid at the Ruby Slipper, I walked into the ladies' room, took out my lip gloss wand, gazed into the mirror and began massaging my lips with it, around and around. I stared into my reflected eyes, marveling at my lovely, tanned, blond image. Candi batted her eyelashes back at me, looking deeper and deeper into my soul. *You are so beautiful,* she said, *a stunning creature. Truly breathtaking.* At the same time, another inner voice taunted me: *John, you're nothing, a vacuum. Just a shell.*

That night I told myself, "When my mother dies—but only when she dies—maybe I will pursue getting a sex change. Why should I torture myself forever, continually coming down from the glorious feeling of being Candi? Being John is just too painful; Candi is who I really want to be. In fact, isn't Candi my real personality—outgoing, gregarious, with no inhibitions?"

One night, Candi bumped into Howard at Imaginations. He had no idea who I really was, and I decided to tell him the truth at my next appointment.

I squirmed a bit on the couch before letting it out: "Howard, there's something I have to let you know. I'm a drag queen. In fact, I'm Candi."

Howard jumped a little in his chair. "My gosh, I'd never have known it! Why, I saw you just last week at Imaginations. I've been hearing about you for months. I think you're absolutely beautiful."

I could tell he meant it, and I was touched close to tears that he thought so. "Thank you, I really appreciate it . . . and . . . and that you know but you're not rejecting me."

"Reject you—why would I? But tell me. How did you ever get to be Candi?"

I told him what had happened, and before long we were discussing some of my possible underlying motivations for doing drag.

"Howard, I guess the main reason I do Candi is that I'm good at her. And I've never really felt as good at being anything else." Howard nodded, but I could sense he wasn't totally persuaded by my oversimplification. At the same time, I wasn't eager to hear any deeper conjectures he might have. I cherished three things in life right then—drag, drinking, and dropping acid—and I wasn't about to become sane enough to give up any of the three.

Nevertheless, the revelation that I was Candi began opening new doors for Howard and me to talk in greater depth about my relationship with my mom and dad. Part of my inner turmoil, Howard said, must have to do with my upbringing and my relationship with my parents. Until we resolved some of those issues, I would probably continue to feel conflict within myself. Would I be willing to trust him enough to explore those kinds of issues? I said I would.

As we probed my past in coming weeks, Howard and I went deeper into my history of feeling abandoned by my father, the admiration and resentment I felt toward my mother, my childhood feelings of rejection by the world around me, and the self-rejection with which my past had injected me. "You have to start learning to accept your father as the person he is," Howard said, "someone who has reacted negatively toward you out of his own hurts and rejections in his growing-up years." Conceptually that made sense, but at the moment I couldn't imagine laying aside the rage toward him and the hurt I felt inside. I told Howard that I didn't know how, but maybe my feelings toward my father might change someday. In the meantime, I felt good as a drag queen, but lousy out of drag. Howard said he was willing to work through those issues with me if I was willing.

For the time being, I made up my mind that drag was where I would continue to spend my quality time. That decision made, I concentrated on drag like a craftsman. I bought glamour magazines and analyzed the models on every page: how they carried themselves, how they dressed and wore their makeup, their eyebrow shapes, their eye shadow colors, their lip shapes, the way they wore their blush, their hair—all to learn what made them so feminine and beautiful.

Then, in the bars I studied feminine women: How they moved, held their drinks, stood, walked, sat, crossed their legs, and held cigarettes. I asked myself questions: How do women drink beer—from bottles or glasses? Do they drink cocktails with their lips or through straws? How do they powder their noses, hold their purses? Do they toss their hair, or run their fingers through it? There were endless details to observe. But I didn't want to be a mere caricature, or even a superb illusion, of a woman. I wanted to be the real thing, indistinguishable from the most feminine woman alive.

Susan was disgusted at my drag habit and eventually showed signs of being furious about my shameless thievery. Her anger and revulsion caused our relationship to deteriorate rapidly. One night I came home in drag and heard a party going on in her apartment, so I went up and knocked on her door. She opened it and screamed, "Get away from here!" Then she slapped my face. Through my stinging lips I seethed, "Hit me all you want. I'm still prettier than you'll ever be!" I got my pert nose out of the way just before she slammed the door.

Undeterred by waning friendships or advancing therapy at this point, I continued to hone my drag skills to the degree that I began thinking about making moves into society at large. I was passable enough as a woman in gay circles; could I also fool people in the straight world? To find out, I started taking walks in straight neighborhoods, even flirting with straight men. It gave my ego a huge boost to make a man vulnerable, to put him on my level, to know he was begging for my body.

Though as John Paulk I preferred gay men, when I was portraying a woman, there was something in Candi that desired intimacy with straight men. And being Candi was the only way I could get straight men's attention, even if I gained it solely on phony premises.

I assessed the jeopardy I might be putting myself in: At the least I risked being beaten to a pulp by straight men for impersonating a woman; at worst, I could be killed for my masquerade. But the excitement of trying to attract straight men was irresistible—once I was fortified enough with alcohol and/ or acid to venture out into the streets.

One night I headed toward the "strip" near my apartment where straight men often looked for cheap female companionship. I'd had a great time in drag earlier in the evening with Jennifer, Gretchen, and Velveeta. They'd dropped me off at my place, but I was still flying high on acid and was anything but sleepy. I thought, *You worked too long and hard tonight to transform yourself into a beautiful woman to waste this great buzz and your perfect looks just stripping out of drag and bedding down.*

As I sauntered down the street, cars gunned their engines and guys leaned out, honking at me. "Hey, babe," yelled one guy, and his friends whistled approvingly. Several men driving alone pulled over by my side of the road, rolled down their car windows, and tried to pick me up.

That night I was wearing a teal-blue rayon skirt, a white T-shirt and a matching teal-blue jacket with three-quarter-length sleeves. My blond wig was combed smoothly back and fell gently around my shoulders. I was the very portrait of an Ohio State sorority girl. Using my most feminine voice, I gave them all a demure, good-little-girl routine: "Why in the world do you want to talk to me?" I felt in complete control. I alone would choose if, when, and with whom I would have sex.

I could see my golden-blond locks sparkle in the overhead streetlight glare as I passed Papa Joe's bar. A few male customers still stood outside on the sidewalk, smoking and nursing beer bottles. As I swayed toward these guys, I locked eyes with one blond hunk and fluttered my eyelids at him. *He's interested in me,* I thought. *I think I'll play with him.*

After I'd walked a couple of yards, I turned my head slowly and looked over my left shoulder. He was watching me, all right. I raised my left eyebrow, smiled just slightly, turned my head away, and threw the slightest bit more hip roll into my walk. Soon I heard footsteps closing in, and I reached the corner just as the stoplight changed red. Perfect! Now he'd catch up with me. A few seconds later, his tall, lean frame sidled level with my right hip. His tousled blond hair advertised a night of hard bar-hopping, his face boyish enough to be a college student's.

"How's it going?" he asked.

I faced him slowly and looked him straight in the eyes. "What's it to you?"

"Don't mean to bug you," he said, raising his palms up by his shoulders apologetically. "Just trying to be friendly. What's your name?"

"Gretchen" was the first that came to mind and mouth.

"How'd you like to come over to my place for a beer, Gretchen?"

"Oh, I can't—I'm on my way home."

His eyes widened with anticipation. "Well, could I walk you home, then?"

"No, I don't think that would be proper. My boyfriend wouldn't like it."

"Oh, you have a boyfriend." His face drooped.

"Yes, I do," I said softly and sweetly, "and he doesn't like strange men coming on to me."

"Do I look strange to you?"

"No comment, sir," I said. He flipped his head to shift his unruly bangs over his left eye. I noticed the light had turned green, and I started walking across the street. I gave him just a hint of my profile and said, "Good night." I heard his footsteps head in the opposite direction and breathed a huge sigh of relief. What if he'd tried to pressure me to go home with him? I wanted to attract him but not quite that close!

I walked down to Fifteenth Avenue, stopped and let myself sag against a brick wall for a few moments. Then I took a slightly roundabout way home. Now that the tension had broken, I did feel a strange euphoria. I'd gotten at least one straight man very interested in me tonight! That made the evening a smashing success. But it would be some time before I put myself through such a nerve-wracking ordeal again.

Several weeks later, Parker called me, obviously distressed. His relationship with Don had gotten so bad he couldn't take it anymore. Could he stay with me until he found his own place? I told him that would be fine. Actually, it would be a huge break for both of us. My leased furniture had been repossessed, and I had no idea how I was going to pay the landlady. "You're just in time," I said heartily. "My whole dining room is empty, just waiting for you to move in. Besides, you can pay half the rent, if that's all right." We decided he'd move in that weekend. I was thrilled that he'd broken up with Don; I hated to see him hurt.

He moved into the dining room, where his things fit snugly but comfortably. It turned out our work schedules coordinated perfectly for minimal friction: Parker worked evenings as a hospital orderly downtown, coming home around eleven o'clock, just about the time I went to bed weeknights. Parker was quiet, he didn't have a host of noisy friends, and I thought I was doing him a grand favor by letting him move in.

Thankfully, Parker paid the deposit on the gas bill, so I had hot water again. Plus, I had someone to keep me company. Parker was a breeze to live with because he already knew my habits and quirks and I knew his. We had only one small problem. As the weeks passed, Parker showed signs of having difficulty dealing with my drag life. But generally nothing I ever did could really shock him, so things stayed cool.

It was April 13, 1984. Gretchen, Velveeta, Allen (a new friend), and Jennifer took me out to the Garage to celebrate my twenty-first birthday. We decided not to go in drag, because I told them I was hoping to find a birthday trick. On the way I dropped the first acid I'd ever taken as John, not Candi.

The evening passed pleasurably, and we bantered and danced ourselves into the new day. About 2 A.M. Jennifer disappeared, but the rest of us continued on, tripping our brains out. Rhonda Real, another drag friend, slipped me two more hits of acid via French kiss after Jennifer left, so I was now soaring on three hits of blotter—one more than I'd ever dropped before.

Gretchen and I were gyrating on the dance floor when my eye caught a man, standing alone in a corner of the bar, who looked like he'd just ridden a horse off a Marlboro billboard. About six-three, with a muscular build that wouldn't quit, he seemed rock-solid—as if Michelangelo had just finished chiseling him from marble. I elbowed Gretchen. "See that man over there? I'd crawl through broken glass without a stitch for him."

"You'd crawl through broken glass for a new pair of pumps."

"Oh, quit!"

Mr. Marlboro approached the dance floor and rested his sinewy arms on the railing. On three hits of acid I had no inhibitions whatsoever. I walked right over to him, flashed a huge smile, and told him it was my birthday. Before long I was saying goodbye to Gretchen and the other girls. Mr. Marlboro put me on the back of his Harley-Davidson outside, wrapped my arms around his chest, and roared down North High Street to my apartment.

Parker was away, so we had perfect privacy. The rest of that night was one of the most passionate experiences I'd ever enjoyed. After Mr. Marlboro fell asleep next to me, I lay wide awake, still excited and tripping. As the night's blackness turned to gray, I snuggled close, wrapped inside his arms.

Tonight I'll be going out with my mom to celebrate my birthday in a whole different way, I thought. *Life with my family is a totally strange existence.* Even thinking about it was like watching a movie of someone else's life. Or was gay life the movie? I wasn't sure anymore.

As the night's acid wore off and my own weariness inevitably wore on, I felt a sense of remorse. I'd hidden a lot of my life from my family, especially from my mother. There was so much we'd never talked about. She would probably be devastated if she knew about this other life of mine. I was gay, that was obvious, and I would never be any different. But I couldn't help wondering: What might my life be like if I hadn't been drawn to men, if I had never gone to the K when I was eighteen, if my life had by some stroke of fate taken an entirely different course?

I had always wanted boys to like me when I was little. Well, now I was "one of the boys," though in a totally different way from what I'd imagined. I had found my niche in the gay world. Forces utterly beyond my own control had brought me to this point, and I was making the best of it. And life wasn't perfect for anyone, was it?

I must have drifted off to sleep again, because suddenly a crack of sunshine was stabbing my half-closed eyes. I opened them full and saw the Marlboro Man, standing by my bed, dressed and waiting to say goodbye. He leaned down, brushed the hair off my face and gave me a lingering kiss on the lips. "Happy birthday," he said. "Hope last night was a present you'll never forget."

"You bet I won't!" I moaned, in my still raspy voice.

Mr. Marlboro grabbed his denim jacket and gave me a quick wave as he walked out the bedroom door. I could hear his footsteps tap down the stairs. His motorcycle roared to life, loud at first, then fainter as he sped off into the distance. Another handsome stranger had come and gone. I'd enjoyed our time together, never fooling myself that we'd have a relationship. I suppose that was progress of sorts for me—at last I was able to fully enjoy sex without a smidgen of love.

That night, my new friend Allen joined Mom and me for a birthday celebration at Lindy's, one of our favorite restaurants. He winked at me when my mother said I was now old enough to order hard liquor. Soon we ordered dinner and sipped a first round of rusty nails. Our conversation was light and fun, but I was quaking inside. For weeks Allen—and Howard—had been urging me to tell my mother about my homosexuality. Allen had decided that this, my birthday night, was the perfect occasion, and I knew he was bound to spring the subject sometime before we left the table. At last, over after-dinner drinks, Allen could wait no longer. "John, isn't there something you want to tell your mother?"

My throat turned dry. Mom's whole attention focused on me as our eyes met.

"Yes, well . . ." I stuttered, "there is something I've been wanting to tell you for a long time." I swallowed hard and went on. "But I've been afraid . . . of how you'd react." I could feel my heart pounding.

"What is it, John?" My mother smiled warmly.

"Mom, I . . . I'm gay." The whole world seemed to go into slow motion as the words came from my mouth. "I felt like I needed to tell you. I want you to know who I really am."

My mother extended her right hand across the table and rested it on top of my left, her eyes never leaving mine. "I knew you were gay, John." Her voice was very soft and gentle. "I never talked about it because I was waiting for you to tell me. I knew it was something you alone would know when you were ready."

Instantly I felt immensely relieved. I had done it somehow, and I was still alive and breathing! Allen leaned back, his arms folded and eyes gleaming with anticipation.

But there was still one important question I felt I had to ask my mother. "Please, tell me the truth. How do you feel about it, Mom?" I held my breath, waiting for her reply.

She looked at me steadily. "John, you are my only son. Nothing you could ever do or ever be could make me love you any less." She paused, her eyes misted over, and she glanced down at the table. "I may not completely like the fact that you're gay, but that's who you are. I want to keep having a relationship with you, and that means I need to accept you for what and who you are. But being gay is a lonely existence, John. I do worry about who'll take care of you when you're old."

I was happy with her answer—and her honesty. And I could scarcely believe the tenderness, the true unconditional love and acceptance that throbbed so obviously beneath her words. She hadn't thrown a fit or grown hysterical. She was concerned, but she wasn't angry, horrified, or sick about my gayness. She accepted me. I decided that I would always treasure her response in my heart and remember her every word and draw strength from those words in the days and years ahead.

Smiling calmly, she said again, "John, I will always love you, no matter what." I knew she was leaving no room for doubt that she meant it completely. I didn't resent her remark about my growing old; that eventuality seemed far from my present youth and vivacity. I appreciated her concern. It was about me. She did care. All of the hidden resentment my heart had held toward her seemed to dissolve in those moments.

Suddenly Allen emitted a volcanic sigh; he seemed even more relieved than me. "Well, that's over with," he chirped. "Let's have another drink." He snapped his fingers for a waiter, and we all switched to Cape Cods.

My mother and I never talked about my homosexuality again; she seemed to accept it as a given in my life. She graciously accepted my gay friends, even inviting them over to dinner with me on Sunday nights. Coming out to my mother made it easier for me to let her into my life and tell her more about what was happening to me. I never told her, though, about my escort experiences, nor the fact that I was a drag queen.

ELEVEN

A T MY NEXT SESSION with Howard, he asked me how my relationship with my father was going. I told him I'd be able to give him a better answer at our next session. I reminded Howard that this was the weekend I was flying with my mom and grandmother to Portland, Oregon—where Dad now lived—for my sister Vicky's high-school graduation. This would be the first time I'd seen my dad in a couple of years, and I was anxious about it. A year previous, Dad and Nancy had divorced, and Dad plummeted into months of deep depression. But slowly he began pulling himself out. Now, after Vicky's graduation, Dad and I were supposed to drive together to Reno, Nevada, with his new girlfriend.

"I'm scared about the whole thing," I told Howard. "I'm not sure I want to be alone with him after we've been apart so long. You know how, whenever I'm with him, I feel reduced to a bumbling imbecile."

"Just try to relax and enjoy yourself," Howard advised. "Concentrate on being happy for your sister. She's the main reason you're going. And John, I think it's good that you'll be spending some time with your dad. You're changing, and you'll probably find that he's changed some, too."

Howard was right on all counts. Vicky's graduation was wonderful. She was valedictorian of her class, and I was very proud of her. In the fall, she'd be going to Georgetown University. My little sister had finally grown up. And so, it seemed to me, had my dad, just as Howard had predicted. Being around Dad did make me self-aware about some of the effeminate mannerisms I'd acquired since we'd last seen each other. But they didn't seem to bother him— at least, he said nothing derogatory about me.

Following Vicky's graduation, Dad and I spent several hours together alone in his apartment the night before I was to fly back to Columbus. I was pleased to find his company more comfortable than ever. We thumbed through old photo albums, reminisced about my growing up, about our trips to the Park of the Roses, about picnics, and camping. Dad was gentle and affectionate, and I really wished for more time. I felt closer to him than I ever had before.

The next morning we stood near the check-in counter at the airport. I was choking back tears. "Dad, can you come to the gate with me?"

"John, I can't," he said, barely above a whisper. "Goodbyes are too hard for me. Let me just leave you here, if it's all right." Tears dropped from his eyes as he hugged me tightly. Tears streamed down my face, too, as I watched him disappear and then walked to the gate alone. I had some time to spare, so I went to a pay phone and called Parker to see how he'd been during the week I'd been gone. It didn't take me long to find out.

"Where are you? And what the heck have you been up to?" I had never heard such venom in Parker's usually soothing voice.

"I've been in Portland. Geez, what's wrong?"

"You have to ask me? Two days ago, the door banged—loud. Two straight guys. They asked me if Susan was available. They weren't very happy."

My throat was instantly dry. I had become increasingly reckless in drag. One night during the previous week, after coming home drunk, I'd had some sexual play with two guys outside my apartment building. They had no idea of my true gender; I'd told them I was "Susan"—the first name that popped into my head when they asked.

Of course, I hadn't breathed a word of this "adventure" to Parker, who continued yelling at me. "Did you know they live in our building? They found out you're a guy! They told me you had sex with them the other night and said you were Susan. They came to our door so they could beat you up."

"Parker, I'm so sorry. Did they do anything to you?"

"They almost broke the door down before I convinced them you were out of town and I wasn't your lover."

"Parker, how can I apologize enough—"

"You can't. Why can't you keep your crazy, screwed-up life separate from mine? I'm sick to death of this crap. I'm sick of coming home from work five nights a week and seeing your stinking drag makeup strewn all over my bathroom. I'm sick of you locking yourself out of the apartment, walking up the fire escape, flinging up the window, and bringing streams of drag queens traipsing through my room. I'm sick of your wild acid trips and your total irresponsibility. I can't take it anymore. I'm moving out."

I was immediately panic-stricken. "Oh, no, please don't go. Wait till I get home. We can work this out."

"Forget it, John. Your lifestyle is too crazy for me. I'm moving in with my brother." The phone clicked dead. I was trembling all over. I felt so ashamed, embarrassed, and sorry for what I'd done.

Six hours later I opened the door to my apartment. The dining room was empty; all of Parker's belongings were gone. My stupidity had forced Parker—the only constant I'd ever had in my gay life—to walk out on me. I put my suitcase down and sat on the floor, my head in my hands. And what about Susan? I'd gotten her involved in this, too. How was I going to face her? Once, I had been Susan's knight in shining armor, her trusted friend. Now I had betrayed her trust in a multitude of ways, even to the lowest depths of using her name to have sex with two strangers. I unpacked my clothes mechanically, thinking only that I needed to get to a bar and get blind drunk to numb the pain. When I had finished unpacking, I walked all the way to the K, found a seat in the darkest corner of the bar, and lined up a half-dozen double Scotches.

Through the smoke-filled air, I stared at my reflection in the dirty bar mirror for what seemed like hours. *What an utter, complete failure you are,* I thought. *I hate who you are, I hate everything about you.* I wondered if I could somehow rig some sort of IV to my arm and fill my veins with an endless stream of Scotch on the rocks, so I'd never have to come back down to reality. It was obvious my life was now completely out of control. What had happened to the values I had once held? What had happened to my belief that sex and love should be inextricably linked together? What had happened to my friendships? Why did I feel like I needed to drink all the time to make myself feel better? What had happened to that innocent boy named John Paulk? What was left for me but mere survival, pushing on forward day by day, lay by lay? What was I good at anyway? What did I have that I could hold on to? Candi was all I had, the only good part of me, and she wasn't even real.

I swallowed another Scotch, wobbled off the barstool, hitched a ride back to my apartment, and stumbled up the stairs. By my bed I found a half-pack of cigarettes some trick must have left and lit one up to calm my nerves. I noticed a piece of unopened mail on the end table. The return address read Office of Admissions, Ohio State University. I fumbled with the envelope and finally got it open. The combined grades from my last two quarters were so bad they weren't going to admit me again. One more failure. I wadded up the paper and tossed it at the wall. I reached into my pocket for my keys, which included one to Susan's apartment. I entered her place and found her in bed, her eyes shut. "Susan," I whispered, "it's John. Are you asleep?"

"Not anymore. What do you want?"

"I know you must be furious with me. But would you mind if I slept on the couch tonight? I'm feeling really lousy."

"I'm too tired to throw you out. There's a blanket at the foot of my bed." She turned over, breathing a sigh that smelled like slightly stale toothpaste.

"Thanks. Good night." I reached over and kissed her on the forehead. I bounced from wall to wall down the hallway to the kitchen. In the furthest cupboard on the right I found a bottle of Scotch I'd stashed there long ago "for my bad nights." I unscrewed the cap and swigged at it, not even bothering to look for a glass. In a few moments my body seemed to go into a kind of automatic pilot. I sat down on the floor, reading over and over again, "Hiram Walker, Hiram Walker, Hiram . . ." Every now and then I took another pull on the bottle. I relished the Scotch's sear in my throat and sting in my nasal cavities.

Then, without thinking, I used the wall to pull myself to my feet. I drifted into Susan's bathroom and set the Scotch bottle on the lowered toilet seat lid. I opened the medicine cabinet and reached for Susan's plastic bottle of Midrin. TAKE ONE ONLY FOR HEADACHE, the label said. I took one, then gazed at the rest of the bottle. Still holding the Midrin, I closed the medicine chest and caught sight again of my reflection in the mirror. A rage of self-loathing seethed through me. I took the bottle and emptied the contents into my right hand, admiring the pile of shiny, dark, blood-red pills. I brought my right hand to my mouth and deposited the pills onto my tongue. They filled my mouth full with their gelatin smoothness. Two forced swigs of Scotch rammed the lot down my throat.

I looked at myself in the mirror. I felt nothing. *So this is what it feels like to die.* I turned off the bathroom light, threw the pill bottle into the sink, gripped the Scotch bottle tightly, swayed into the living room, and plumped down on the couch. I was drifting, . . . drifting, . . . watching the digital clock in front of me slowly change green numbers.

As the moment 3:29 dissolved into 3:30, a sudden wave of shock rose to my throat. A voice deep within me seemed to say, *"You don't really want to die, John. What you really want is to be rescued. Someone to help you, someone to be there for you, someone to love you and care for you."*

Could it be God? I wondered. God? How profoundly embarrassing it would be to call for His aid now. But I did recall hearing about suicide hotlines. Through the blur, I spotted Susan's phone near the couch and, with difficulty, managed to dial 0.

It took awhile, but I persuaded the operator who came on to connect me with someone who answered, "Suicide Prevention." I wasn't very cooperative with the counselor, but he tried to find out from some books whether I'd taken a lethal dose of Midrin—especially in conjunction with the quantity of Scotch I'd drank. When he'd located the drug in his reference book, he told me what some of its physical effects might be if I lived. I thanked him sarcastically. He did persuade me to go and dump the rest of the bottle of Scotch while he waited on the line. When I got back he asked if I had a relative or girlfriend they might call. I told him I didn't want to talk to any relatives, and I had no girlfriend. "I'm a queer," I said. At last I gave him Dr. Bryant's name and the number where I was.

Howard called a few minutes later. After ascertaining that I still had some presence of mind, he said, "John, I would feel a whole lot better if you'd let me call an ambulance and let them have a look at you, just to make sure you're OK."

"No," I mouthed. "I have no insurance, no money. I don't want a big scene here—flashing ambulance lights, the whole neighborhood waking up."

"You might have considered that before you took the pills."

"Spare me, will you? My only regret is not being in full drag, wearing a black dress, rhinestones, and a Marilyn Monroe wig. I'd like to be remembered that way. Who knows? Properly dressed I might have gone through with it."

"If you won't let me call an ambulance, at least Suicide Prevention suggests trying to make yourself throw up. Mix some dish detergent and warm water, drink it, and you should vomit. Then let me call you back."

I agreed to try, but I couldn't even swallow a sip of the sickening mixture. Howard rang again. I told him I hadn't vomited, and he said, "Don't worry. I've just called a doctor friend, and he doubts that you've taken a fatal dose. You're probably safe to just lie down and sleep if off. We're pretty sure you'll wake up tomorrow." In any event, I felt myself fast fading toward oblivion and figured I no longer had any choice but to fall asleep, whether I ever woke up again or not.

Howard's voice broke through my daze: "John, I want you to know I do care about you and what happens to you. You're important to me. Sleep that drug out of your system and call me tomorrow. I want you to come first thing in the afternoon and see me." I hung up the phone, collapsed onto the couch, and instantly passed out.

Many hours later, I awoke. Someone's hands were clutching at my shoulders, shaking me violently. Then I heard Susan's voice, rife with desperation. "John, will you please wake up?" With the greatest difficulty I forced my eyes open; it felt as though they'd been glued shut.

Susan's face sagged with relief. "It's past eleven, and I've been trying to wake you for an hour. You look horrible. What in the world have you done to yourself?"

"Hmm?"

"A Dr. Bryant is on the phone."

I slowly sat up and pried my lips apart. "Could I have a glass of water?" My tongue felt like a slug sliming out from under a rock. Susan nodded and walked toward the kitchen. I tried but failed to stand up. My head felt four feet thick. I glanced down at my arms. They were bright red and flushed; all my pores looked puffy and bloody. I managed to get up, make it over to the phone, sit down on the rug, and hold the receiver to my ear.

Howard's voice felt like a bowling ball shattering my skull. I did hear him tell me he was glad I had awakened. I told him I appreciated that, but I didn't feel like talking. He asked if I could come to see him about two o'clock. I said if Susan would drive me and hung up. I got up again and shuffled down the hallway to the bathroom. My face in the mirror was bright red and splotched. I reached my hand up to touch it. My skin felt gluey, like somebody had covered it with rubber cement. Susan walked in with a glass of orange juice and a host of questions. They sounded like somebody was breaking a pool rack inside my head.

"You tried to kill yourself . . . here in my apartment? . . . How could you be so selfish and thoughtless? . . . I'm so sick of you and your craziness! . . . You took my medication. . . . What did you think I was going to tell the cops when they came for your body? . . . Do you realize they might have accused me of murder? . . ."

I could only keep saying over and over, "Susan, why are you mad at me? This didn't have anything to do with you." She hurled the empty plastic Midrin bottle back in the sink; it bounced out and clattered onto the tile floor. Then she continued her tirade: She was sick of my mooching from her, sick of my self-centeredness, get out of her place, get out of her life. . . . I staggered out her door and skulked down the hall to my apartment. She'd never even given me a sip of that orange juice.

I don't remember how I got down to Howard's office, but somehow I made it to the appointment. I knew that as long as he had managed to save my life I felt obligated to see him. I told Howard the whole sordid story—the Portland trip, my dad's behavior, Parker's leaving, about Ohio State's rejection, the pills, Susan's tirade about what I had done to her last night.

Howard sounded sympathetic. "No wonder you were so depressed, with all those things happening at once." He hesitated, then leaned forward. "John, I want you to do something. Will you pay a visit to a friend of mine at the Community Mental Health Clinic in downtown Columbus?"

"Why?"

"I think it would be good to have you looked at by someone else. I'm concerned that you might try to take your own life again."

"Hold on. I didn't really want to kill myself, I just saw no way out." I began to cry. "I just have no stability in my life, nothing permanent I can hang on to. Everything slips through my fingers; it's the same thing, over and over again."

"If you look at your problems as a whole, they seem overwhelming. We can't deal with everything at once. We can only deal with things one at a time." He put a hand on my arm. "For the time being, I want you to stop drinking. I'm starting to see a clear pattern in your life: Again and again, you tend to abuse alcohol to escape your problems."

"Come on! Alcohol is no problem for me. I can stop drinking whenever I want. Besides, everybody drinks, don't they?"

"Not like you do. Let me make a suggestion, all right? Do a little experiment, just to see if it's a problem or not. Will you stop drinking for now?" I promised I would, if only to get Howard off my case about it. I also agreed to visit the person he'd suggested at the Community Mental Health Clinic.

For the next couple of weeks I did stop drinking. And I felt better, almost as if my life were taking an instant upswing. I called Parker at his brother's and apologized profusely for what had happened. He said he would forgive me, but he thought it was better for now if he stayed with his brother and didn't move back in with me. I kept the Mental Health Clinic appointment.

They said I wasn't really suicidal, but I should continue my therapy with Howard and follow his advice to curb my drinking.

I didn't keep my promise to Howard for long. But as the next few weeks passed, I tried drinking a bit less. Sometimes I actually began to feel pretty good about myself, aided in part by my discovery of still another new guy named Doug, whom I met in the aerobics class I joined along with Parker.

TWELVE

"T HIS TIME, TAKE IT SLOW," Howard said, after I told him about Doug. "Don't let yourself fixate on this man. Don't get completely absorbed in him. When you take a relationship slow, it has more potential to last longer." I knew he was right, and I promised him I would try. I felt confident making the promise because I was feeling better, even if only because now I had a guy on my arm when I went to the bars.

But deep down I had that same, aching feeling. I knew it wouldn't last. Sure enough, after about six weeks Doug was calling me less and less. Then it became obvious that he wanted to avoid me altogether. I couldn't understand it. Hadn't I tried to follow Howard's advice?

Well, I always had Candi to fall back on. I had now solidified my drag identity as being on a par with Crystal Carrington of *Dynasty*. I wore beautifully tailored dresses and suits, designer Nolan Miller ensembles, pillbox hats, and smart clutch purses. Everything was subtle and understated. My reputation was growing by leaps and bounds around central Ohio. Yet in a seeming paradox, I was also getting slightly sick of it all.

At the beginning of one of our sessions, just before Christmas, Howard started peeling off another layer of my personality. "John, tell me what it's like to be Candi."

I thought for a long minute. "It's really hard to describe. *Euphoric* comes to mind. When I'm Candi, I feel like I can really be more of myself."

"What do you mean?"

"When I'm Candi, I'm not afraid to be who I really am on the inside. I can be fun as Candi; I can be outgoing; I can be sarcastic; I can be loving. I'm bold, I'm anything I want to be."

"But John, don't you see it? You're using Candi as a mask for yourself. But she's not really you, she's just a part of you."

"Howard, I don't think so. I mean, I couldn't survive without Candi."

"But John, you are part Candi, and she's part you. You're both the same person—but more than the sum of the both of you—existing under the same skin! You couldn't be Candi if the fun, sarcasm, love, and courage she embodies weren't parts of you. She's just a costume that makes you see yourself as two people instead of one."

I had to agree that he had a good point. As much as I loved being Candi, I felt a disparity when I came home from the bars at night. Dressing as Candi was like taking a drug. When I took her off, I came down from the high.

"Howard, by the end of the night, I'm craving to be myself again. I'm actually losing the desire to go out as Candi. But I don't know how I can go out all the time without her. . . .

"It's hard to explain," I continued. "But there are times when I think of getting rid of Candi altogether—throwing away all my dresses, wigs, high heels, and makeup."

Howard raised his eyebrows. "What do you think that would do for you?"

"It seems like all my drag friends go through phases. All of a sudden they want to get away from drag. But everybody who stops doing it eventually comes back."

"John, I think we're hitting a nerve here. Alcohol might not be your only crutch—Candi might be one, too." It was true: All my life I'd been looking for some sort of identity. I hadn't fit in with straight boys; and my mother's consolations ("different is good") hadn't made me feel better about myself, either.

Maybe if I'd been around my dad more often, things might have been better. Now, due to the geographical distance between us, real closeness wasn't happening on a steady basis, either. "My dad's trying hard," I told Howard, "but he never seems to say enough of what I need to hear. So I'm on my own, and I've got to prop my ego up with something. I guess I do use things for crutches, and maybe Candi's part of that."

Howard leaned forward. "Let me ask you another question I've been wondering about. You've told me all about your mother—she's glamorous, popular in society, and an elegant hostess. I'm wondering something: Could part of your motivation for being Candi lie in an attempt to re-create your mother?"

I thought a minute before responding. "I don't know, it sounds pretty farfetched. Really, I don't know what to think about that. I think I just picked up drag because I was good at it."

Howard wasn't convinced. "I think there's much more to it. You've taken most of your identity from your mother, not your father. I think you're vicariously re-creating your mother's identity as Candi."

"Whew, I'm going to have to think about that one for a while!"

And I did. While Christmas came and went and 1985 swept in, things were continuing to look up for me. I was promoted to assistant manager at the copy shop, which gave a boost to my self-esteem as John.

But Howard's questions kept nagging me: How much of my identity had my dad given me? Why hadn't he given me more? My dad and I hadn't corresponded much since my trip with him to Reno, so early in 1985 I was surprised to receive a letter from him:

Dear John,

For a long time there has been an unspoken tension between us. Some of this was bound to arise, since neither of us has made much effort to maintain communication. I'm making an effort to change that from my end. If there are other reasons on your part, I would like to see them slip away.

If part of the problem is that you think I don't care, then put that feeling aside. I do care. You are carrying a burden, because you have not chosen to tell me that you are gay. And I would like to address that.

It is not necessary for a son to have approval from a father to be able to go forward with life. What does make a difference is that two people accept each other, with individual rights, ambitions, and choices.

I accept you as an individual. You are your own man. But you are still my son. All I ask is your acceptance in return. We don't have to be the same kind of men to love each other. I love you. Don't let bitterness about your life interfere with living it.

Love,
Dad

Beads of sweat ran down my forehead as I read the letter. I was totally out of the closet now! But I could hardly believe this man. I was trying so hard to like him. How dare he announce so bluntly that he knew I was gay. He didn't even have the decency to call and ask me. And how did he find out? I picked up the letter and read it again. I had to admit that I did sense love behind it and my father did seem to accept my being gay. All he was asking was for me to accept him in return—exactly what Howard had told me I needed to give him. I thought a lot about my dad's request. I tried to accept him in my heart. But I just couldn't. Not now. Would I ever be able to?

Every Sunday, I joined Mom and Jerry for dinner. She didn't love him enough to marry him, but they still dated, and he treated me wonderfully. Altogether, things were better than they'd ever been with my family, except that I discovered word was spreading like wildfire about my being gay. Early one morning my sleep was shattered by unexpected phone jangles. To my amazement, I heard an aristocratic voice with a slight Texan accent. "John, this is your Grandpa Jack. I just want you to know that I heard you're gay. I've seen it in you since you were a small child. I knew you'd eventually turn out that way.

"But I also want you to know it's OK. I accept it, the whole family accepts it. I've talked to your mom and dad. And I want you to know that if you decide to get back into school, I'll help you pay for it. I want to help you make something out of your life." He didn't say much more, and I was almost speechless. My seventy-year-old grandfather had known about my homosexuality and yet never said a word to anyone! And now he was informing me, with cold bluntness, that he knew the most sensitive thing in my life. How typical of the male Paulks!

By that summer, Candi was famous and enough of an expert to be a drag mother to several budding new queens. I was now near the top of the Midwest female impersonator world, but I still wouldn't do drag shows or pageants. I didn't have to; my notoriety preceded me everywhere I went. Often during a drag show, the mistresses of ceremonies would ask, "Is Candi in the house?" Then the spotlight would turn on me as I took my bows and acknowledged the wild applause and wolf whistles.

But even while my popularity skyrocketed, I was painfully aware that the attention was for Candi, not me. The more famous she became, the less highly regarded John Paulk seemed to be. Once, coming down from an acid trip, I asked a drag friend of mine, "Why don't people take drag queens seriously? We're real people with feelings, just like everyone else."

"You're not a real person, you're a drag queen," she retorted. "We're only the party favors of the bars. Why should anyone take us seriously?" I had no answer. And what she said kept gnawing at me. Didn't I deserve genuine, unconditional love and acceptance from anyone?

Then another gay friend told me, "If you could be Candi—not in drag, but when you're just John—I think the whole world would fall in love with you."

"How's that?"

"If you could act just like Candi when you're not Candi but John, everyone would love you."

At first I was deeply offended; later, I realized this was a terrific compliment. At our next session, I told Howard that after the Gay Pride parade I was going to try quitting drag.

Gay Pride Columbus, 1985, was a festive day. Of course, I planned to attend the parade in full drag. Gretchen had made me a luscious white satin, 1920s-style, drop-waist cocktail frock, splashed with sparkling rhinestones, and a white chiffon sash to flow over each shoulder and into the wind behind me. We would march the whole way in pumps, blisters and all, as high on acid as we could be. During the march, I looked stunning enough to be approached by a sponsor of the Miss Gay America pageant (although I never followed up on his overture). Lots of supporters were watching from the sidewalks; there were also numerous Christian fundamentalists holding REPENT! signs and shouting anti-gay slogans. I kept smiling but thought, *Why can't these hateful people just leave us alone to live our lives as we please?*

As the summer wore on, I began to increase my drinking, and the number of times I blacked out also increased. Often I'd start drinking and wake up the next morning in bed with a total stranger. I'd have to find his wallet when he left the room, just so I could pretend to remember his name. I wasn't especially distressed by these predicaments; they happened so frequently that they seemed almost normal.

I didn't quit drag immediately after Gay Pride, but I still thought a lot about it. One thought kept bugging me: John and Candi were well known as being one and the same person, and John was tired of not being taken very seriously because he was also Candi. I felt an urge to reestablish my John Paulk identity. As a drag queen, I just couldn't be the "husband material" I wanted to be. What gay man would want to settle down with Candi?

Meanwhile, Howard kept chipping away at my drinking and drag habits. "I'm asking you again," he said at one session, "would you be willing to limit your drinking to two or three drinks a night? You're showing clear signs of being an alcoholic."

"I have no problem with drinking," I insisted. "I can control my alcohol intake, and I will." That Saturday night I was able to follow Howard's prescription. At the next session I crowed about my accomplishment, and Howard told me to keep it up.

As I got more sober, I took a break from Candi, packed my drag gear and makeup into a big box, and put it high on a closet shelf. Of course, all my drag friends and daughters thought I was being ridiculous.

"How can you stop doing drag when you're one of the most popular drag queens in town?" Gretchen asked me.

"I can't spend the rest of my life as everyone's party favor," I retorted. "I've got to find someone I can spend the rest of my life with. I'm never going to do that as Candi."

A few nights later I had a weird experience I couldn't explain. I went to the K as John and totally blew my self-imposed, three-drink limit. Before long I was ready to let the night take me where it would. Out on the dance floor, the lights were going crazy, the poppers were passing freely, and several kinds of intoxication were swelling my brain. Suddenly the music surrounding me seemed to stop in midnote.

I looked around, and it seemed as though I was completely alone in the center of the floor while everyone else stood frozen a hundred feet away. Light spattered like snowflakes all around me. I felt as if some kind of unseen hand was tilting my head up toward the discotheque's ceiling until I was looking intently at the spinning mirrored ball overhead. Then I heard a voice speak straight out of the mirrored ball and into my brain. It was gentle but firm: *"John, I want you back."* I looked around. No one was anywhere near me. It came again: *"Come back to me. I will set you free and change your life."*

It felt eerie, to put it mildly. The mysterious voice had cut through my highs, my euphorias, through the bar's raucousness. And I knew exactly Who was speaking.

Instantly I was fifteen again. One girl in my eighth-grade class had developed a crush on me. Heidi said she was a "born-again Christian." She had told me all about Jesus and how He had a "plan of salvation" for me. We spent hours talking about it, and somehow she convinced me that I needed to "get saved" so I would be ready when Jesus Christ came back to earth.

Soon after that, I had been alone in my room, thinking about my conversations with Heidi. I opened my window and knelt down by the sill, then prayed and asked God to come into my heart. Afterward, I had been so enthusiastic that one of my friends became a Christian, too.

But my parents were puzzled about my Christian experience. When I started going to church, Mom took my Bible away and pressured me against it. Gradually I drifted away from church and the youth group I was attending. Six months later, I had no connection with any of it anymore, and I gave no more thought to religion of any kind—until now.

For a brief moment I was bathed in an overwhelming sense of peace and security, just as I had felt years ago after praying to become a Christian. As I gazed into the spinning ball overhead, I thought, *But I don't know how to get back to You. I've drifted so far. Being the way I am is all I know.*

I lowered my head—and the brief vision tinkled to pieces like a dropped Christmas ornament. The music throbbed and the person dancing in front of me handed me a popper bottle. But as the popper's rush flushed through me, I thought, *What just happened? What could it matter to God how I'm living my life?* That I should hear from God made no sense whatsoever. Whenever any straight person began to talk about God, I became furious. Any time a gay person brought up the subject of God, I simply got up and left the room. God, for all practical purposes, meant less than nothing to me. Still, for the rest of the night I felt this dull, persistent ache in the pit of my stomach. And I knew it wasn't just something I'd eaten.

Six weeks went by, and I still hadn't done drag. Howard and I were now zeroing in on my relationship with my mother. We explored the hypothesis that, growing up, I had seen myself internally as an extension of her personality. We probed the feelings of my childhood—that I didn't really exist and that in my small universe only my mother was important. Outside Howard's office I had some good talks with Mom. She was able, much to my relief and joy, to validate some of the things Howard and I were discussing, and even took a measure of responsibility for my growing-up problems.

I sensed my mom was never thrilled about knowing I was gay. But I knew that she and other family members were responding in an atypical—even remarkable—way to my homosexuality. Their reactions lacked the hysteria and judgmentalism of many families, and I was grateful.

Unfortunately, I wasn't able to hold onto the psychological progress I'd achieved with Howard. Toward the early autumn I fouled things up royally. Mom broke up with Jerry, whom I loved dearly, saying they were just not compatible. Angry with her, I hit the bars as John and got totally plastered.

My friend Allen drove me home, but I asked him to let me out about halfway there; I wanted to "cruise the meat rack." Near Larry's bar a guy drove up alongside me and asked me to get into his car. I kept telling him no, he kept asking, and then I blacked out.

When I came to, I was standing in the middle of North High Street, with cars whizzing past me on all sides. Terrified, I worked my way through the busy traffic to the sidewalk. Then the same persistent guy walked right up to me. He told me he'd parked his car nearby, and somehow he coaxed me into going back to my apartment with him. We went inside and sat down to finish some wine before I blacked out again.

When I woke up, I was lying facedown in my bed. As I opened my eyes, stark sunlight seemed to set off a hangover explosion in my head, and I felt pain throbbing over every inch of my body. My clock said it was 3:00 P.M. My chest felt sticky. So did my hand as I raised myself to a sitting position. I looked down at a wide pool of blood smeared across my sheets. From the ravaged way I felt below my waist, I realized the blood had to be mine—I had been raped.

I picked up my wet sheets and wadded them into a gooey ball. I could hardly walk, but I did manage to get to the bathroom, where I immediately vomited. When I had cleaned myself up, I looked around my apartment. My watch and money were gone. So was a fourteen-karat-gold, diamond and amethyst ring. With the family crest engraved in the amethyst, it had been a treasured heirloom inherited from my grandfather. I knew I'd never see any of the stolen things again. But far worse than losing things, part of me had been ruthlessly taken, and I had no idea how to get back that severed slice of myself.

I told Howard about the rape during my next session, and he confronted me. "I've worked with you for two years. Although you've come a long way, I simply can't help you any further until you do something about your drinking." He referred me to Drummers, a local gay meeting of Alcoholics Anonymous. Then he looked at me with tears in his eyes. "I'm sorry to say this, but I will not make another appointment until you have been to at least one Drummers meeting."

I knew beyond question he was serious. I was so distraught, I had to do something to make myself feel better. That weekend I pulled Candi down from the shelf and got back into drag.

THIRTEEN

I T WAS A USUAL Saturday night, and I went out as usual to the K with Gretchen. We were both in drag as usual. I had half a dozen drinks, expecting to get the usual buzz and make the usual spectacle of myself, to the usual adulation. But this night things just didn't turn out as usual. For reasons I couldn't fathom, the liquor didn't seem to have its customary effect. I felt almost no buzz, and I felt awkward, *trying* to be a barely plastered Candi. As the hours went by, nothing unusual happened to spice things up for me, and the whole night was turning into a long, crashing bore.

I decided to dance and put my purse down by the rail at the edge of the dance floor. After a couple of numbers, I came back—and my purse was gone. That meant everything I valued at that moment—my lipstick, keys, money, ID, compact, driver's license, lip liner—had all disappeared. I was stunned. I felt as if I had been invaded somehow. I ran to Gretchen, frantic. "My purse is missing!"

"Candi, haven't I told you never to leave your purse lying around?" she scolded.

"But I can't carry it with me and dance relaxed."

"I don't care," she said, "you always need to keep it with you. When will you ever learn?"

We went to the ladies' room, and I found my purse, stuffed behind a toilet. I took it out in back of the disco and sat down on a step. My purse had been thoroughly rummaged. I started to sob and quickly flew into a terrible rage.

"Candi, collect yourself!" Gretchen hissed.

"Somebody has invaded me," I wailed. "Somebody stole my identity. This is who I am—this is my purse."

She put an arm around me. "I know just how you feel. A woman's purse is part of who she is."

When I got home that night I thought, *Why did I even bother going out?* Then I thought about the scene I had made. I hadn't felt drunk, yet losing my purse had almost ripped me apart at the seams. In that moment I made a momentous decision: I decided to quit drinking.

Nothing more dramatic than that. No huge ordeal, no rock-bottom experience, no green snakes or pink elephants. Not even a great revelation that, like a stroke of lightning, told me I had too many symptoms of a drinking problem. It was simple: I'd had enough booze. When I woke up the next morning, I decided to attend my first gay AA meeting.

The Drummers met at St. Mary's Catholic Church. I took a bus downtown and walked up the long driveway leading to the basement where the meetings were held. I had no clue as to what I would find there. I did feel a strong compulsion, which I resisted, to turn around and walk back to the street. As I passed through the church parking lot, I saw several familiar people getting out of their cars. *Why should you be surprised?* I thought. *This* is *a gay meeting.*

I opened the door and looked into a smoke-choked room dominated by a long, U-shaped table bordered by folding chairs. Two large coffee urns, with some twenty-five to thirty people congregated around them, weighed down one end of the table. Most people there seemed to know one another. They stood talking and laughing together as if they were at a bar. Only the absence of pot, poppers, beer, hard alcohol odors, and disco decor indicated that the gathering had a serious purpose.

I tried to avoid eye contact with anyone I thought might know me. I did notice a few people standing around the outskirts who seemed ill at ease. They were new, I surmised, and I shuffled into their loosely defined ranks. But I wasn't allowed to feel alone for long. People kept detaching from the "inner circle," coming up, shaking hands, and introducing themselves. They were trying their best to make me and other newcomers feel comfortable, but I was just too nervous to really relax.

A few minutes later, a handsome man with salt-and-pepper hair sat down at the far end of the room. The scattered conversations lulled, and he said, "I'd like the meeting to come to order. Hi, folks! My name is Tom, and I'm an alcoholic."

The rest of us took seats around the table as the room chimed back, in unison: "Hi, Tom!"

At the age of three and a half I loved my baby sister, Vicky, but she cried at my attempts to be affectionate!

My first "official" photograph was taken in kindergarten.

Second grade brought my parents' divorce and growing insecurity for me.

Starring in *Anything Goes*, at Ft. Hayes School, just before meeting Parker.

My 1981 high-school senior picture.

I love this picture of me and Vicky, taken three years after my coming out.

Candi, in 1986, during a "rare" performance.
Greg took the photograph.

Candi in 1983 as 1st runner up in the Miss
Ingenue pageant.

Greg and Candi out at the K during a gay formal.

In 1988, while at Love in Action. I was a Christian, struggling, but changing.

Anne in fifth grade. Her tomboy image was evident.

Dad visited me while at Love in Action. Our relationship was steadily improving.

Anne struggling with her orientation. Feeling comfortable as a woman was still a few years off.

This is the only photograph of my sister, mother, father, and I all together. Today my parents are friends.

Anne blossomed like a rose. In 1991 we were engaged and so much in love with each other.

Mom and I after my wedding. She and my stepfather, Tom, became Christians a few hours after this picture was taken.

The happiest day of our lives, July 19, 1992.

Timmy's 1997 Christmas picture, surrounded by Winnie-the-Pooh!

Mommy holding Timmy during a trip to Multnomah Falls.

My son Timmy is the joy of my life.

Therefore, if anyone is in Christ, he is a new creature; the old things have passed away; behold, all things have become new.

— 2 Corinthians 5:17

"I'd like to welcome everyone to the Drummers meeting of Alcoholics Anonymous. Let's bow our heads for the Serenity Prayer."

I glanced around as the group recited the famous AA prayer. Most people didn't look like down-and-outers, weirdos, or winos. The group spanned the whole age spectrum from late teens to sixties. After the prayer, a Latino-looking guy sitting at my left elbowed me and whispered, "Hey, aren't you the guy who's Candi?"

"Yeah," I said. "So what? I think I've seen you before, too."

"Maybe last June at the Gay Pride parade. You were with Jennifer and Gretchen, right? This your first time?"

"Yeah. I'm not sure what the heck I'm doing. Maybe just here to listen."

"Hey, that's cool." He didn't seem the least bit judgmental about my presence. I also noticed several other attractive guys in the group. *Maybe there's opportunity here for more than just listening,* I thought.

Just then Tom asked if there were any first-timers, and a few people raised their hands. Slowly I slipped mine up, and the whole room broke into applause. As Tom glanced at me, I put my hand down. I was embarrassed but pleased that the group seemed glad I was here.

As the meeting proceeded, various people talked about how drinking had rendered their lives unmanageable, leading them to do things they'd never dreamed of; . . . how they had tried controlled drinking but found they couldn't control themselves; . . . how they had ended up going home and having sex with people whose names they didn't even know; . . . how their lives had turned nearly insane.

Their experiences all sounded familiar. Before long I felt like I belonged—especially because everyone was gay. I could totally relate to their explanations of why they drank: to escape insecurity, to take the edge off, to meet new people, to forget their problems, to avoid unpleasant family situations.

"How do you know you're an alcoholic?" Tom asked. "No one can decide whether you're an alcoholic but you." At that moment I knew I fit the portrait they had been painting. And I finally admitted to myself, *Yes, I am an alcoholic.*

I learned that various AA meetings were held all over Columbus, nearly every day of the week, at all hours of the day and night. Now that I'd admitted to being an alcoholic, I decided to check out other meetings. During the next several weeks, I went to nearly every AA meeting I could find. But I felt most comfortable at Drummers since everyone there was gay.

The first time I shared at a Drummers meeting, I could scarcely get the words out. "Hi, my n-n-n-name's John, and I-I'm an al-al-alcoholic. . . ." I learned at AA that if I gave up drinking, I was going to have to relearn social life all over again. Like many other alcoholics, I had become so addicted to booze highs, I didn't know how to talk to people, how to have fun, how to live "with the edge," how to face reality without a buzz.

People at Drummers assured me that I would learn how to enjoy life again. Reality was much better than being out of touch, they said, and I believed them. I wanted the serenity these AA people seemed to have, and just being around them made me feel good, like I was climbing out of a deep, dark barrel. At AA they talked a lot about "your Higher Power," that is "God, as you understand Him to be" (or, ". . . as you understand *her* to be," as the lesbians liked to say). It was really the power of God that kept us sober and restored us to sanity, they explained.

It was strange to be around a bunch of gay people who talked about God. I felt nothing but discomfort with the idea. But some of the people I admired most in the group talked about God the most, so I listened to what they had to say: "You need to find your Higher Power in God. Now, God can be whatever you want Him to be. For you, God could be nature. You might find God in someone else. Your Higher Power might be AA meetings themselves. God just needs to be something outside yourself that's bigger than you."

Howard was pleased with my progress, and he encouraged me to attend as many meetings as possible. It was going to take quite a while for me to get my system cleaned out, he said. After fifteen sober days, I admitted to him that I still craved liquor. In fact, I shook whenever I even thought about it. But, as AA advised, I was sucking on candy whenever I got the cravings, and it helped a lot. "Keep going, one day at a time," Howard said, "and you'll find your life changing fast."

At the Drummers meeting on November 4, 1985, Tom asked, "Are there any anniversaries or sobriety milestones today?"

I looked around the room and said, smooth as silk this time, "Hi, my name is John. I'm an alcoholic, and today I've been sober for one month." The applause was as wild as anything Candi had ever received. Tom asked me to come to the front of the room. He gave me a bronze medallion with the inscription: ONE MONTH OF RECOVERY. I felt hugely proud of myself. *I may still be dreaming about alcohol almost twenty-four hours a day,* I thought, *but I've been able to live without it, I'm still here, and I'm still sober.*

My sex life, however, had come to a grinding halt. Since I didn't have alcohol to numb the fear and help me be spontaneous, relating to strangers in a gay bar was suddenly very difficult for me. But not only me. Lots of gay AA people shared how hard it was for them to go bar-hopping, because so much drinking went on. But, because gay bars were the only kind of social outlet most of us really knew, we still felt we had to keep going there.

Of course, I still had Candi to think about. I had to maintain her reputation, and that could only be done in gay bars. In the nearly three years I had been Candi, however, I had never stayed sober for the entire evening. Being Candi and completely sober felt really strange. But even though I was more inhibited and dancing was harder for me when sober, things weren't all bleak: I was now able to recall casual acquaintances' names, I was recognizing faces from week to week, and I wasn't having blackouts or experiencing time gaps anymore.

During a session with Howard in late November, he suggested that I ask my mother to come the next week with me. She agreed, and I decided the time had come to tell her I was an alcoholic. Because of my involvement with AA, it had been weeks since I'd joined Mom for Sunday dinner. She looked puzzled when she offered me some wine and I turned it down. I took that as my cue and, lapsing back into a stutter again, told her I was an alcoholic.

She refused to believe me at first. "I'm so surprised that you would say that about yourself," she said. "I've never seen you drink that much—and I've never seen you drunk." She knew I'd been promoted to the position of manager at work, and she had never smelled alcohol on my breath when she had dropped by to see me. Nor, she said, had I ever had more than a glass of wine or two when I came to dinner.

I explained to her that you don't have to drink every day to be an alcoholic. And if I'd had only a little wine when I was at her house, it was because I saw no sense in just drinking a glass or two when I mainly drank in order to get stone drunk. She looked at first as if I had slapped her across the face. She seemed far more upset to hear I was an alcoholic than she had been to learn I was gay. But she was relieved to hear that at least I was in recovery, and that made me feel good.

When we went to see Howard, Mom spoke with remarkable openness about our past together. For the first time, I heard her admit to someone other than myself the responsibility she felt for some of the anguish of my growing-up years. One of her regrets was a rather loveless marriage with my dad. At the time she gave birth to me and Vicky, she admitted, she was imma-ture and unprepared emotionally to have children. As she talked, my mother demonstrated with every word her love and concern for me, and I felt com-pletely able to receive her love.

"John, it's OK now for you to let me know who you really are," she said. "You can tell me your wounds and hurts. I won't put you off or put you down or not listen to you the way I used to. I'm here for you." All three of us shared happy tears together that day. And my mom has been there for me ever since.

In my session right after New Year's Day, Howard told me, "I think it's time for you and me to take a break. You've come a long way in the past few months. AA is giving you a lot of support, most of what you need right now. Why don't we take six months off? Of course, if there's any emergency, I'll always be available."

I thought about Howard's suggestion and decided he was right. As man-ager of my own copy shop, I was finding that I could handle responsibility. I was successfully supervising a staff, making schedules, keeping records, pay-rolls, hiring, and firing. My boss, the regional manager, was emotionally aloof and difficult for me to get along with; he reminded me a lot of my dad. But I was able to handle that challenge, too. I was even budgeting my money bet-ter. Yes, I told Howard, I felt I could stand on my own two feet now. He was delighted that I wanted to try.

On April 3, I received my six months' sobriety medal. I could scarcely believe the time had gone so fast. I was getting used to the pleasure of waking up every day without a hangover. I was getting used to going to bars, getting cruised by guys, and cruising back without worrying about falling down, stumbling drunk. And, once I had broken the sober-sex barrier (it didn't take long), I enjoyed going home with guys, having sex, and being able to remem-ber their names the next morning.

I still did Candi, but I found that even her personality was changing now that she wasn't drinking. She was actually starting to turn into a civil, even respectable, woman—instead of an ice queen, who'd fly off at the mouth and hurl cutting obscenities at the slightest provocation. Candi hadn't lost all her spice, but most of her verbal jabs were now affectionate, rather than cruel.

About this time, my mom began going to alcoholism support meetings. After several weeks, she was able to admit that she was an alcoholic. Of course, I wasn't surprised; her father had been an alcoholic. All my life I'd seen her drink, and I was an alcoholic. So it all seemed to fit. I still hadn't told Dad, so a few weeks later, I wrote him about my struggle with alcohol and that I had been in recovery for seven months. Later I talked to him on the phone; he never mentioned my confession, which upset me. It seemed as if he was slighting me, as though he hadn't even heard me. When he failed again in his next letter to address the issue, I asked him in my reply why he hadn't. I also wondered to myself why we only seemed to have good conversations in letters.

At last he wrote a response that included these paragraphs:

> John, it was a fine gesture on your part to disclose your alcoholism to me. It is understandable that my not mentioning anything before could lead you to think that I was either shocked or, for some reason, did not know how to deal with the situation.
>
> In fact, I was concerned in my last letter that you know how proud I am of how you are trying to work through things rather than highlighting the obstacles you have faced. John, nothing in life shocks or even really surprises me. There is little I have not been exposed to. I'm very aware of the human condition.
>
> I do not mean to sound like I am downplaying the problem of alcoholism. It is real and does not just go away. Some people are more susceptible than others. Whether this is due to allergies, chemical reactions, or social dysfunction is not important. If alcohol is wrong for you, then you are fortunate to recognize it and darn lucky to take steps to protect yourself.
>
> John, all my love and best wishes to you. Life is a long time. Find out what is important for you and grow in the joy.
>
> > Love you,
> > Dad

Dad also mentioned that he had a new girlfriend named Vicki, similar to my sister. He hoped I could take a trip to Portland soon and meet her. From his description she sounded like a really nice person.

By late May I was gay, sober, and content. I was totally "out" to my family. They accepted me and my gayness as well as any family imaginable, and they, too, all seemed to be getting their lives together. I was on my own, performing well at work, liking myself, clearheaded and sure footed. I wasn't doing acid or poppers anymore. I'd even made up with Susan, after asking her to forgive my insensitivity. Maybe, just maybe, now I was ready at last to meet the man of my dreams.

FOURTEEN

L ESS THAN A MONTH LATER, I met Greg. It was a Saturday night; Gretchen and I were in full regalia, dancing up a storm at the Garage. I looked across the packed dance floor and was dazzled by a familiar sight: a particular male dancer in the spotlight, swiveling seductively in perfect time to the pounding rhythm. He had sky-blue eyes, golden tan, velvet tufts of blond hair curling from his muscular chest. On a daring impulse I shouted, "C'mon, Gretchen, let's scoot over next to that guy."

"I thought you weren't interested in picking up anyone tonight," she yelled back.

"I'm not, but I can have a little fun, right?" I wiggled my way over to the blond hunk, and he flashed a beautiful white keyboard of teeth. "Hey, Candi, how are ya?"

"Hi, Flawless."

"Name's Greg."

"Hi, Greg," I hollered, my hips wildly revolving. "I've been watching you for about a year." I leaned over to Gretchen. "Oh, Miss Thing, have you ever seen anyone so gorgeous?"

"Get over yourself. Let's go, I'm bored."

"You are such a drag." I smiled at Greg, then Gretchen and I headed off the dance floor. We walked two blocks to the K, and I paraded in to the usual adulation. After a stroll around the bar, I headed for the ladies' room to fix my hair, powder, and lipstick. Glancing around at several lesbians, I thought, *I'm more woman than any of you will ever be.*

As I walked out of the ladies' room, standing before me was none other than Greg! "Hi, Candi." He flashed another big smile.

"My, my. What brings you here?"

135

"I followed you from the Garage. Can I buy you a drink?"

"No, thanks." I felt myself blush. "I don't drink."

Greg took a step toward me. "You know, I've been watching you for years." I blushed even deeper as he continued. "You're by far the most gorgeous drag queen I've ever seen, and I'm an amateur photographer." He cleared his throat just a bit shyly. "You know, I would love to take some pictures of you."

What drag queen could possibly turn down that kind of offer from this hunk? I told Greg that would be wonderful, and he gave me his phone number.

"Give me a call," he said, then he whirled around and ran onto the dance floor, shedding his shirt as he went. Gretchen and I ended the evening early, and she took me home.

During the next week, I almost forgot about Greg and his offer. At this point in my life I wasn't looking for a boyfriend; I was busy enough managing the copy shop, going to AA meetings, and being Candi. I had also joined a gay therapy group Howard had started with another therapist.

Two weeks later, Gretchen and I were enacting our customary Saturday night dress-up ritual when the phone rang. It was Greg, wondering if he could go out to the bars with us. "I never drive when I go out to do serious drinking," he explained. "And you don't drink. So, if I go out with you, we'll both be safe."

"Gee, that would be great." I tried to sound cool while my heart was doing flip-flops. He lived in my neighborhood, and I gave him directions.

"Would you believe it?" I called to Gretchen after hanging up. "Greg remembered me. And not only did he remember, he got my phone number somewhere and called me! He asked if he could go to the Garage with us. He's on the way over."

Soon I heard a knock at the door. I swung it open and there stood Greg, wearing cutoff jeans and an Ohio State T-shirt, just as scrumptious as the last time I laid eyes on him. We piled into the car and in a few moments strutted into the Garage. But Greg only hung out with Gretchen and me for about twenty minutes and then disappeared. We looked around for him the rest of the evening, but he was long gone. *He just drank his fill and forgot all about me,* I sighed. I was hurt but decided not to bother giving Greg another thought.

Another two weeks went by. Then one night the phone rang. It was Greg again—but this time he seemed very soft-spoken and downright embarrassed. "John, it's taken me awhile to get up the nerve to call you. I–I'm really sorry. . . ."

"About what?"

"Running out on you and Gretchen the other week. I want to apologize. I'm afraid I had a little too much to drink. I just lost my head and forgot who brought me."

"That's OK, I understand completely. No big deal—although I was a little worried about you."

"Is there any way I can make it up to you?"

"Well, you did say you wanted to take some pictures of me. Are you still interested?"

His voice brightened. "Absolutely. I didn't think you'd still want me to. Hey, I can't wait to get you in front of the camera."

Greg called me at work the following Wednesday and invited me over that night to watch *Dynasty* with him.

I felt a sharp pang of disappointment. "I'd love to, but I've called a staff meeting after my store closes. We won't be through till about ten."

"That's OK, I'll save the show on my VCR. Then we can watch it together when you get here."

"Great idea! Where do you live?" Greg gave me his address, and I sensed something was up. After we hung up, I realized something very significant: Whenever I was in drag, Greg always called me John—though he always remembered to call me Candi when anyone else was nearby. And he had called me John today. Maybe he was really interested in *me* and not just fascinated by the funny, outrageous femme I portrayed to the rest of the world. Maybe there was more to this guy than I'd thought.

After the staff meeting that night, I ran home, changed clothes, doused myself with cologne and quickly walked the two blocks to Greg's place. He lived in a rooming house with several other people, but he rented the whole top floor. Like Greg himself, nothing in his living quarters distinguished it from a straight guy's, though I did find his king-sized waterbed a standout feature.

"Would you like a drink?" he asked after I'd settled on the couch. He fixed me a Diet Coke with ice, then got a Scotch and water for himself. After turning on the TV and VCR, he invited me to lay down next to him on the waterbed. As the next hour passed, Greg got up a few times to refresh my drink and his own; every time he came back, he moved a little closer to me. Tingles of anticipation began tickling the back of my neck. For the first time since I'd been sober, I was seriously attracted to another man.

Greg immensely intrigued me; he was extraordinarily handsome yet never seemed preoccupied with himself or his looks. He was fun and seemed genuinely interested in getting to know me at a deeper level. Yet he hadn't tried to jump into sex with me. In fact, we hadn't yet come close to being physically intimate. We were actually getting to know each other first, and I liked that. For the first time in months, I was being gently pursued. I wasn't having to take the lead, and that felt great, too. Before I realized what was happening I grew so relaxed I drifted off to sleep.

When I awoke about an hour later, Greg had snuggled close to me and wrapped his arm around my waist. His even breathing told me he'd fallen asleep. I snuggled close, careful not to wake him, then returned to sleep. When I woke up the next morning, I knew this was the start of a great relationship.

Greg and I spent a week together before we had sex, just talking and cuddling and hanging out. He was shy about his homosexuality, and it usually took him a few drinks to loosen up. But that didn't matter to me. From that first night on his waterbed, I was a total goner. I loved Greg beyond reason. He treated me wonderfully: with respect, with sincere love for John—and he loved Candi almost as much. For Greg, going out with me when I was in drag was pure joy. Candi didn't threaten him; he didn't even think Candi made John effeminate. Greg accepted all sides of me completely, which was amazing.

During the next few weeks Greg and I spent every available moment together. We went to movies, ate out, danced at the bars, and just plain enjoyed each other's company. He also took some wonderful photos of me in drag at several bars. I couldn't have felt happier.

Only one major problem loomed over our relationship: In less than three months, Greg was moving to Florida. He was finishing his degree in nursing at Ohio State and had already accepted a nursing position in Naples, Florida. I had no idea how I was going to handle our parting. The mere thought that we'd ever have to be separated made me ache deep inside.

Greg's having to leave didn't make any sense. After all, everything else in my life was getting better in big strides. I was pleasantly accustomed to going without booze. My personal reputation was fast improving; people now enjoyed having me around, not just because I was outrageous, but because I showed them respect and consideration, too.

Things also continued to go well with my mother and father. Mom was blossoming in her own recovery process. My dad wrote me from Portland that he and Vicki had decided to get married, and they both wanted me to come for the wedding. I hadn't seen my dad since my sister's graduation, and I was thrilled for him.

When Dad and Vicki's big day arrived, I flew to Portland. The minute I met Dad's bride-to-be, I fell in love with her and told her, "Vicki, you look like one of us!" She was warm, compassionate, caring, and very motherly; she had no children of her own, but took to all of us immediately.

Dad and Vicki had a small and quaint ceremony in a tiny church. The service was lovely, and we had a wonderful family reunion. I flew back home feeling deeply fulfilled, despite the aching memories the marriage brought back of my own long-faded dreams of a little house and a white picket fence.

My therapy group was a big support during this time. They encouraged me to face up to my upcoming parting with Greg, and I came to a decision: I would look at this relationship as something incomparably rich and pleasurable, even though it might end soon. I told Greg that I wouldn't try to put any strings around his neck. We'd just stay together as much as possible before he had to leave.

One night while Greg and I were at the Garage, Nathan, my longtime bar buddy, came up and looked me over. "Candi," he said, "I think I told you this once before, but I'd like to say it again."

"What's that, sweetie?"

"I've been watching you carefully for the past few years. And I've become convinced that if you could just act like Candi while you're still dressed as John, the whole world would fall in love with you." Then he turned and walked away.

He had said those words before, and they reminded me of something Howard had told me not long ago: "Candi is just a part of you. John and Candi are the same person. You only feel less inhibited when you're in drag because with Candi you have someone to hide behind." At that moment I realized that they were both saying the same thing. Candi exhibited some of the best parts of my personality, aspects I seldom revealed as John. If I could combine Candi's best sides with John's best sides, I would have one wonderful personality. It was a thought I'd ponder often in the coming months.

Over the next several weeks, Greg and I had many wonderful days enjoying each other and basking in the glow of our mutual affection. Greg set his departure date back for our sakes, and his apartment lease ran out earlier than he was ready to go. So he asked me if he could live with me until he moved. I couldn't have been more thrilled, and when he moved in, it felt just like we were married.

At last, here was my longtime dream come true: Greg, the joy of my life, sharing the same space with me. We were a couple, both madly head-over-heels in love with one another. I thought about Greg all day and dreamed about him all night. How could he leave and walk out of my life? Would I really find myself alone again?

Columbus's annual Gay Pride and Freedom Day was fast approaching, and I asked Greg if he would stay just one more week to escort me in the parade. He agreed, and I was thrilled. Until now Greg had never marched in a gay pride parade because he hadn't wanted to be openly out. But now that he was leaving Columbus, he said, what difference would it make? We decided to rent a candy-apple-red Mustang convertible for the parade, and Greg would dress as Candi's chauffeur. It would be our final hurrah together.

It was a glorious day for Gay Pride—the sky cloudless and balmy temperatures in the mid-70s. Greg had decorated the car with streamers, balloons, and Christmas garlands. It was a little gaudy for my taste, but he'd had such a great time doing it that I never breathed a complaint. As we were waiting for the parade to begin, Jennifer Heart came to my side wearing a strained smile. "So, Missy," she sneered, "what makes you think you can ride in a convertible all by yourself?"

"I'm Candi," I said with a laugh, then turned my back on her to greet fans who begged me to autograph their T-shirts. When it came time for us to enter the parade, Greg took my hand and helped me step up onto the top of the convertible's back seat. Then we left Victorian Village's Goodale Park and drove slowly down North High Street toward downtown, where the parade was to end in a rally at the amphitheater on the other side of the Olentangee River.

Mischievously, Greg had bought six big packages of starlight peppermints for me to toss to the adoring crowds. Whenever people cheered "Candi, Candi!" I would have a fun time blowing kisses and throwing handfuls of the mints.

The Stonewall Union, Columbus's gay activist group, had assigned some burly members of the gay/lesbian community to wear pink armbands and serve as guards along the parade route. Some of these "honor guards" walked beside my car. As we started to cross the bridge over the Olentangee and make for the amphitheater, I found out why. A strange silence seemed to hang in the air ahead. I noticed a different-looking crowd of several hundred people amassed in the distance on either side of the road covering the old, curved concrete bridge. It was the Christians again!

One man, dressed in black and wearing what looked like a priest's collar, held up a sign that read, GOD HATES FAGS. Other people, dressed in Sunday-best clothes, held signs saying, TURN OR BURN, FLIP OR FRY, QUEERS GO HOME, and ALL GAYS GO TO HELL. Another sign said, REPENT! THE KINGDOM OF GOD IS AT HAND, with the words surrounded by hellish-looking flames.

"Right-wing, fundamentalist Christians," I told Greg through gritted teeth and a forced smile. The Christians yelled, "Repent, you queers!" and waved black leather Bibles. Some looked angry. Some wept openly. Others looked like they were praying.

Chills of revulsion and fear washed over me. The right-wingers' screams were ruining our festive atmosphere. *I hope I'm ruining their day,* I thought. *Let them shriek, while Candi, the most prominent drag queen in Columbus, drives right past them.* Still, I couldn't help but feel naked and exposed some-how. All too vulnerable—and terrified. These people looked like they might attack us at any moment.

I reached down and tapped Greg on the shoulder. "Step on it! Get across this bridge fast. I hate these people."

"Things are at a standstill up ahead," Greg answered over his shoulder. "Just relax and keep calm."

I felt like a bug in the middle of a circle of Raid cans. The right-wingers didn't move, but it seemed like they were pressing in on me. To my horror I recognized one of the trainers from the health club I attended. He'd always been so kind to me. What in the world was he doing with this despicable bunch of Christians?

"Why would anyone want to follow a God like theirs?" I asked Greg. "Why can't they just leave us alone? We're not hurting anyone." I wanted to scream, "I was born gay, so just leave me alone!" But I was afraid they would storm the convertible, and our gay guards wouldn't be able to control them.

Finally, after what seemed like an eternity, our red Mustang lurched for-ward. We reached the other side of the bridge, leaving the fundamentalists behind. I let out a deep sigh. "Boy, am I glad to get away from them," I muttered to Greg. Aside from the Christians, the remainder of the parade was great fun. Greg and I forgot the ugliness on the bridge and settled into enjoy-ing the high spirits of the amphitheater rally. But every time I looked at Greg,

I felt stabs of sadness. How could he be moving so far away, just when our relationship was getting so good?

I helped Greg pack during the next three days, trying to look brave and happy the whole time. But after a tender and loving last night together, the inevitable and fateful morning came. I awoke at the earliest dawning light and watched Greg sleep beside me. I knew this would probably be the last time I'd ever set eyes on him this way. My eyes lingered over him from head to toe. I breathed in his scent. I tried to remember every moment we had ever shared. I never wanted to forget a single detail of him.

Why does this best relationship of a lifetime have to end? If Greg really loves me, why doesn't he want to stay with me? Why hadn't I ever worked up the courage to ask him either to stay or to take me with him? Perhaps I was too fearful that his saying no would be even more painful than his leaving. In any case, he seemed to be content to move on and leave me behind.

Later that morning we packed up Greg's silver Chevette, and he drove us a couple of blocks to a restaurant where we had a late breakfast. Afterward, we stood together in the parking lot. At last the time had come to say our goodbyes. To my shock, Greg threw his arms around me, right in public. "Greg, aren't you worried about what people will think?" I said anxiously over his shoulder.

"No." He was choking with emotion. "I don't care what anybody thinks anymore. I love you, and I'll miss you so much. There's no one like you, John, and no one ever will be." I had no words to answer him. We clung to each other for long moments, and Greg kissed me tenderly on the mouth. Then we held each other at arms' length.

My lower lip trembled, and I bit it hard, trying to hold back the tears. "Goodbye, Greg," I whispered. "I'll never forget you. I've had the most wonderful time of my life with you these last months. I love you. Don't ever forget me." After final goodbyes, he got into his Chevette and turned to me as he started the motor. He shot me one last wink, then he drove off.

As I lost sight of Greg's car, I felt like some powerful vise seized my heart and began to squeeze the life out of it. I stumbled back to my apartment, closed all the curtains, and fell face down on the floor. I wept uncontrollably for the next four hours. I wept for having at last found someone I loved so deeply, only to lose him. I wept for the life pouring out of me now that he was gone. I wept for the years I'd spent trying to find him. I wept because I was alone again.

For the next three days I never left my apartment. I called into work "sick." I refused to answer the door or the phone. I shut all the lights off. I didn't eat; I hardly even moved. I let the television run unwatched, and I cried even after there were no tears left.

As the first rays of light snuck through my curtains on the third day, I heard a soft knock on the door. Then another. Still another. I don't know why, but this time I moved. I opened the door a crack and saw Parker's troubled eyes peering at me. "John, what are you doing in there?" he said. "You haven't been at work, haven't answered your phone. What the heck have you been up to?"

I opened the door wider, and his eyes also widened. "You look horrible," he said, putting his arms around me and hugging me tight as I shuddered out more tears. "C'mon, let's get out of here for a while."

"I don't want to go anywhere," I sobbed.

"Come on now. Let's spend the day at my brother's place." I didn't want to go, but I felt too weak to resist. He guided me firmly to the bathroom, where I showered and dressed. We left my apartment, and for the rest of the day Parker did his best to distract me from my grief.

The next morning, Parker gently prodded me awake. "John, you've got to get up and go back to work. Greg is gone, and you have to move on with life."

I dragged myself back to the copy shop. Then, day after day, one day at a time, I forced myself back into the grind of running the store. The next few months passed in a blur. I let myself go numb with the sheer routines of life. Most nights I'd stare blankly at the TV screen. I slept a lot but kept going to AA meetings and group therapy. I was just going through the motions, but at least I was moving. And somehow I never fell back into drinking. By October, I had made it to my first full year of sobriety. I got up at Drummers AA and gave my lead, the story of my recovery so far. And, for those moments at least, I had fun.

People tried their best to comfort me after Greg left, and slowly my spirits began coming back to life. Friends would manage to get me out to the bars, but these jaunts were painful at first. Everyone would call out, "Hey, where's your scrumptious boyfriend?" and I'd fall into depression all over again. Greg did write and call me when he could. But he never suggested that I come down and move in with him. *If he only would,* I kept thinking, *we could make it together.* But it never happened.

During the last months of 1986 I graduated from group therapy. I had become one of the leaders there, and my surviving Greg's departure without going completely to pieces seemed to convince everyone that I really could stand on my own. I had no idea what life might still have in store for me, but at least I knew by this time that I was going to carry on somehow. I no longer needed the group, everyone said: "Once you're part of the solution instead of part of the problem, you no longer need to be in the middle of the problem."

In late November, Gretchen came over and tried to talk me into going out in drag with her. Finally I gave in, more to shut her up than anything else. But there was no more sparkle left for me in either the drag ritual or in being Candi. That night as we left the K, a blond guy sitting out front in his car yelled to me, "Hey gorgeous! Come on over here!" I was lonely, and it had been forever since I'd had sex. He was beyond handsome, so why not check him out?

"Candi," Gretchen said, "don't mess with that guy. He's one of those straight guys who likes to sleep with drag queens."

"So what? He's a live body." I walked over to him.

"Like to take a ride in my car, girl?" he smirked.

"Sure, why not?" I told Gretchen I was going home with this guy.

"It's your thing," she said. "Call me in the morning." I got into the blond guy's car, and we went to my place. I went through the motions of acting interested in him, but before long I knew Gretchen was right: He was one of those basically straight guys who, for some reason, got excited making it with drag queens. With me still in drag we had a dull sexual encounter. Then he really blew my mind: He asked me if I would put him in drag.

Somehow his request totally disgusted me. *Buddy,* I thought, *you straights think we gays are sick. But I've never met anyone like you.* With a sneer I told him, "Get out of my apartment—right now!"

As he walked toward the door, I yanked my wig off and hollered, "Here's what I really look like, you sicko!" He made no attempt to hide his revulsion, and I slammed the door behind him.

The next morning, I found a huge cardboard box in the basement, brought it up to my apartment, and opened my voluminous closet. I looked at four years' accumulation of Candi's wardrobe and accessories: dresses, pantsuits, skirts, blazers, evening gowns, sportswear, wigs, hats, gloves, pumps, purses, earrings, necklaces, rings, bras, boots, underwear, pantyhose, and makeup. I stuffed every single article into the box and taped the lid shut. Then I hauled the box down the fire escape and heaved Candi with all her gear into the open dumpster.

I felt like ten tons had just fallen from my back. As I looked at the drab exterior of the box, I thought to myself, *Candi, I loved you. You've been a great friend to me. I've had lots of fun with you. But, dear girl, I don't need you anymore. Goodbye!*

I turned away and climbed back up to my apartment. I felt as if a new day in my life was dawning. My personality had at last merged with Candi's. I was now confident enough to be just John from here on. I phoned Gretchen, Velveeta, Jennifer, Miss Action, and Lauren and told them what I had done. None of them took me seriously. Miss Action clucked out the same old line, "Candi, you'll be back. Once a drag queen, always a drag queen."

"You're wrong," I said. "I don't need to be Candi anymore. That's not who I am—and I'll never do drag again as long as I live."

Howard and I had our last session together in January 1987. I thanked him for giving me all the tools I needed to stay sober and deal with my issues. I was now what he'd always hoped I would become: A well-adjusted gay man with every prospect of future happiness. He had every confidence that whatever issues I might still encounter, I'd be able to deal with myself as life brought them to the surface.

I asked Howard if I could check back with him in a year, just to let him know how things were going. He said that would be great, but he fully expected me to report that I was still what I was today: a happy gay man.

"Howard, how can I ever thank you for the past five years you've spent with me?" I said as we hugged. "Thank you for being here for me."

"You've changed so much," he said. "I can't tell you how proud I am. If I could ever have a son, I'd want him to be just like the man you are now." I barely managed to make it out of Howard's office before a flood of tears began flowing.

FIFTEEN

I LEANED ON THE BATHROOM counter and looked into the mirror. My brown eyes, looking dull and tired, stared back at me. *I'm happy as a gay man, but something is still wrong.*

I had just finished having sex with Jack—someone I didn't even know, except from the two other times we'd been intimate. He had never called me after either of our encounters; not even tonight had he made the slightest attempt to learn more about me. After our last time together, I said to him, "You know, we should get together some night for dinner or something."

"Oh yeah," he replied. "That might be fun." But it never happened.

So why am I here with Jack again? At the K tonight, when the closing lights flashed and everyone still there was caught standing around, Jack and I happened to be facing each other and also happened to know each other slightly. But why bother with these types of relationships? I was supposed to be well adjusted now. Candi and I were at last one person. My distinguished psychologist had assured me I was ready to embrace a successful future. He should know, shouldn't he? He had found happiness as a gay man, even living with the same partner for years. Of course, even his long-term relationship was "open," with both men seeing other people on occasion. Was that the best the gay life had to offer?

Engaging in sex while sober was getting more difficult again, as my inner core of modesty reasserted itself. I had never completely gotten over the nervousness of gay sex.

Why do I still need to have sex to make myself feel like I'm worth anything? Maybe having someone's arms around me in a bar proved that I was worthwhile—and kept the gossip from wagging behind my back that I had lost my appeal. I had been sober for over a year, and had friends in AA who really seemed to care about my well-being. But something was still wrong.

I was twenty-three years old, but I felt like a washed-up old man. I was too well known—and too old—in the gay community ever to be an exciting "new face" again. It was time to face reality: No Prince Charming was going to ride up and sweep me onto his shining white horse and off to Happily Ever After. Greg had looked and acted like my prince, but I couldn't keep him. And what about Bob, my "big buddy," who had also left me? Or the hundreds of men with whom I'd had sex over the years? Faceless people in the dark. Men I brought home when I was drunk and never even saw again the next morning. Being able to attract so many men should have made me feel good about myself. But my whole life seemed dead and empty.

I splashed some cold water on my face. Is this all my life would ever be? Just looking forward to finding my next trick and having a few minutes of sexual pleasure? At AA, I told everyone I was going cold sober, ready to face reality. So why didn't somebody tell me what reality's face was going to look like? I was glad to have stopped drinking, but there had to be more to life than this.

I crawled back into bed with Jack. He was already asleep, and I just lay there; I had no desire to snuggle close to him. After tonight, I'd probably never see him again, and I honestly didn't care.

At work the next morning, I saw a quirky—but friendly and unassuming—couple who were regulars. *Good customers,* I thought, *even if they do run some kind of religious thing at Ohio State.* Whenever they came in, I gave them personal service and went out of my way to show them ways to improve the layout on their material. Was it because they always seemed upbeat and enthusiastic about seeing me, and I was just responding in kind? In any event, I enjoyed talking with this couple—Thor and Linda Nelson—whenever they came in with a copy job.

Actually I seemed to keep running into them outside of the copy shop, too. On my lunch breaks, sometimes I'd walk down to Wendy's, and they'd be there having coffee. They'd invite me to join them. Or I'd grab a city bus to head for a bar, and they were on it, so I'd sit by them and chat. One day I went with my mother for a picnic in the park, and they were there. *Weird, I can't seem to get away from these people,* I thought.

At the same time, I didn't really want to get away. In fact, one day Thor came over to the cash register, ready to pay for his copies. He smiled, and suddenly I felt overwhelmingly moved, like I wanted to cry. There was some power, some force coming from him, not menacing but something warm and trusting. I didn't cry, of course—with a store full of customers, I maintained my professional demeanor. What did Thor want from me? Nothing, it seemed. *I can't see why he and Linda always seem glad to see me . . . me, with my bleached-blond hair, swishy mannerisms, and campy wit.*

I decided to return to school. Maybe that would get me out of the doldrums. I petitioned the university, and they responded, "We want to see some evidence of change in your life that might lead us to believe you'll succeed here this time." I got Howard and my AA sponsor to write letters saying I had been in therapy for five years and in successful alcoholism recovery for eighteen months. Thus encouraged, the school said I could re-enroll. I had lost my desire to study music but decided to aim for social work. Maybe I could help other people rebuild their lives, the way Howard and AA had helped me.

Thor and Linda kept coming into my store. Sometimes they dropped off jobs instead of doing their own copying on the spot. While I did their jobs, I read some of their material. They seemed to be spiritual spooks of the "born-again" stripe. Ugh! But at least none of their stuff seemed anti-gay.

I got sick and missed a couple days at work; somehow Thor and Linda found out where I lived and brought food over to me. They showed me other kindnesses, too. *What's with them?* I wondered. When they left, I didn't want them to go.

Then Thor came in to pick up some copies and said to me, "Would it be OK if I come by your apartment sometime and talk to you?"

"What about?"

"Well . . ." He hesitated. "I just want to talk to you as a friend."

Oh, no. This whole thing has been some kind of setup. I know exactly why he wants to talk. He wants to convert me to his religious beliefs. I wasn't the least bit interested; I'd seen too many times how Christians felt about gays, and I wanted no part of whatever he was peddling. Despite my reservations, however, I found myself blurting out, "Sure, I guess that would be OK."

"Great! How about tomorrow at 4:00, after you get off work?"

"That sounds fine." As I watched him walk away, I debated whether to call him back and tell him I forgot about a doctor's appointment or something. But another customer was waiting in line, and I decided it wouldn't be that bad. *Let him come tomorrow. I'll get rid of him quick enough.*

After work the next day, I was in my apartment when the doorbell rang. I looked out my bedroom window and saw Thor standing there with a smile. I had tried to forget about his "friendly talk," but it obviously hadn't slipped his mind. I sat for about fifteen seconds, hoping he'd disappear back down the stairs. But he knocked again, harder. I heaved a sigh and went to answer the door.

Thor came in and found a seat on the couch. After a few minutes of small talk, he got to the point of his visit: "John, I want to talk about something serious. I want to tell you about Jesus."

I knew it. Well, bite your tongue and let him talk. The sooner he says it, the sooner he leaves. He started to speak—but each word began to slow down and drift strangely into my ears, like a portable tape player on low batteries: "John . . . every . . . time . . . I . . . see . . . you, . . . you . . . look . . . like . . . you're . . . carrying . . . suitcases . . . that . . . are . . . too . . . heavy . . . for . . . you . . . and . . . you . . . need . . . somebody . . . to . . . help . . . you. . . ." His words seemed to thump into my brain, dull and heavy, like slogging through knee-deep wet snow. They stunned me, because somehow I knew what he said was true. *But how does he see what I feel and have tried so hard to disguise?*

Thor's next words penetrated my thoughts: "John, I know somebody who can carry your 'suitcases' for you."

My mind was blank. *Why don't I have some glib response? I should—there's one somewhere near the tip of my tongue.* But Thor's voice was so quiet and assured, and I was so close to tears, that I couldn't say anything.

Thor continued. "This world isn't right, and we're not right, either. There's something written here . . ." he pulled a small Bible from his jacket pocket, ". . . that I want to read you." He thumbed through the book's crinkly pages and read, "For all have sinned and come short of the glory of God." He looked at me. "That's you and me, John. And without Jesus in our lives to forgive us, we feel like we're lugging heavy suitcases onto a train going nowhere."

His words pierced me—and made perfect sense. "I've felt like that," I said to myself, but I also heard myself say it aloud.

"That's OK," Thor said. "Jesus can forgive us, because He took those suitcases—what was wrong with us and what we've done wrong—upon Himself. And He died for us, so we could get off that train to nowhere. He did that because He loves me and you, John."

I knew I'd done many wrong things. I had lied and stolen from people plenty of times. Could I really be forgiven? This Jesus didn't seem much like the one represented by those sign-shaking Christians on the Olentangee Bridge. Or was He?

What difference did it make? If Thor was a Christian, no matter how nice he seemed, he would hate me, too. *It's time to get rid of this guy. Out with it, John.* "Thor, I need to let you know something. I'm gay. God can't love me."

He looked puzzled. "Whatever gave you that idea?"

I didn't expect that response. What could I say? "I'm not sure, but I think it was from Christians. I mean, that's all I've ever heard. God hates queers, so He can't love me."

Thor lifted a hand. "Hold it just a minute. Let me read you something else. 'And while we were yet sinners, Christ died for us.' John, this is saying that, before you or I even knew we needed to be forgiven, He forgave us." He flipped a few more pages and kept reading. "Neither fornicators, nor idolaters, nor adulterers, nor the effeminate, nor homosexuals, nor thieves, nor the covetous, nor drunkards, nor revilers, nor swindlers, shall enter the kingdom of God."

I looked at him, puzzled. "You just read it yourself, Thor. I can't get to heaven, so why are you talking to me?"

"I wouldn't be honest with you if I didn't give you everything God says about being gay. But there is good news after the bad news." He turned some more pages in his little book. "Other places in here say clearly that homosexuality is wrong. Here's one that says, 'You shall not lie with'—that means have sex with—'a male as one lies with a female; it is an abomination.'"

"I thought you were gonna tell me some good news."

"If you accept God into your life, you accept everything about Him. Here is Jesus speaking, 'If you love Me, you'll keep My commandments.'"

"Thor, if He says don't be a homosexual, I can't do it." I knew I loved God; He had helped me through AA. But even in AA, I couldn't claim to love God and continue to drink. *Maybe loving God does have to come with some sort of price tag.*

"Listen, John, this is the good news," Thor said. "The Bible says homosexuals won't inherit the kingdom of God. Then it goes on to say, 'And such were some of you.' In other words, the apostle Paul was talking to people who *had been* homosexuals—but they weren't involved anymore. They had changed.

If we make the decision to accept Jesus into our lives, He comes to us, then His love changes us. John, you don't have to stay the way you are."

"What do you mean? I was born gay. What other way is there for me to be?"

"You weren't born gay," Thor answered softly. "Let me read you something else, from the very beginning of time: 'And God created man in his own image . . . male and female He created them. . . . And God saw all that He had made, and behold, it was very good.' The man and woman God created were named Adam and Eve. If another man could have been the suitable helper Adam needed, why didn't God make another man instead of a woman?"

What Thor said made sense, like turning on a light switch. Male and female *were* different—but made for each other. And God said that was very good.

Suddenly Thor stood up. "I think I've said enough for today. Linda and I have to go out of town for a week. When we get back, I hope we can talk again." He smiled, then turned and left, shutting my front door quietly behind him.

Thor's words haunted me over the next few days. I'd wake up in cold sweats and have trouble concentrating at work. One thought ran over and over in my mind: *I don't have to stay the way I am.* I had a terrible sense that something was wrong, not just with my behavior, but with me. According to Thor's little book, God loved me—whether I was gay or not—but He desired to change me and give me a new life. If that was true, I had a decision to make: Either forget this Jesus business and stay the way I was, or let Jesus take my life and change it.

Thor said Jesus was someone who would never leave me. A lover who never leaves? *If that is really true, Jesus is the person I've been searching for all my life.*

Suddenly I remembered a time many years ago, when I was ten. One Easter Sunday, I watched *King of Kings* on TV, the movie about the life of Jesus. None of my family members were religious; Dad, Mom, and Garry never went to a church of any kind, even at Christmas and Easter. We didn't pray at meals, and I never saw a Bible in the house.

But I was so entranced by the movie's characterization of Jesus that I began to walk by myself on Sundays to a church nearby. I decided that I wanted to be a minister when I grew up. I even set up an altar under the stairs in the basement, with some candles and a cross I made of wood. I put a bedspread around me like a priest's robe and gave communion to an imaginary congregation. Mom and Garry got a great kick out of it.

I also thought back to the time when, as a teenager, I had prayed to invite Jesus Christ into my life after talking with Heidi, the born-again Christian in my class. What had that experience meant?

And what about that strange night out on the dance floor at the K? Time had stood still and I had heard a voice saying, *"I want you to come back to Me. I can free you from all this and change your life."*

Could God really change anyone? I had to admit, God had helped me give up drinking; I knew that for sure. That was one suitcase He had taken from me. I also knew, if I asked Jesus to take my life and change it, I was going to do it all the way, whatever it meant, or not do it at all.

After pondering these kinds of thoughts for several days, I made up my mind: *I will accept Jesus. I'll do it.* But what was the right way? On impulse, I got down on the floor by the foot of my waterbed. "God," I prayed, "I don't know what You're going to do to me. And I don't know how to get out of homosexuality. I have no idea how that's possible. But I want to give my life back to You. I will trust You, and I'll never turn away from You again, whatever happens."

I stood up slowly. It was February 10, 1987. *I guess I'm a Christian now. . . . But I still feel gay.* Was I a gay Christian? Could there be such a thing? I wasn't a bit changed as far as I could tell. I had no idea what to do next.

Linda and Thor came back from their trip, and I called to tell them what had happened. "Now what?" I asked, and Thor said he would come right over.

When he arrived, he told me, "John, you were honest with me. Now I'll be honest with you." He paused. "Linda and I first saw you on campus and then at your copy shop about six months ago. We've been praying for you ever since. Right from the beginning, we knew you were gay. But we also knew that made no difference to God. And we felt sure that, sooner or later, you would come to Him." I was dumbfounded. They had cared so much for me all this time; I knew there was something special about this couple!

At Thor's urging, I dug out an old Bible and began reading it, starting in the Gospel of Matthew. Every day I took it to work with me and read on my lunch hour and breaks. Then I brought it home and read some more.

It was an eye-opening experience. In this book I saw a man, Jesus, Who was totally unafraid to be seen with, Who even embraced, everyone: high people, low people, sick people, weak people. He was equally at ease among ordinary folks and highly educated socialites. He was gentle with children, women, even His followers when they acted stupid. Yet He was unafraid to stand up and oppose kings, even religious people who probably would have been the anti-gay sign-wavers of His day.

Most important, He let Himself die—not for His own wrongs, but to pay for mine. Then He refused to stay dead. "I have power to lay my life down and to pick it up again," He said. And He rose from the dead to give me a new life in place of the one I'd been living.

As I read, His warmth and wisdom radiated from the pages. And I became certain that, in Jesus, I had met someone capable of loving me more than anyone else ever could. Yet He wanted nothing from me; I didn't have to perform for Him. He was delighted with my kind of flamboyant personality. *There's nothing I could ever do to make Him love me any less,* I realized. *He loves me, simply because I exist.*

During the next week, Thor and Linda spent hours answering my questions about the Bible, about Jesus, and about what it meant to be a Christian. One evening I went to their house for dinner. As they were preparing the meal together in the kitchen, tears ran down my face. There was an innocence about them, a purity and a harmony that I found very moving.

By now, Thor and Linda had essentially adopted me. We'd go to the grocery store or the laundromat together. If they came over and I was gone, they'd thumbtack a note on my door: "Come over for dinner any night you'd like!" They didn't talk about homosexuality or tell me to stop being gay. They didn't treat me any different than the way they treated each other. They openly loved each other, and they openly loved me.

Meanwhile, my gay life went on but in jumbled fashion. I wasn't really sure yet how to live any other way, and Thor and Linda hadn't told me directly to stop. My drag sisters were still my friends, and the bars were the only social world I knew. But now I found that my gay life, which already had begun to seem tedious, didn't have any of the old excitement. I would go from Thor and Linda's house to a bar downtown and immediately be aware that the innocence and purity of motive I'd just left were simply not there. It seemed no one was innocent in a gay bar; everyone was just looking for self-gratification.

I sensed something like an invisible curtain slowly descending between me and the life and friends I had loved for so long. It was a curtain I could still push away if I wanted, but I had no desire to resist it. *I don't even have any strong desire for sex right now. Strange . . .*

I called my mother and told her, "You're not going to believe what has happened. Do you remember when I was fifteen, and I joined that Christian youth group?" She said yes, and I blurted out, "Mom, I don't have to be gay anymore. I wasn't really born gay—"

I heard her take in a sharp breath. "I can't believe it," she said. "I was just praying, 'God, if You are out there and if there is some way you could help John not be gay anymore, would You do it?'"

"You're kidding! You said that to God?"

"Yes."

"Just now?"

"Uh-huh." She sounded as stunned as I felt inside.

"Mom, I don't even know what's going on, but something is changing inside me. I can feel it."

We were both amazed, confused—and happy.

I continued to spend most of my time alone, reading through the Bible and crying as though I was being rinsed out from the inside. It was almost like a nervous breakdown, except I wasn't anxious. I was finally at peace and felt inner pain dropping from me like an icicle melting in the winter sunshine.

But I still harbored many doubts. *I have no idea how I can ever live the way the Bible says I should. But I want to, even though I can't see how.*

Parker was the first person in gay life I told about what was happening. He smiled. "John, at this point, nothing you could do would surprise me. You're so dramatic, and you've gone through so many different changes in your life. This is just another one of them—one more phase."

"No, this isn't a phase. It's never going to go away." He just shook his head and kept smiling.

One major question kept looming in my mind: What about being Christian *and* gay—was it possible to be both? Thor had said I wasn't born gay. *But since I am gay and I know God loves me, can I stay gay?* I decided to ask someone other than Thor or Linda, just to see what someone else had to say about it. Several weeks later, without telling anyone, I went to a local Metropolitan Community Church where I had attended some AA meetings. Arriving at the church, I was ushered into an office where a middle-aged man sat in a wheelchair. He pushed himself out from behind a desk and introduced himself.

I didn't even try to catch his name but got right to the big question on my mind: "Sir, I need to let you know something. I've given my life to Jesus Christ. I've become a Christian. And I am wondering, can I be a Christian and stay gay as well?"

"Oh, sit down, sit down!" he exclaimed, directing me to a chair. "Of course you can stay gay. Jesus has absolutely no problem with that!"

I persevered. "But I'm reading parts of the Bible that tell me it's not cool for a man to sleep with other men. I've also read that I wasn't born this way, that God created male and female to be together."

"Son, let's look at the Bible and see what it really says. I think you'll be pleasantly surprised." He took a Bible from his desk and, pulling his wheelchair closer to me, proceeded to read several passages in the Bible that spoke about homosexuality. All of them condemned the behavior, or so it seemed. But this man had a "reinterpretation" of why the passages actually were neutral—or even supportive—of gay behavior.

For instance, he turned to the first chapter of Romans, where the apostle Paul spoke of men "exchanging the natural use of the woman" and burning "unnaturally" in their hearts toward one another and also women acting "unnaturally" and sleeping with other women. According to this part of the Bible, both behaviors were "detestable."

"That seems pretty clear—" I started to say, but the minister interrupted me.

"The men and women mentioned here were heterosexuals who engaged in homosexual behavior. You see, they were engaging in unnatural behavior—for them. But it is natural for *gay* men and women to love members of the same sex. So you can see why this passage doesn't say that homosexuality itself is wrong."

I wasn't convinced and told him about my growing conviction that God created me to be heterosexual.

"You were born gay," he retorted. "There is strong scientific evidence to prove it. You've probably felt gay from your early childhood, right? Don't let anyone tell you different!"

The more he talked, the more convinced I became that he was wrong. I practically skipped out of his office that day. It seemed strange, but I wasn't upset with what I was coming to believe. I knew in my heart that Thor had been telling me the truth. I had no idea how God could possibly change me. But I had the desire to see Him do it. I didn't even know what was wrong with being gay. There were still a lot of unanswered questions, but I knew the answers would come in time.

That night, I went to the Garage. Looking across the dance floor, I saw the gay minister from MCC in his wheelchair. I caught his eye, and he looked away. *You're a minister in the church—and you're sitting in a gay bar?* I wondered. *Mister, what are you doing here?* Then another thought startled me even more: *Come to think of it, what am I doing here?*

SIXTEEN

I WAS AFRAID TO ATTEND a straight church, and Thor and Linda didn't pressure me. But something was becoming very clear. The contrast I felt between the heaviness of gay life and the lightness I sensed at Thor and Linda's was a dissonance that couldn't be easily resolved.

Still, I kept going to gay bars and Drummers AA meetings. One night at Drummers, a struggling young lesbian alcoholic asked, "Do gay people go to heaven when they die?" It was a rather odd question for the setting, but at this particular meeting people were allowed to talk about whatever they wanted.

We went around the room, and everyone expressed an opinion—mostly that if you were a good person who helped other people, you'd get to heaven. I began to get nervous; I knew I wanted to say something else, but I wasn't sure just what it would be.

When my turn came, I stammered, "I-It's immaterial whether you're gay or not. If you accept J-Jesus Christ as your Savior, you'll go to heaven." I couldn't understand why it had been so difficult for me to say those simple words. There was dead silence. Everyone looked at me with slack jaws and pie-eyes, as if to say, "What in the world is up with you?" After all, I was a fixture—a celebrity—in gay life. Had I lost my mind?

Right after I said those words, I thought more about them. Thor had told me that when people first accept Jesus, their character doesn't change instantaneously. But they begin to go through a gradual process called *sanctification*, during which their character is molded by God, to be more like Him.

When the meeting was finished, I went and introduced myself to the girl who had raised the heaven issue. She was about twenty-one and obviously troubled about her lesbianism. "Kelly, I need to tell you what's happened to me," I said, then described how I had accepted Jesus Christ.

"I don't think it's right to be gay," I added. "There is another way. I'm not sure how to get to it, but God has something better for us than being gay."

She was perplexed but interested. She came over to my place, and we had several long conversations. She was so sweet, so young, and so confused about lesbianism. But after a few weeks, she stopped coming over to talk.

I had become friends with several other gay people at AA. One of them named Chuck invited me over to his apartment to enjoy some new gay, X-rated videos. We had done this before, but this time I said, "No thanks, Chuck, I don't want to see them."

Chuck's voice over the phone burned with sheer rage and astonishment: "John, what's wrong with you? Who are you? This isn't you!" I had no answer, just the knowledge that the videos represented something I didn't want in my life anymore.

Then Parker called. "My hairdresser and I were talking about this religious thing of yours. Doug wants to come over and set you straight—no pun intended." About half an hour later, Doug walked in with Parker and we covered much of the same terrain I had traveled with the gay minister. Before long Doug was visibly trembling. Suddenly he excused himself, leaving me and Parker alone.

"How do you feel about what I'm saying?" I asked Parker.

"Like I want to run out of the room and cry."

"Why?"

"I don't know."

I smiled at him. "What I'm saying is true, and you know it." He was silent, and I asked, "Will you reject me as a friend because of what's happened in my life?"

"No, John, I'll never do that."

I sat down next to him on the couch and looked him in the eyes. "If I didn't care about you so much, I wouldn't be sharing these things with you. And I want you to know that you'll reject me before I'll ever reject you."

I realized after Parker left that the more people argued with me, the more convinced I became that the Bible was true. I couldn't explain why I knew, but I had this inner certainty; I just couldn't be swayed.

During the coming weeks, I was glad for the hours I spent at my job. They provided me with the distractions of plenty to do and lots of people to interact with. I even felt less like going out to the bars anymore. But I was accustomed to my home phone ringing off the hook, and now it wasn't ringing much at all.

By May, I felt I had reached a point of no return to gay life, even if I didn't yet feel straight. I decided to mail a letter to fifty of my closest gay friends explaining my departure from gay social life. This letter marked a turning point for me. After it went out, I pretty much withdrew from gay society for the time being. Not one person to whom I'd written ever responded. I stopped going to bars and changed my phone number. No one told me, but I realized that to really break free from homosexuality I would have to leave all of its influences—at least for a while.

I felt comfortable letting Parker remain my only gay friend. He told me that not long after I wrote my "Dear friends" letter, he'd been standing outside a gay bar one night, and a carload of drag queens pulled alongside him. "Parker," a shrill voice shrieked, "tell Candi that if we ever see her again, we'll kill her!" I didn't ask him who had been in the car, and he didn't offer to tell me. I didn't really want to know; I wasn't sure if the words were a joke or serious.

Cutting loose of gay life brought me face to face with a vacuum of loneliness that my social activities had covered over. But the loneliness I felt was different from what I'd known before. It felt more like an ache for human company—but not for sex with men. I felt deeply loved by Jesus, although I longed to find another group of friends who seemed familiar. My whole living environment had become so unfamiliar.

My apartment had always been filled with gay erotica. Now I got rid of the explicit photos, porno magazines, and videotapes; one by one they went into the same dumpster where Candi had disappeared. As I purged my apartment of these things, Thor and Linda got me replacements: Christian books, pictures, and plaques that reminded me of God. They told me about radio stations where I could hear Christian programs and recommended Christian music tapes. They all helped—but the inner ache persisted.

It was becoming obvious that I needed more help than Linda and Thor were equipped to give me. If I was going to really get out of homosexuality, I needed to find other people who had made the same journey. Then, in a Christian bookstore, Thor and I found a book that promised to shed some light on my struggles. *Beyond Rejection* by Don Baker told the story of a man raised in a Christian family who married, struggled with homosexual feelings, and found the kind of freedom I was looking for.

At the back, the author mentioned an outreach called Exodus International, and I wrote them for information. Since I knew no more about changing my gayness than I had right after becoming a Christian, I eagerly read the ministry's material when it arrived in the mail. Exodus, it turned out, was involved with helping people leave homosexuality behind. By now I felt I really wanted—if it was at all possible—to get away from homosexuality. I found out that one of their oldest ministries, called Love in Action, was located in the San Francisco area. Thor and Linda were due to take a trip to the West Coast to see their parents; they decided to take a detour to Love in Action and look things over for me.

When Thor and Linda returned, they told me Love in Action was a residential ministry for men and women who struggled with homosexuality. It was headed by a married couple named Frank and Anita Worthen. Frank had left homosexuality in 1973; he and his wife had been married for several years. Linda and Thor sensed deep emotional healing going on at Love in Action, and they requested that my name be added to the ministry's mailing list. I went home and wept for joy that some place existed where I might meet others like myself and find freedom.

Thor and Linda held church services on the Ohio State campus, but only a handful of people attended. I kept saying that I needed companionship of some kind, so Thor took me to a much larger church. But I was terrified there, panicked about what people might think if they knew what my life had been all about.

One day I got a postcard from Greg. "Greetings from sunny Panama!" he had written. I reminisced for the rest of the night about our times together. I thought, *Maybe I should see some of my gay friends again—just as friends—to ward off my loneliness.* I could still think of a few gay friends to whom I hadn't sent my letter.

I called one of them, David, and went over to his place for pizza and a video. We had fun, but being around him made me almost forget I was a Christian. He reminded me too much of Greg.

Meanwhile, Love in Action continued to send me material, and I hungrily read Frank Worthen's book, *Steps Out of Homosexuality,* which offered more hope that I might be able to change. Even amidst all my inner turmoil, I could feel my relationship with God continuing to grow. I devoured the Bible and spent many hours thinking about its words and concepts.

Thor also helped me understand some basic things about what the Christian life involved, regardless of whether a new Christian was gay or straight. But I still found myself wrestling constantly with compulsive masturbation, stirred up by the years of gay fantasy backlogged in my memory banks. Perhaps the people at Love in Action could tell me how to deal with this issue. I hoped someone could.

With all my uneasiness, I still had to admit that my twenty-fourth birthday was the most precious I'd ever known. Thor and Linda invited me over for dinner, with all the trimmings and a big birthday cake. Afterward, we sat down in the living room and they prayed for me.

"God," Thor began, "You know how special John has become to us. Thank You so much for bringing him into our lives." Their deep, fervent prayers went on for many minutes, and I felt so loved and embraced by their tender concern. They prayed that God would keep me on the right path and that I would continue to pursue my relationship with Him. And that God would give me answers to all the questions I was still asking about homosexuality.

Soon after that night, I decided to move from my apartment altogether. Every nook and cranny was full of memories, especially of Greg. I found another place in a different area of Columbus and got an unlisted phone number. With all the transitions occurring, I decided I would benefit from less job stress. So I asked to be transferred from manager of my own store to assistant manager at another location.

By June, I'd been a Christian for nearly six months. I'd stopped going to gay AA meetings; in fact, my involvement with AA had greatly decreased. I still went to occasional meetings but only straight ones, although sometimes I saw gay friends there, too.

I finally started school again—summer quarter at Ohio State. I worked out a part-time class schedule that didn't conflict with my job. I guess the stress of my life-change was obvious, because my mother, Parker, and some AA friends picked up on it. They shared their opinions that maybe the Nelsons were exercising too much control over my life, and I began to think maybe they were right.

One night, I suddenly had an overwhelming urge to go to a gay bar and pick up someone. I almost experienced real physical pain as I resisted. Finally I got down on the tile floor in my bathroom and cried, "God, I beg you, keep me from going to a bar! I can hardly resist. . . ." Somehow I found the strength to stay home.

I faced a dark time; I fought repeated, agonizing temptations to go back to gay life. Masturbation continued to trouble me, most of all because the accompanying fantasies kept perpetuating the feeling that I was hopelessly gay. And I had to admit it: Much as I didn't want to anymore, I still felt gay, and I couldn't seem to stop feeling that way.

Early that fall, I called Love in Action and asked them to send me the application form for their one-year residential program. At the time, LIA was the only place offering the kind of twenty-four-hour care that I knew I needed. I quickly returned the completed application, banking all my hopes, prayers, and dreams on getting into their program. I knew that people from all over the world were applying for just sixteen openings. So I began to pray that God would get me in.

My sister, Vicky, asked me to drive her to Washington, DC, to enroll for her fifth semester at Georgetown. While I was there, I told Vicky for the first time that I had become a Christian. I also shared with her my plans about going to Love in Action. "Don't do it, John," she said. "You were born gay. You're only asking for trouble. Ten years from now you'll come to your senses and realize you were really gay all along—if you don't kill yourself first."

I tried to assure Vicky that I hadn't been born gay and that I could change. She just shrugged. "Well, you'll have to do whatever you're intent on doing. But don't say I didn't warn you."

In late October I was overjoyed to receive the long-awaited notice: I had been accepted to Love in Action! In early December I gave notice at my job and to my landlord, sold most of my belongings, and moved into my mother's apartment. Two days after Christmas, I packed two suitcases and prepared to leave. Thor and Linda drove me to the airport; my mother couldn't bear to go with us.

Just before I left her apartment, I cried in her arms. "John," she said, "I'm so proud of you and what you've done with your life."

"Mom, I didn't do anything; it was all God. I only had Him to lean on. It's Him you should be proud of."

At the airport, in a flood of mutual tears, I hugged Thor and Linda and thanked them for all they'd done for me. As my plane lifted above the clouds, I felt my spirit also soaring, confident that the help I needed was waiting for me in California.

When the plane arrived in San Francisco, I got off and caught a bus to San Rafael, twenty-five miles north. I had been told that someone would be at the bus stop to meet me. They would know me by the picture I had sent with my application.

"San Rafael, son," the bus driver said when we stopped. As I clambered down the steps with my two suitcases, I caught sight of a man about sixty years old, waiting on the platform. He looked at me and smiled. "John! John Paulk!"

I walked up to him, and he opened his arms and wrapped them around me. "I'm Frank Worthen. Welcome home!" He held me tight for several minutes while I cried tears of joy.

SEVENTEEN

A S FRANK PULLED UP to New Hope House, one of three residences run by Love in Action, I was excited but a little scared. "Here we are, John," he said with obvious satisfaction. "Your new home, and one of a kind."

Love in Action indeed was unique—at that time, the only residential ministry on earth exclusively devoted to helping men and women come out of homosexuality. We parked in front of New Hope, and Frank said, "Let's get your bags! This is where you'll be staying, you and the other new guys. I'm sure you'll all be great support for one another."

As we carried my bags into New Hope, Frank explained that each house had a leader and one assistant to oversee its basic running. My house leader, John Smid, had himself come successfully out of homosexuality. New Hope's eight new men would share the house's chores—including cooking meals from New Year's Day until the following December while we immersed ourselves in the Steps Out program.

"As a resident," Frank continued, "you'll take part in classes, Bible studies, meetings, and counseling—all created to help you discover the root issues behind your homosexuality and provide you with the necessary tools to live a victorious life." His words filled me with expectation and hope; somehow I knew the next year would be a pivotal one in my life, a twelve-month period that I would never forget.

I also knew some big hurdles lay straight ahead. Life here would not be easy. Love in Action expected every resident to find a full-time job as soon as possible to help meet personal expenses, plus the cost of room and board—about five hundred dollars a month.

But that didn't concern me. I had already lined up a job in advance with a Kinko's near Love in Action's administrative offices. What did worry me a lot was that all of us would be required to attend Church of the Open Door, a nearby nondenominational fellowship that had supported Love in Action almost since its inception in 1973. "Frank," I said, "I really haven't been very comfortable at the bigger churches I've been to."

"Not to worry, John!" Frank reassured me, smiling. "You'll find Open Door's congregation remarkable for the deep and compassionate way they accept people trying to overcome homosexuality. I guarantee you'll feel as much at home there as you do here!"

We walked through the large living room and into a back hallway, which led to several bedrooms. Frank opened the door to my room, joined me in putting my bags on the floor, then gave me another hug and left me to unpack. I found my room small but pleasant; it looked out into the back yard and a small patio surrounded by bamboo trees through which afternoon sunlight played. As I unpacked, I realized I hadn't seen anyone other than Frank since he'd picked me up. I wondered what kinds of people I would be meeting at supper. I'd never met any of them, yet I'd be stuck living with them for the next twelve months. I mentally pictured a square, nerdy group wearing horn-rimmed glasses—the dregs of the gay world. Hopefully I'd find one or two with something in common to make my stay tolerable.

Once I finished putting my things away, I ventured back out to the living room—and was somewhat stunned. Other New Hope men began trickling in: some young, some middle-aged. Not only were they most unnerdy, they were sharp and witty. We had come from all across the USA, including Texas, Florida, Nebraska, Georgia, Tennessee, Kansas, and other parts of California. I soon learned that the majority of the men in the program were my age, college educated, mostly from middle-class families, and quite physically attractive.

After dinner that night, which was New Year's Eve, all of us sat around the dining room table and prayed that God would enable us to complete the program successfully—together. From that night on, every Tuesday and Thursday when we gathered for prayer, we earnestly repeated that same request to God.

The other men's residence, El Shaddai (which means "God the All-Powerful One") was also home to eight new men. A couple of days after my arrival, the two houses got together for a social. Right away, one man in particular caught my eye. When I first saw Randy, he reminded me of Greg: blond, blue eyes, smooth skinned, and attractively built. Almost immediately, I felt an overwhelming sexual attraction toward him.

During the evening, I managed to engage Randy in conversation and discovered that he was from Toronto, capital city of Canada's Ontario province. Soon we were talking about how cold winters got in that part of the country. When I told Randy I was from Ohio, he said, "That's only a few hours' drive from Toronto. You should come and visit me when the program is over." The invitation sounded more than mildly interesting.

Over the next few days, I could hardly get Randy's face out of my mind. I was completely fixated on him—his looks, his body build, his warm personality. Suddenly I felt everything I'd learned as a young Christian melting away like snow on a hot California highway. I thought, *Why did I ever move thousands of miles to the West Coast? Who cares about some old program, anyway?* All I could think about was connecting with Randy. I wanted him sexually, like I was under a powerful spell of emotional and body-wrenching desire. It had been so long since I'd felt sexual attraction this strong to someone; it felt really good, kind of energizing and exciting. And to make things even more intriguing, it soon became apparent that my attraction to Randy was no one-way street. He gave off subtle signs that he was also drawn to me, which made me feel wonderful.

The next Sunday I walked into Church of the Open Door for the first time. They held services in a slightly run-down union hall, not a "real" church building. But, in spite of the plain surroundings, I almost immediately felt a warm, caring atmosphere. It certainly felt strange, however, to be surrounded by two hundred people who knew exactly why I had relocated to San Rafael. We weren't a hard group to spot: We all sat together among the rows of folding chairs—two whole rows of new single men—looking a mite insecure and timid among the congregation's chatting and friendly men and women. I felt rather uncomfortable. After all, how could I really be sure that these straight people—especially the men—would accept me?

I felt a little better when the senior pastor, Mike Riley, stood at the pulpit and welcomed the men and women of the 1988 live-in program. I was surprised when everyone burst into enthusiastic applause. They actually seemed pleased to have us there. *Interesting . . .*

It was at church that I first noticed something unusual. After the service, as people introduced themselves, several looked from me to Randy and said, "Hey, you know what? You two guys could be twins!" I didn't say so, of course, but I kind of liked that. I didn't stop and think about it then, but if I had, I might have realized that my usual pattern was about to click in—to seek out other gay men who resembled me but who also seemed somehow better than I was in some way. Why was this? Did I somehow feel that if I could attract these "better" persons, being with them would raise my own self-esteem? Whatever the possible motivations, I really couldn't have cared less just then. All I wanted was to get to know Randy better, and I sought out his company at every opportunity during the coming days, all the while being careful not to let my infatuation become known to any of the other men in the program.

The second weekend, Frank Worthen decided to introduce all of us to his favorite city, and we all drove into San Francisco for a walking tour of Frank's must-see spots. Before setting out, we divided the group into several clusters, and I quickly paired up with Randy and a few other guys. Soon we were walking around Fisherman's Wharf, looking at the outdoor markets with their impressive displays of fish, lobster, and other seafood. Then we spent some time looking through Ripley's Believe It or Not museum, before heading a few blocks west to Ghirardelli Square for ice-cream sundaes.

Along the way, I began playing eye games with Randy: I let my gaze linger on him as we walked, just so he knew in not-so-subtle ways that I was interested in him. Things escalated between us during dinner awhile later. I purposely sat across from Randy at the long table, then let my legs lean against his under the table where no one could see. This contact left me wanting more. By the end of the meal, we had both taken our shoes off and, unseen by the others, were caressing each other's feet.

Later, we strolled through Pier 39, a collection of cute shops on the waterfront overlooking San Francisco Bay. Randy and I were about to pass a dead-end walkway with dim lighting. No one else was in sight, and I knew this was my perfect opportunity. With no hesitation, I grabbed him by the front of his shirt, pulled him close to me, and began kissing him with passionate abandon. I was completely mesmerized. At that moment I didn't care who saw us or what the other program members would think. As our lips separated, we stood gazing deep into each other's eyes, not saying a word. We didn't need to; we both knew exactly what was happening inside. I could see my own emotions mirrored in his eyes.

A little later, the other guys in our group headed back toward the cars waiting in a parking garage a few blocks away. "I want to tell Randy something," I called after them casually. "We'll catch up with you in a few minutes." We ducked into another dark alley between two attractions on the Pier and locked ourselves into another long, lingering kiss. My heart was pounding; my body flushed with passion. I had only one thought, *Maybe not right now, but I'm going to have sex with you, Randy—soon!* I couldn't wait for the moment to come.

Randy and I realized we had better hurry on, so we quickly walked down the street and caught up with the others before they reached the cars. Then we began driving north through the city streets toward the Golden Gate Bridge. As we drove through the Embarcadero, Randy and I were sitting in the back seat, with two other program members up front. On impulse I said, "Hey, why don't we check out Golden Gate Park?" We'd passed it earlier that day, and who knew? We might stumble into a dark corner of the park where Randy and I could get out for a casual "stroll" under the stars before returning home.

Randy and I were holding hands, discretely rubbing each other's palms affectionately. *Those guys in the front seat don't have a clue what's happening here,* I thought with excitement. Suddenly Drew turned around in the front passenger seat and announced, "There is something going on in this car that I'm not comfortable with."

Randy and I started giggling, and I said with mock innocence, "Everything's fine. What're you talking about?"

Drew didn't laugh along with us. "We need to turn this car around and go home because otherwise something might happen that someone would regret."

Suddenly his words penetrated the shiny veneer of what I was doing, and the truth of the situation hit me: I was playing with fire, and I was about to get badly burned. It had been almost a year since I'd had sex with another man. Here I was, willing in a moment of foolish passion to throw it all away, to go against my deepest beliefs and my strongest commitment.

David turned the car around, and I abandoned all plans for a midnight walk in the park. Suddenly we were on the Golden Gate Bridge headed home. Randy and Drew got off at El Shaddai, then David and I went to New Hope. As soon as I walked in the front door, I went upstairs and told my house leader exactly what had happened: Randy and I had kissed, we'd groped each other when no one was looking, and we'd been heading straight toward a sexual encounter. Then, through one of my new friends, God had intervened, and I had stopped just short of falling into sin.

As I confessed what had happened, I started to cry. I was distraught; I was disappointed in myself. But, most of all, I was confused. I had never in my wildest imaginings about Love in Action anticipated being so quickly and powerfully attracted to another program member.

John listened to my confession, then began giving me some surprising words of wisdom. "Don't be surprised that you're attracted to somebody," he said. "This program is all about learning where your attractions come from. This is the best place for you to work through these things."

The program leaders responded quickly to my situation with Randy by putting restrictions around us: We were not to be alone together for the next ten days. My immediate reaction was misery, like a love-sick teenager pining away for a lost love. And Randy and I acted like teenagers: We wrote each other notes and managed to convince the other program members to sneak them back and forth.

Then the unthinkable happened: One of the other men in the program, a handsome man from a wealthy family in Florida, decided he was attracted to Randy and wanted to pursue him—and Randy had signaled his encouragement. Just like that, I was caught in a love triangle. All three of us had come from cultured families and had acquired a certain arrogance. Up to this time we'd been like a little snobbish clique too good for anybody else. I'd thought they were both my friends, but now they seemed to be turning against me in the most vicious way imaginable. *How dare they carry on right in front of me! It's obvious, isn't it? But why isn't anybody else catching on to their little love affair?* I was hurt and feeling very left out, frustrated beyond words. But, most of all, I was furious. Betrayed again by so-called friends—just like so many times before in the gay life. Would it never end?

Even in the midst of my insane jealousy, I recognized that I was regressing badly. Not only was I ready to jump back into bed with the first attractive man who came along, I was emotionally going to pieces with possessiveness. When was I going to learn my lesson?

Though I didn't realize it at first, God was certainly getting my attention, even in the midst of my painful emotions. As the days passed, I continued feeling miserable. Yet even through the turbulent emotions, a deeper realization pushed through: *This is not what I really want anymore.* I began to see more clearly. Hadn't I been through emotions just like this enough times for enough years? Did they ever bring me lasting fulfillment or satisfaction? Could I face them now and start dealing with the underlying reasons why I wanted to go down another dead end?

First, I had to face the reality that two parallel worlds were warring inside me. On one hand, I felt like a gay person, with all the typical emotional urges and sexual desires for other men. On the other, I was a Christian who wanted to do right, who wanted to be righteous and live a pure life pleasing to God. Here at Love in Action, I was being given a new chance to choose which side would win. The structure around me, the whole live-in program and everyone connected with it, were external supports to help me choose the right path—the one I knew I really wanted to pursue. But the ultimate choice was up to me. All the programming and external support in the world wouldn't change my life unless—and until—I began making right choices in how I related to men, no matter what my initial feelings and attractions might be.

After I had been at Love in Action for several weeks, something significant happened one Saturday afternoon when I was sitting at the kitchen table. John, my house leader, was sitting within eye's view in the nearby living room. A moment later, he walked into the kitchen, his brows knitted together.

"John," he began, "I think something very significant has just happened, and I feel I need to tell you. As I was looking at you a few seconds ago, all of a sudden it seemed like you changed dramatically. You didn't even look like you are now, but your appearance completely changed. I didn't even recognize who you were—but you were healed from homosexuality. There was a feeling of peace all around you, like you had become a man completely comfortable with yourself."

As John spoke, I was deeply moved; he'd given me hope to know that God was actually going to change me. I just needed to hang on and let Him do it. From that moment, John Smid's vision became my goal.

At the end of January, all the members of the Love in Action program went on our first weekend retreat. We traveled about two hours from San Rafael straight north on the main freeway, then headed west through apple orchards, hilly vineyards, and groves of towering redwoods until we reached the northern California coastline. Finally, we reached our destination, a rustic farm in the Mendocino hills with spacious acreage and over a dozen cabins dotting the landscape, many of them hidden by thick underbrush and trees.

We drove up the gravel driveway to a small parking lot next to the main house, a two-story structure with gables and chimneys that looked like something from a Grimm's fairy tale. Inside, the cozy living room was dominated by a hand-hewn stone fireplace that stretched floor to ceiling. Hand-carved chairs and other furniture beckoned invitingly. The upstairs bedrooms had a large assortment of beds, bunks, and floor mattresses. It was certainly a unique, attractive atmosphere for our retreat.

The weekend had a specific purpose: This was a time to get to know one another in a deeper way, apart from daily routines, and to begin the bonding process of forming a "family" together, something that would carry us through the entire year. Huge chunks of time were set aside that weekend for confession and sharing among the group. Each man had one hour to tell his entire life story while the rest of us sat and listened. We confessed the most personal details of our lives, especially how we had first become aware of homosexual leanings and how we had responded to them. How we had perceived our family situation, especially our relationships with our parents and closest loved ones. How, for most of us, we had acted upon our homosexual feelings by pursuing relationships within the gay world. How we had become disillusioned with homosexuality, and why we had ended up at Love in Action, seeking change.

Listening to these stories for hours that weekend was a fascinating experience. I began to see common factors among many of the men as the weekend progressed. Two patterns became especially clear to me, and sounded very familiar to my own life: Disrupted relationships in early life with men, especially absent or detached fathers, and disrupted relationships with other boys—inferiority, being feminine and "different" from other boys. Some of the guys had been sexually abused by older men, which had confused and frightened them and left them vulnerable to having more physical intimacy with men as they grew older. Others, like myself, had taken refuge in alcoholism and drug abuse from the pain we'd grown up with.

As these men talked, I was astonished by the stark disparity between outward appearances and inner turmoil: Outwardly, they looked "together," attractive, fully functional, and mature. Inside, once the facades were torn away, they were like hurting little boys still looking for unconditional love and approval, especially from other men.

When my turn came to sit in front of everyone and tell my story, I started crying before I could even say one word. I felt so empty on the inside, like a huge container that had been dumped out and was waiting to be filled again—but with what? It seemed strange to be feeling this way after Howard, my therapist, had "graduated" me from therapy, telling me that I was now self-sufficient and self-confident, a "happy gay man" ready to face whatever lay ahead.

As I talked, once again I had to face all the pain, the disappointment, the despair of growing up. Perhaps most painful, I had to face the fact that I had lived my life very differently from how the Bible instructed me to live. I had plunged into all kinds of evil, and now I was reaping the consequences. As I neared the end of my story, I confessed my deepest desire for the coming program year: "All I really want, more than anything else, is to know that I am loved. I want to really know it and feel it. I've been told all my life that others loved me, but I have never really felt loved at all."

I could see it so clearly now: My life's whole theme had been rejection. My parents divorced, then my stepfather and mother divorced, then my mother didn't marry Jerry. Ultimately, I felt deserted by all my most significant homosexual lovers. I felt rejected by almost every significant person in my life. "My heart cries for permanence, to know that somebody—no matter what happens—will never walk out on me. I'm just beginning to discover Who God is and what His character is really like. I have to learn to trust Him, to really know He won't ever reject me for the rest of my life."

Finally, I was done. Then Frank reached over and gripped my shoulders. With a huge smile, he said, "I know you belong here. And I want you to know how deeply you're loved."

Then all the men gathered around me, put their hands on my head and shoulders, and prayed fervently that God would pour out His presence and blessing upon my life during the coming months. They prayed that I would be healed from the wounds of rejection, that I would be open to trust them to show love and acceptance to me during the coming year.

The retreat was wonderful, but soon it came time to get back to the real world of work, evening meetings, and the struggles of living with so many other men under one roof. By this time, Randy and I were allowed to see each other again, but with one stipulation: There always had to be a third person present. In a way, it seemed so juvenile, like I was a teen being grounded for staying out late. But, as I was to learn, I was acting like a child in many ways, especially in my emotional attachments to other men. I needed some firm structure to help me grow up and find more mature ways of dealing with my emotional needs.

But my inner turmoil over Randy and David's relationship continued. I wanted to seek revenge on them and make them as miserable as I felt. I began gossiping about them at every opportunity, trying to turn others in the house against them. I also found myself wanting to run—maybe to go home where I was safe and everything was familiar. But, even as I seriously considered the thought, I knew that was not the answer. I had nothing waiting for me back in

Columbus. I felt like a tiny raft plunging down the Grand Canyon rapids; I had no place to go but forward, come what may. I would have to stick it out, persisting and trusting that God would, somehow, become more real to me and provide His strength for the temptations that were bombarding me every day.

One of the main features of Love in Action was the evening meetings each Monday and Thursday, when Frank taught about the various aspects of overcoming homosexuality. He spent the first weeks laying a foundation, including the Bible's perspective on this issue and how God desires to come into our lives in a personal way and begin changing us inside to become the men He created us to be. It would take many months for me to begin clearing up my distorted concepts of God, His character, and His intentions toward me. I had never experienced—or been able to receive—unconditional love from anyone. It was foreign to begin understanding what that meant and how God could offer it to me.

I also struggled to see God as a loving Heavenly Father. I had perceived my own father as being emotionally detached and seldom available when I needed him. So, even though I knew in my head that God loved me, it didn't yet touch my heart to the depth that I longed to experience it.

"Your primary source of love and acceptance must come to be God Himself," Frank told us one Monday night. "God will never reject you, and you need to derive your primary sense of belonging and acceptance first from Him, and only then from other people."

I understood the concept, but I struggled to live it out in daily life. My emotions still pulled me strongly in Randy's direction, and I had no idea how to let God fill those emotional needs I was trying to fill in homosexual patterns. But I realized these ways of looking to other men to fill my inner needs had been firmly established over years of living out a homosexual way of life. It only made sense that unlearning such habits would take a long time. How could I expect my same-sex attractions to vanish overnight, or even in a few short weeks or months?

One of the ways I began learning to deal with my infatuation with Randy was to seek out other relationships with straight men at church. They thought nothing of greeting each other with a warm hug, something I longed for but was also a little afraid of. I had never met men outside of a gay bar who were so open and loving with each other. But slowly, I found myself beginning to look forward to Sunday morning church services, where I could chat with the growing number of male friends I was making outside of the LIA program.

As the weeks passed, Randy and I at last felt we could spend time together on occasion. We might go out for breakfast or drive to a nearby park and feed the ducks in the huge pond encircled by a walking path. By this time, I felt quite sexually detached from Randy, though the distance was also aggravated by strong feelings of rage I felt toward him.

I did find myself able to talk more freely about my feelings toward Randy with others in the house. One man in particular, whose body was quite ravaged by AIDS, spent all his time at home because he was too weak to work. Bob really appreciated my company during the long hours he lay in bed, too weak to do anything but rest. We spent hours talking in his room about my frustrations with Randy and David, and he encouraged me to persist through the feelings that were raging inside me. While Bob encouraged me, I could also encourage him just by spending time with him and keeping him from being isolated.

As the other men in the program opened up, I realized that I was not the only one struggling with old habit patterns. During a meeting a whole series of confessions came out: One man confessed to having had sex twice in a week; another had snuck off to San Francisco for a sexual encounter; my roommate had gone out the previous weekend and gotten drunk. I had recently avoided sex but spent $80 on shoes and cologne I didn't need, just to make myself feel better. Afterward, we all prayed for each other and promised to support each other when the temptations came back.

As I became more involved in church and a weekly Bible study, I noticed something else that encouraged me: All around me were men and women who'd graduated from the program in years past, some of whom were now married with families. My Bible study was led by a man who'd been through Love in Action about ten years before. He was now happily married with two children. What a powerful encouragement, to see others around me who had successfully navigated the road down which I was embarking!

Things at work also went smoothly. One of the other men in the program got a job at the same Kinko's where I worked, and we met together before work every day for a short time of Bible reading and prayer. He also struggled with old drinking habits as well as homosexuality, so we had a lot in common to talk about. We also began to leak little bits of our stories to other coworkers and even customers, as opportunities came up to explain why we had both relocated to California.

Other indicators told me my mindset and self-image were gradually changing. One Friday, I took one of the guys in the program out to lunch for his birthday. We were stopped at a red light when another car pulled up beside me. The two guys inside whistled at me suggestively, then started laughing. For a split second I felt weird, and my immediate reaction was, *You guys are barking up the wrong tree!* Then, a second later, my old feelings kicked in, and I found myself wanting to jump into their car because they were cute.

All that day, I struggled with thoughts about running into San Francisco that night and cruising a bar. Instead, I stayed home that night and went to a support group meeting for men struggling with homosexuality who weren't living at LIA. I met a man who had left his wife and kids to pursue a homosexual way of life, then had come back to his family and was trying to make his marriage work. After the meeting, we went out for coffee and spent several hours talking about our lives and how God was helping us. I had a wonderful time and realized that God knew my needs for some personal attention. And He provided exactly what I needed in His way, rather than in my old ways. Maybe He was someone I really could begin trusting with my deepest needs.

Anita Worthen confirmed this thought during a house meeting one night when she turned to me and said, "John, until you stop running from your problems and completely surrender to God's work in your life, you'll never change." As she spoke I realized that I had been leaving a back door open in my mind, a way of escape back to gay life if things got too hard. Then the Lord reminded me again of my ironclad commitment a year previous: *No matter how hard things get, I will never turn away from You again.* Right then and there, I prayed silently that God would help me live up to that commitment. Deep inside I knew that change would come if I would stick it out, though I still had little idea of how it would happen.

In our Monday night Steps Out classes, Frank explained some of what made change so difficult: "Essentially, all the major components of deeply established homosexuality—sexual behavior with other men, adoption of a homosexual lifestyle, and entrenched homosexual personal identity—are rooted in the same-sex attraction commonly known as homosexual orientation."

Frank went on to explain that the underlying attractions toward men were a symptom of deep, unmet needs for love and approval from members of our sex. They were not inborn or genetically caused, but due to the influences of many complex life experiences. "Love in Action exists to give men like you tools of insight into your sexual orientation that can help you move toward change. But remember: It took you many years to get the way you are, and you've got to have patience with yourself, because dramatic change simply isn't going to happen overnight!"

As the weeks passed, I received lots of encouragement from others in the program. I also had additional support from Thor and Linda, who kept regularly sending me letters and cute cards, which cheered me up just when I needed it.

"Your faithfulness in writing is another sign of your love for me," I wrote them in one of my letters. "You have proven yourself faithful to me like no other humans. I am learning that God's love is commitment to others. I just want you to know that your devotion to me never goes unnoticed or unappreciated." Even on the difficult days, I was beginning to catch a clearer glimpse of God's love coming through faithful friends.

At the end of March came another milestone in our year: the annual Love in Action night at Church of the Open Door. This was the night when we would be officially introduced and welcomed as members of the church. This service was an annual highlight for the church, and many relatives and previous LIA grads attended. At the end, program members stood at the front of the congregation and each announced their name and home city. Then people were invited to come up and pray with a specific program member, then they could commit to pray for him or her during the remainder of the year.

I was overcome with emotion as a young couple stood over me and prayed that God would change my life and help me be faithful to Him. In their words I felt an overwhelming sense of love and acceptance. After that night, I noticed an even stronger desire to be part of the church. I had gotten over the feelings of being an outsider; now I felt accepted by others. They would come to talk when I walked in, putting a hand on my shoulder or patting my back and telling me how glad they were to see me. I felt loved and supported; the church was like the extended family I'd always wanted but never had.

I also enjoyed getting to know Mike Riley, the senior pastor. Mike was quiet and reserved but also warm and nurturing toward me and the other LIA men. He was gentle but carried a firm authority I found most admirable. Over the months, as we got to know each other, Mike began to take on a father image; I really looked up to him, and we started developing a close relationship.

All throughout the year I continued to communicate with Parker. We called and wrote each other regularly, and he seemed very interested in what was happening with me. From his perspective, though, I was part of some strange California cult he didn't really understand. By this time, he'd developed a dating relationship with another man. At every opportunity, I kept telling him what was occurring in my life and how, even through my struggles, God was changing me a little at a time.

By this time Parker and I had been friends for about ten years, and I appreciated the longevity and security his friendship represented in my life. Although our lives were going in divergent directions, we were mutually respectful and even supportive.

As the months passed at church, I began to notice something new: Gradually I was feeling more secure around the straight men. I could walk right up to other men at church and engage them in conversation, instead of avoiding them out of fear or insecurity. I was feeling more "equal" to them, like two brothers who had a good friendship. Feeling comfortable with men who were not gay was a totally new experience, and it felt wonderful.

But my attraction continued toward Randy for many months. And, even though the power of the attraction seemed to dissipate over time, I still struggled with romantic thoughts about him. I would dream about walking through a nearby park with him, both of us deep in private conversation. Or I would imagine us sitting on the cliffs overlooking the Pacific Ocean, which stretched to the horizon, enjoying another glorious California sunset as we snuggled close.

But an even greater problem was lingering sexual fantasies about other men, especially men I'd known and had sex with in the past. When these fantasies plagued me, I began praying that God would show me the underlying needs and desires triggering them. Frank Worthen taught us about common emotional triggers that stimulated sexual desires toward other men, such as depression, loneliness, disappointment, and frustration. The evening classes helped me pinpoint further connections between my homosexual feelings and my self-image. Growing up, I had always felt inferior to other boys, almost like I was on the outside of masculinity looking in on a foreign and fascinating world of men.

Especially with the help of Frank's teachings about the dynamics of homosexual attraction, I began learning how to analyze my own temptations as they were happening. One day I was in the neighborhood supermarket in the produce department. Another man a short distance away was examining the lettuce, and I found myself examining him: blond hair, muscular build, smooth skin—all the elements that had drawn me to other men in the past. But this time, instead of allowing myself to lust after him and picture ourselves in a sexual encounter, I asked myself for the first time, *What is it about him that you're drawn to?*

Surprising answers flashed into my mind. I found that I was envying his physical appearance. My attraction could be put into these words: "If I looked like him, I would feel better about myself. But if I could have sex with such an attractive man, I would also definitely feel better about me." In a flash of insight, I saw the underlying motivations for the attraction: my self-image. I was envious of what I perceived was lacking in myself. I wanted something he had. And I wanted his approval.

I was forced to think back on the hundreds of sexual encounters I'd experienced. I had attracted and seduced dozens of wonderful-looking men. And, in the midst of the sexual excitement, I had felt better—temporarily. But inevitably those feelings had vanished like a morning mist. And I'd been left, thirsting once again, for intimacy and connection with other men.

I remembered an insight Frank had shared: "Why are many gay men so promiscuous? Because gay men use sex as a counterfeit for genuine feelings of intimacy and affirmation. They think sex will secure these things for them. But because gay men tend to be so lacking in affirmation, they seek extraordinary amounts of sex in a vain effort to be affirmed. Having vast amounts of sex creates addiction, which only leads to seeking even more sexual gratification."

In gay life, I had almost unconsciously been trained to worship the male body. Strength, muscles, golden hair, blue eyes. I worshiped what someone looked like, but had little concern for his inner person. I wanted my needs fulfilled, no matter what the priorities and concerns of the other individual.

That day in the produce department, I started counteracting these old thoughts with some new ones: "You know, I'm not bad looking. I have a nice build. I have people who care about me. I have friends who are straight men." And a smile crept over my face because, for the first time, I realized that I didn't need the attention of that attractive man to make me feel good about myself. I pushed my cart down the next aisle with a spring in my step, feeling freer than I had felt in a long time. In that experience, I had a flash of insight that maybe there was a glimmer of hope: I could conquer this thing called *homosexuality*. With God's help, I was going to make it!

But, one night in church, I was discouraged about my ongoing attractions toward Randy. Although my feelings for him had abated considerably, they still persisted enough to bother me. At the end of the service, Pastor Mike invited anyone who was experiencing problems in their relationship with God to come forward for prayer. I went forward and knelt down, then cried my eyes out. I hadn't been able to cry since our first program retreat, and it felt good to let it all come out.

John Smid came over, wrapped his arms around me and prayed for me. "Lord, I pray that You will minister Your comfort to the hurting places in John's heart tonight," he began. As he prayed, I realized that I was still trying to control my behavior through my own actions, rather than relying on the Lord's strength. *I don't even know how to lean on the Lord,* I thought, *but at least I can confess my weakness to Him Who forgives.*

The same week, I sent away to an organization called Focus on the Family for one of their books, *Parenting Isn't for Cowards* by Dr. James Dobson. I wasn't sure exactly what motivated my purchase. But when it arrived, I knew it would always be sitting on my bookshelf, waiting for the time when I perhaps might have a son of my own. I found growing in me a new longing: a deep desire to become a husband and father. On the discouraging days, I only had to nurture that dream for a few minutes before I found the strength to keep on toward it. And that book served as a tangible reminder to me, something I could see to nurture the hope that my life would arrive at my dream's destination.

Toward the end of April, my father called me; it was the first time we'd spoken by phone since I had arrived in California four months ago. Our conversation was quick and seemed a little awkward. I felt sad after hanging up. *I don't really know my dad at all.* The thought hit me like a solid punch in the stomach. Even though Dad and I could exchange words, I felt like we were still emotionally separated by a gulf. I still was not identifying with him.

But my dad had given me this news: He and Vicki would be coming down to San Rafael from their home in Oregon, and we could spend a few hours together. When they arrived, I introduced Dad and Vicki to everyone I could. Afterward, we drove to San Francisco and walked around the waterfront before dinner. It was a beautiful spring evening, and we had a good visit, though conversation was a little strained between us. Perhaps that was to be expected; after all, I hadn't spent more than a few days at a time with my father since I was about fourteen years old.

As summer approached, I noticed my attitude changing toward other gay men I saw on the streets—especially when we visited San Francisco on the weekends. One Saturday, a group of us were walking around Union Square, in the heart of the downtown shopping district. As we walked out of Neiman

Marcus and paused for a red light at the corner, I noticed a guy nearby looking me over closely from head to toe. Immediately an indignant feeling rose up inside of me. *How dare he check me out! What gives him the right to look me up and down like I'm a piece of meat?*

Another time I was in the downtown San Francisco Macy's, a mecca for gay male shoppers. I walked up to the cologne counter and was smelling some samples when a clerk asked if he could help me. From his voice and mannerisms, I could tell he was gay and proud of it.

Rather than falling into my old pattern of giving off gay vibes, I had a completely contrary reaction. *Do whatever you can to make him think you're straight,* I thought. *Watch how you walk and talk—and ignore the signals he's giving off!* As I walked away from the counter I suddenly realized, *I don't want to identify with being gay anymore! Things must be changing at a deep level in my life.*

I began to have opportunities to share these changes with others. An ongoing part of the Love in Action ministry was evening rallies, when the men in the program would travel to other churches around the San Francisco Bay area to present our ministry and talk about the changes happening in our lives.

I enjoyed standing up in front of hundreds of people and presenting our unique and exciting program to others. I was aware that, in almost every church, there would be men secretly struggling with homosexual thoughts and desires, men who needed to know that support was available and change was possible. After one meeting, I remember saying to myself, *I think I want to spend more time in front of people. This is something I really would like to get more involved in.*

One of my most exciting sharing opportunities came later that year, when a small group of us traveled all the way to Eugene, Oregon, to talk about the ministry in a church near where our director's wife, Anita Worthen, had lived years before. I was especially excited because, now that she had graduated from Georgetown University, my sister Vicky was living a short drive away in Portland. I called and asked her if she'd like to drive down to Eugene to see me at the church. She said she would.

During that church service, we introduced the men from the program, and one of them told the story of how he had left gay life and become involved in Love in Action. Then I got up and sang a song called "Can You Reach My Friend?" I glanced down at my sister as I sang. To my surprise, she was weeping openly. When our presentation was over, I approached her, gave her a big hug, and asked her why she had cried.

"I realized as you were singing that something in you really is changing," she replied. "You're not being brainwashed, as I told myself you would be. You're truly not the same person. I don't know what's happening to you, but it's beautiful and profound."

I had to leave Vicky for a moment to greet another person in the audience who wanted to thank me. After this brief interchange, I was about to return to Vicky when Anita gently took my arm. She whispered, "Who's the girl you were talking to, the one who's crying?"

"That's my sister. She came from Portland to hear us tonight."

Anita didn't want to interrupt the moment to be introduced to Vicky, but she gave me a suggestion, "Perhaps you should take Vicky off alone and ask her if she'd like to receive Jesus into her life."

I said, "Anita, I'm not sure. No one in my family's ever shown any interest in becoming a Christian."

"But my brother led me to the Lord, John," she responded. "Think about it."

I walked back to Vicky and asked her if she'd like to come outside with me. We went to the parking lot, and there she sobbed in my arms for a while. When her tears had subsided, I told her that it was God's power working in my life that had enabled me to change. After a few moments, I asked her, "Vicky, would you like to ask Jesus to come into your heart?"

"Yes, I would like to," she replied. I put my arms around her again and prayed with her. Then she prayed and asked Jesus to enter her heart. It was one of the most joyous moments of my life. Even my sister believed I was changing. And now there were two of us in God's family—together!

Back home, much to my frustration, my struggles with Randy continued. I felt like a runaway roller coaster, my feelings alternating between love and hatred. Gradually, however, my eyes were opening to see the *real* Randy, inside the veneer of infatuation I had built around him. For one thing, I saw that he was a whiner. He complained about almost anything that didn't please him (and very little pleased him). He complained about the rules and appearance of the ministry houses, about the demands of the program, about aspects of our church he didn't like. He complained about his roommate, about the other men in the program, and that his job was less than fulfilling.

I got really sick of his attitude; our conversations began to wear me down. Randy had come from an affluent family, and nothing seemed quite good enough to please him. *This guy I'm infatuated with sure has some growing up to do,* I thought. I got downright angry sometimes and reminded him, "Look, we're not here for the decor, Randy!"

Not all my struggles were with Randy, of course. Sometimes I battled other facets of my relationships. I remember some of the guys in my house teasing me because I liked the color *dusty rose.* "That's your feminine side coming out," they joked. "John, only women like pink!" I tried to laugh it off, but I was deeply hurt by their remarks.

Next week at house meeting, I shared my honest feelings with the other guys. "Look, I know you're not trying to hurt me on purpose, but I've been struggling with feeling feminine all my life. So it really hurts to hear comments like that coming from you guys. I'd hoped you would be a little more sensitive to these types of issues."

Immediately they apologized for their thoughtless comments, and began affirming me. "You do display masculine characteristics," they assured me. One man was more specific: "John, you are one of the most assertive people around here in terms of how you handle life. And what about the way you have been handling temptation? I've seen you stick for months to praying and reading your Bible, even on the days you haven't felt like it." They also assured me that they admired my ability to confess my faults and ask forgiveness when I was wrong. Not only that, but they said even my mannerisms were changing, the way I carried myself and the kinds of clothes I chose to wear.

By the end of the evening, I felt much better. I was really glad that I'd risked opening up my true feelings. Not only did it make the other guys more aware of who I really was, I ended up being affirmed in sincere ways for the progress I had made since the program's beginning. And as they reassured me that I exhibited outward signs of masculinity, I felt something change inside me. After that night, I felt comfortable—for the first time—saying the simple statement, "I am a man." I had never felt comfortable saying it or even thinking it before.

Another significant event that year was the annual Exodus conference, which was being held at a university in Los Angeles. I was very familiar with this national organization because their offices were in the same suite as Love in Action. At that time, Exodus included about seventy-five ministries around the USA and Canada, and San Rafael served as the North American headquarters.

Often I would go into the office and talk to Bob Davies, the executive director of Exodus, to find out what exciting things were happening around the country. It wasn't unusual for someone in an Exodus ministry to be featured on a national radio or television program. Many Exodus leaders were also being written up in Christian magazines and secular newspapers around the country.

Right from the beginning, I was curious about what God was doing through ministries like Love in Action around the world. So I was excited to attend the Exodus conference, only a one-day drive south from where I was living. One of my most vivid memories was walking into the auditorium for the opening session and seeing a huge sea of faces—hundreds of people from all around the world, most of them coming out of homosexuality like myself. I was elated at the sight; it was a huge encouragement to see such visible evidence that I was not alone.

That week, dozens of us gathered on the front steps in front of one of the administration buildings to be photographed for the very first Exodus poster. The poster featured a cheering throng of people—all of them ex-gay—with the bold headline: "Can homosexuals change? WE DID!" It was wonderful to be part of that historic group, photographed for this exciting project that has been ultimately distributed all around the world.

The Exodus conference in late June marked the halfway point in our year-long program, and I noticed during the next month that the mood seemed to change around our house. Suddenly, everyone realized how quickly the year was passing, and I think they also realized—as I did—how many things we still wanted to learn before December rolled around. Even though it was hard to admit, some of us were disappointed, I think, that our homosexual struggles were still so strong and frequent. Shouldn't we have been at least half-way healed by now? And what about heterosexuality? That seemed distant, unattainable, like standing on the Pacific coastline and gazing out to sea, looking for a distant land that was somewhere across a vast ocean.

Now, after living together for so long, people's facades were crumbling more all the time. All the fronts of maturity and stability were being worn away. Actually, even though it had slipped most of our minds, this phenomenon was one of the goals of the program. As John Smid had reminded me during the first week, now was the perfect time to let down all the walls, to be honest with other people in a way we had never allowed ourselves. Only in being vulnerable and completely honest could we experience unconditional love and acceptance from others. Gradually, I was learning that people loved me for who I really was, not for the false image that I portrayed to the world.

I experienced another milestone that year: taking the HIV test. Several other LIA men had taken it, and I knew it was something I, too, needed to face. Public health officials were strongly encouraging gay men to get tested, then medications could be started to combat the eventual symptoms of AIDS. So, after work one day, I walked down the street with several other men from the program to the free clinic at the Marin County Community Health Department. We sat down on chairs in the waiting room, but I couldn't concentrate on anything; my hands were shaking slightly, and suddenly my mouth had gone completely dry.

Finally the nurse called my number and led me down the hall to a small private room, where she strapped rubber tubing around my upper arm and started to draw blood. Afterward, she began asking routine questions about my possible risk factors. When she asked me about my previous sexual contacts, I felt a wave of shame come over me as I told her, "I've had sex with other men." Then I quickly added, "But I haven't had sex with a male for almost two years."

She paused and looked at me. "That seems very unusual. Can I ask you why?"

"Well, I used to be gay. But I became a Christian two years ago, and I'm here in a program that helps people not be gay anymore."

She looked quizzical but didn't say much in response. I was just glad to leave as soon as possible. Then came the ten agonizing days of waiting. I would wake up at night and break into a profuse sweat. I would toss and turn, playing out worst-case scenarios in my mind. *I've had over three hundred sexual partners. I must be HIV positive by this time!*

Several days later, Mother's Day, I phoned my mom to give her my love. I also couldn't help telling her about the HIV test. I could hear her voice trembling over the line. "Oh, John, now I'm going to worry myself sick. What will we do if you have AIDS?"

"Mom, we'll get through it together somehow," I reassured her. "And I'll let you know the results as soon as they're back."

Finally, day ten arrived, and I went back to the clinic, feeling like I was moving in a mental fog. I felt numb as I sat down in the same room where I'd given blood. The same nurse faced me, holding a folder of papers in her hand. My heart was pounding as she reached out and held my hand. Then she spoke reassuringly, "Your test result is negative."

I felt total elation; suddenly my future had been handed back to me like a gift straight from heaven. The nurse assured me that, since it had been such a long time since my last sexual encounter, I could be certain that I would never develop AIDS. As I drove home that night, I let my imagination run wild about the future. Maybe that dream of a wife, kids, and a house with a white picket fence was to be part of my future after all! I don't know if Mom or I wept more when I phoned her with the good news.

Later, I learned that several other men in the program had also told the nurse at the clinic that they'd stopped having gay sex, and their combined stories began to make quite an impression on her. Eventually she visited our church out of curiosity—and became a Christian! Before long, she was teaching classes on AIDS at some of our LIA church seminars, and she became a good friend of many LIA men over the coming months.

By late fall, with the end of the program in sight, many of the men were feeling anxious about the future. Only one question weighed in each man's mind: "What am I going to do next year?"

As I considered my own options, I remembered what Frank had told us in January: "The goal of this program is not to turn you into a heterosexual by the end of the year. But if you leave this program closer to Jesus Christ than when you arrived, the program will have been a success. The program itself can't change you; it's designed to give you tools of understanding that you can put to use in your life. Ultimately, actual healing and change come from a source outside ourselves: through our relationship with Jesus Christ."

Then Frank made an announcement: "I am excited to tell you that Love in Action is about to launch a totally new program to train future ministry leaders. Those of you in the program who wish can apply for a second year of training."

I knew almost immediately that I wanted to stay, and I applied for that next year. By now I had a strong vision to help others who were struggling with the same battles I had fought in my own life. Even though I hadn't arrived, I wanted to give out of what I did have and what God had done so far. Before long, I received back the good news: I had been accepted for another year!

In December I was experiencing major anxiety about Randy leaving San Rafael to return home to Canada. His one-year visa was about to expire, and there was no doubt that he and I would soon be separated by half a continent. I was torn by two contrasting emotions: one part of me felt like I'd die if he left; the other side of me said, *This is the best thing that could ever happen.*

Then came the year-end retreat. We made the three-hour drive north to the Mendocino coast, where we had held our first retreat so many months before. One huge answer to prayer buoyed all of us that weekend: Not one person had dropped out of the program and gone back into homosexuality. For the first time in the history of Love in Action, everyone who entered the program in January had stuck it out until the very end!

That weekend, I found myself once again sitting near the fireplace in front of the men, telling what the year had meant for me and what I wanted for the future. But even I could tell that there was a marked difference in my life. I didn't fall apart emotionally during my time, but I spoke with confidence. "Everything that I wanted out of this program has happened for me," I told the men. "I wanted so much to feel loved, and I really do feel like I am loved by all of you."

That night, as I lay awake in bed, I felt a keen sense of excitement and anticipation. So much had changed in my life in twelve short months. Yes, I still had many areas where I needed to grow. Saying goodbye to Randy wasn't going to be easy. But I was not the same person who had arrived in San Rafael the previous year. *I don't feel like I've completely changed,* I told myself with a sigh. *But I know that I'm well on the way.*

Then I uttered a simple but profound prayer. "God," I breathed silently, "I would like three things from you. I want to get married—and to a woman who was a lesbian. I want a child. And I want You to use our story to blow the world away." Then, moments later, I fell into a deep and peaceful sleep.

EIGHTEEN

———

JUST BEFORE CHRISTMAS I started feeling depressed about Randy going back to Toronto. During our last conversation, I fell apart and couldn't stop crying. I gave him a hug and couldn't let go; I was still wrapped up emotionally in our relationship. At the same time, I desperately wanted him gone so I could get on with my life. Before he drove off to the airport, we promised to keep in touch.

After Randy left, I went home to Ohio to spend Christmas break with Mom and her new husband, Tom. I really loved Tom; he was also a recovering alcoholic and made me feel like a son to him. He was also incredibly supportive of me coming out of homosexuality. But I was too embarrassed to tell my mother why I was so obviously depressed. I got to see Parker for a few hours in Columbus, and we caught up on each other's lives. Parker hadn't been doing too well. The relationship he'd had earlier in the year had already broken up, and he was wondering where his life was headed. But I did enjoy seeing him and touching base while I was in the area.

As 1989 began, four other men and I began the first leadership training program offered by Love in Action. I was fascinated by the behavior of the new men who arrived on New Year's Eve. I could see how many changes I'd already experienced over the past year. I had definitely matured amid all the struggles I had faced.

Soon my house leader and I were spending time counseling the new guys and praying for them. It deeply satisfied me to be able to tell them how I'd struggled with many of the same things they were facing now and how God had helped me during the past year. I had wrestled with inappropriate feelings and behavior, but I'd been obedient—and celibate. And I could see that, in return, God was beginning to change me on the inside at a level deeper than my previous feelings and emotions.

One of my new responsibilities was helping the house leader oversee various program activities, like the household chores and our weekend social outings. At this time, both men and women were involved in the live-in program. Although we lived across town in separate houses, we shared social activities together. The first outing that year was a day trip to Fisherman's Wharf and Ghirardelli Square in San Francisco, and I was in charge of the group that included both the men's and women's programs.

Some friction developed almost right away between me and one of the women. I'd already met Anne Edward the previous year. She'd been part of the ministry's Friday night drop-in group for people who didn't live in one of the houses. I had been impressed with her commitment: She rarely missed a meeting, even though she had to drive ninety minutes each way from her home in Hayward.

Today, though, I wasn't impressed with Anne. She still seemed to carry a well-entrenched lesbian identity. And she was pushy. She kept insisting that we go to places along the Wharf that weren't on my agenda. "Give us a few minutes to look around this jade shop," she suggested at one point. "This looks like a great place for souvenirs."

"Will you stop?" I said to her in front of the whole group. "We're already late for our dinner reservations. We don't have time. And I'm the one leading this group—not you!"

By the end of the evening, I was more than ready to go home. *I've had enough of that woman,* I thought. *She sure is controlling, and it's driving me nuts!*

As the new program members began attending classes and examining the underlying factors that might have helped push them toward homosexual activities, I found myself inspired to review every letter my father had ever sent me. Maybe looking more closely at how he communicated with me would give me some new insights into our relationship—or the lack of one.

I pulled down a box from the bedroom closet, then took out the envelopes and put them all in order, beginning back when I was in high school. As I spent several hours reading through these letters, I was struck by something I'd never seen before. Throughout his notes, I could clearly see my dad's consistent love and commitment toward me.

Why, I wondered, had I never been able to see this love flowing from my father when I was growing up? I hadn't realized it years ago, but now I could see beyond doubt that my father had really loved me through all the years that we had been separated because of my parents' divorce. He had loved me—in the best way he knew how.

As I read his letters, I felt my heart softening toward him. The anger and bitterness that I had been holding began to fade, and I felt a strong desire to talk with him.

I dialed his number and soon I was blurting out, "Dad, I have to tell you something. I've taken some time tonight to read through all the letters you've written me over the years. And I want to ask you to forgive me for not believing that you loved me." I told him how sorry I felt for my attitude toward him in the past. "I know you probably didn't want to have a gay son," I added. "Please forgive me for not being the son that maybe you wanted to have."

My dad's voice choked with emotion as he answered. "As far as I'm concerned, John, there's nothing to forgive you for. But if you need to be forgiven, believe me—you are. And I'll tell you this, John: Gay or straight, I couldn't possibly be more proud of you as my son."

From that moment, my relationship with my father began to change. I began seeing him in a different, more realistic light. Finally I could recognize him as a fellow human being with all his faults and weaknesses, just like me. I no longer had to compare him critically to some mystical "perfect father," someone who didn't measure up to my needs and expectations. At last I was reaching the point where I could honestly accept my father. It was one of the most meaningful and healing things I'd ever done. I only regret that it took so many years to do it.

Another significant event happened in 1989. I became aware that I was still carrying the image of Candi around inside me, and she was feeling like dead weight, a ball and chain tied around one ankle, holding me back. At its root, the issue was the way others looked at me. I was still having difficulty believing that people would ever perceive me as a normal man. I was afraid that, when they looked at me, they'd always see a drag queen walking around, even if I no longer wore costumes and makeup.

I tentatively thought of myself as a man, but was that how others perceived me? I could even call myself an ex-gay man. But a full, normal heterosexual man? It still didn't seem to fit, no matter how hard I tried.

One day I shared these thoughts with John Smid. His response was direct. "When are you going to cut Candi loose?" he challenged me. "You'll never be completely free until you let her go. Let her die, John. It's in your power to do just that. You're not a drag queen now, and you haven't been for a long time. And nobody around here sees you like that, you can be sure."

John furrowed his brows for a moment, then continued, "In fact, I want you to stop calling yourself *ex-gay*. There's a verse in the Bible that says, 'As a man thinks in his heart, so he is.' Our self-image begins in the mind; that's where changes really are born. The label of *ex-gay* is still connecting you with the past. John, I think you should start connecting your identity with the future, not with who you used to be. You actually said goodbye to Candi several years ago; now you don't need her or anything she represented in your life anymore.

"So, from now on," John continued, "you're not an ex-gay; you're a man. And not just a man, but a heterosexual. That's how everyone sees you. And that's what is going to help you let Candi go—now and for good."

I went back to my bedroom and prayed alone for a while. John was right: I had let Candi go, physically, years ago. Now it was time to sever the emotional connection as well. "God," I prayed, "please show me that I am acceptable as a man, that I am respected by other men. Help me see myself as others do—as a heterosexual man who loves You. Today I am cutting off this chain to Candi. She will no longer be connected to me in any way. And help me never to hide behind her image ever again."

At that moment, I realized that Candi had merely been an image I had created; she had never represented reality. After that prayer, I could look at pictures of Candi and no longer feel any attachment to what she had tried to represent.

Not only was I detaching from my old identity as a female impersonator, I was losing the desire to be codependent upon women or treat them as buddies, as I'd done with Jackie, Susan, Joanne, and other women who had been friends in the past. In my drag identity, I had imitated femininity in an external way, but now I realized that I had never internalized true femininity—nor could I. And, to be honest, I was also realizing that I had great difficulty figuring out real femininity or understanding how women really thought at all.

I began to go through some significant changes in my appearance. Throughout my years in gay bars I'd been fixated on my outward looks. I always kept my weight under control and dressed impeccably in designer clothes. I knew what was fashionable, and I was proud of my sophistication and taste in fine clothing.

Then one night I went to see a Christian play with some of my friends. I was dressed jet black, in Ralph Lauren from head to toe. During intermission, as I walked from the front row toward the rear of the theater, a few women along the way caught my eye. They were staring intently at me and my outfit, studying me curiously, with eyebrows raised.

Suddenly I felt ashamed, like I wanted to run and hide somewhere. Then a clear conviction flashed through my mind: *I should stop drawing attention to myself by what I wear.* As a Christian, I wanted others to be drawn to a reflection of God's character in my life. But, as long as I was dressed to the hilt, I knew that my clothing would simply be a distraction from that higher goal.

I promised myself that I'd go home and get rid of every piece of clothing in my closet with a designer label. It was time to clean up my act at an even deeper level. From that day on, I began wearing plain clothes and felt an incredible new sense of freedom. For the first time, I realized how trapped I had been by the outward identity I had been creating through what I wore.

Another thing happened in terms of my appearance: I found that I was much less concerned about being the "perfect" weight—another factor I'd fixated on in my attempt to attract attention. My weight started to increase, and I found little desire to keep on a strict diet in order to stay fashionably slim. My very appearance was changing; I was looking less and less gay. And I was perfectly happy about it.

By my second year in California, I'd grown a little weary of the old routine at Kinko's and decided to get a job doing something else. So I went to work for a manufacturer of fine, designer chocolates. In my position, I worked constantly around women. But after I'd been there for a few months, Frank took me aside and told me what he thought about this change: "I think you need to take another step away from relating to women so closely, John. I think it would be good for you in terms of your personal growth to quit your job and work in an office where you have to wear a shirt and tie—and where you'll be surrounded by other men."

I had to admit, Frank's challenge of being surrounded by straight men was still a frightening prospect. But I also knew that Frank was right. I had to give it a try.

After some searching I landed a job with a computer software firm. I wore a suit, shirt, and tie to work and ran a computer all day. And since I didn't yet have a car and I knew Anne Edward had a job right across the street from my employer, I asked her—with some reluctance—if she'd let me carpool to work with her.

When she agreed, I thought to myself, *I guess I can get along with anyone for just one hour a day, Monday through Friday!* And Frank was right. Working with straight men turned out to be a challenging and yet increasingly comfortable environment for me. I struck up several friendships with straight, male coworkers. And I was affirmed in my masculinity by the fact that, whether in business dealings or just talking over lunch, no one ever seemed to look at me funny or remarked that I was still coming off like a drag queen in a suit and tie.

Carpooling with Anne turned out better than I'd expected. We clashed less than I thought we would. I guess I was maturing, and Anne—now that she was involved in LIA's live-in program as well—was changing, too. She seemed softer, gentler, much less defensive and self-protective. I found an increasing number of reasons to compliment her on her clothes and her personal qualities as well.

Anne didn't always appreciate my feedback, though. She was still too new at dressing in feminine ways, and being recognized as beautiful brought out her insecurities. She had previously been employed as a physical education teacher; now she worked in an office where she had to wear dresses, skirts, pantyhose, and heels.

I hopped into her car one day and couldn't help noticing the new patent leather high heels she was wearing for the first time. "I just love your shoes, Anne," I gushed. "They look fantastic—and they really go well with your outfit."

I was shocked at her angry response. "John Paulk, I am sick of all your compliments," she snapped. "I don't want to hear any more of them!"

Of course, I was properly mature in my own response: "Well, fine. If that's your attitude, I'll never compliment you again!" And we spent the rest of the ride in stony silence.

Soon, however, we got over our mutual huff and started being civil to each other again. After that incident, however, I was more restrained in what I said to her. And I realized later that maybe Anne felt I was trying to patronize her in some way by my gushy compliments. In ways I'd never experienced before, my hours commuting alone with Anne certainly gave me some insights and firsthand experience in relating to women.

Despite our differences, Anne and I had one quality in common: We both loved to talk about God and our relationship with Him. We were both serious about our commitment to godly change—and every bit as determined to leave behind the old gay life and all its trappings.

One evening, as we pulled up to the Love in Action house, Anne said, "Let's go out and do something together sometime."

I responded casually, "Yeah, that would be OK." But weeks and then months slipped by, and we never did anything except ride together to and from work.

In June, I attended the annual Exodus conference again, and one workshop led me to many hours of self-examination: "Misogyny: Hatred of the Feminine" offered many insights into my past. "Many gay men and women have been emotionally abused by their mothers," the workshop leader said. "For some of us, this has resulted in deep resentment toward all women, and toward femininity itself, together with a distorted image of womanhood."

I thought of my complex relationship with my own mother. Certainly it had improved over the years. But much of my primary sense of identity had been shaped by suppressed anger and fear that she would obliterate me in some deep way. With this internal imprinting, I had always viewed the prospect of bonding with a woman as rife with the dreadful possibility that something would be taken from me. I needed to break through these fears and move past them.

At the end of the class, I went forward for prayer. "I need to lay down my distorted image of women," I told the leaders. Then I asked God to forgive me for allowing false perceptions about femininity to create such fear in me that I could not allow a woman to get emotionally close. I still had no idea what the future held in terms of relating to women. All I knew was that I still held onto a deep desire for marriage and family some day. Certainly this prayer was knocking down one more barrier that remained in place to separate me from my eventual goal.

Another significant event happened at that conference. It was held in Toronto—the same city where Randy had returned after our first program year together. I knew I needed to tie up some loose ends regarding our mutual infatuation that year, so we got together for lunch. As I had suspected, my attraction to him was gone, and none of the dynamics of our relationship were stirred up again. I could enjoy his company like any of the other male friends I had. He was a nice guy but certainly not someone with whom I desired any kind of immoral connection like I had in the past.

Toward the end of 1990, Frank Worthen made an important announcement during a meeting of our ministry leaders: "After seventeen years of directing Love in Action here in San Rafael, Anita and I have made the decision to move to the Philippines and begin a ministry like this in Manila."

Afterward, Frank took me aside. "John, I am interested in having you take Anita's place as administrator in the ministry's office here. Would you pray about it?"

I said I would, gladly, and I saw Frank's eyes fill with tears. "I just can't believe it, John. You've only been here three years, and here you are, ready to take on Anita's job!" At that very moment I recalled the vision my house leader had shared with me soon after my arrival. He'd seen me as a healed man who didn't even look the same! And at this instant I knew the vision was becoming a reality—much sooner than I'd ever imagined.

The changes in my life began to impact other people, even those outside of Love in Action. For instance, although I had almost lost contact with my old friends from the gay world, I continued to maintain my friendship with Parker back in Ohio. Each time I went home to visit my mother, I would always get together with him. And somehow my growing relationship with God always seemed to crop up in the middle of the conversation.

I went back home for Christmas, and this time Parker acted troubled, quiet, and withdrawn when we got together. I couldn't get him to tell me what was really going on in his life. After I returned to California, I decided to phone him and probe further.

"What's going on?" I insisted gently. "You seemed totally out of it when I saw you last week."

Finally he admitted the truth. "Being with you really makes me sad. My life is going nowhere, and it's obvious to me that you are onto something important. I can see the peace in your face, and I don't have to look hard to see that you're actually changing—and not just on the outside. Something's happening deep inside you, John. I know part of it is spiritual, and it's something I want very much, too. But I have no idea how to get it." He confessed that, in the midst of his difficulties, he longed to find some of the peace he saw in me.

I decided to be bold. "Parker, I'm so glad that you can see the changes in me. Yes, something significant has happened to me in the past few years, and my life is taking a whole new direction that's exciting and deeply fulfilling. But it's not just for me. Parker, you can have it, too." Then I asked him if he'd like to accept Jesus into his life.

"Yes, I think I would," he said softly.

I prayed with him as joy swelled up from deep inside me. I could hardly sit still; I was so excited. After Parker asked Jesus to come into his life, I promised to send him a Bible so he could begin learning the same principles and insights that had been so helpful to me as a young believer. "Maybe you'll even join the Love in Action program someday," I told him, and he agreed to think more about it after he graduated from college.

By this time, I had been sexually abstinent for four full years and completely sober for more than five years. And a curious new development was occurring in my relationships with other people at church. I noticed I was losing the desire to hang around with just men. I still wanted to have other men as friends, but I was starting to find the sole company of men rather boring.

Then, at a Bible study one night, I found myself noticing something in particular about one girl in the group. Bonnie was sitting on a sofa near me as we sang some songs at the beginning of the meeting. A nearby lamp was shedding a soft light on her head, and the delicate sheen from her blond hair caught my eye. I was transfixed by the highlights of Bonnie's hair as her head swayed through the lamp's rays in time to the music. Suddenly a realization struck me: Never in my life had I felt such a sense of pleasure in contemplating any attribute, physical or emotional, of an actual woman. But now, without my being able to control it, my heart was being drawn toward the sight of Bonnie's soft feminine beauty.

That night, as I lay in bed, my mind tried to sort out this strange new experience. Women had always fascinated me in an objective way. I had made a major study of their appearance and mannerisms so I could imitate them. But before tonight, never had I felt such a sense of excitement and pleasure aroused by a flesh-and-blood woman.

Again I remembered Bonnie's hair and allowed myself to enjoy the memory of her loveliness, so different from anything I had contemplated before. What was this kind of beauty made of? Softness. Gentleness. Roundness. Quietness. Stillness.

It wasn't masculine, made up of strength, muscles, sweat, and violent exertion. I felt no envy relishing this beauty, because it was nothing that I craved to internalize or imitate. Though I longed somehow to connect with Bonnie, I did not have any desire to be engulfed in her, as I had with the masculinity I saw in attractive men. Rather, this lovely feminine beauty was something I wanted to shelter and protect. I realized that I had experienced a genuine attraction toward a woman. I longed to look at Bonnie again and get closer to her in order to know her and become her friend . . . and maybe more than just her friend.

Immediately I tried to act on this crush I felt for Bonnie. In fact, I was so zealous I almost threw myself at her. A few days later, I left a single rosebud on her doorstep with a signed card to let her know of my interest. In return, she expressed an interest in me, and we began spending time together, going out for coffee and having little chats after LIA meetings. One day we went window-shopping together and spent time admiring some elegant wedding gowns.

But, despite my boyish enthusiasm, my budding relationship with Bonnie soon began to sour. I was so excited about this totally unexpected physical and emotional attraction that I had no idea how to handle it; I proceeded to bumble toward Bonnie with far too much intensity.

When I was around her, I felt excitement—but I also felt a growing fear. I felt nervous and inadequate in my new role. I had been pals with women but had never allowed myself to get into any kind of romantic relationship. In the past, my friendships with women had been too uncomfortable as they got deeper. Women would become mothering, suffocating me. What would happen if I allowed Bonnie to get too close?

Soon, I felt so tense I could hardly keep up a decent conversation with her. Only a few weeks after our relationship began, I broke it off, though I wasn't able to explain the real reasons why. Bonnie was crushed, and I felt devastated, too. Would I ever be able to function in the world of heterosexual relationships?

After a few weeks had passed, I gained some perspective on the whole situation. I realized it would be wrong for me to blame the breakup entirely on me or on the lie that I still might be gay. Some understandable insecurities had contributed to the problem, and it was my first boy-girl romantic relationship.

First, I realized that I'd been feeling the same kind of puppy love that overwhelms teenage boys. "What you're experiencing, John, is almost like a second puberty," Pastor Mike told me affectionately. But other factors played a part, too. Bonnie had reminded me of my mother in a number of ways. Perhaps that was why I instinctively backed away: I feared she would become an emotional drain on me. In any event, I decided it was better for now to stay within the safety zone of male relationships. Certainly I had lots of challenges in that area to sort out. But regardless, a new and startling change in the way I saw myself and the other—feminine—half of the world had begun to emerge from the depths of my being.

By this time, I was thoroughly enjoying my full-time involvement at Love in Action. During the day, I worked in the LIA office, answering the phone and helping men and women across the country find the answers they were seeking in coming away from homosexuality. I also continued to screen incoming applications for the live-in program, which was now attracting interest from potential applicants around the world. During evenings and weekends I was leader of New Hope House, the live-in residence where my own healing journey at LIA had begun. Only now, instead of arriving as a shaky, first-year participant, I was assuming charge of twelve men from all over the country. They looked to me for help and support, to learn how to work through temptation and adjust to their new living situation in California.

Two men in particular stood out for me that year. Mike came to Love in Action so sexually addicted that he'd been reduced to having sex with several strangers every day. He was so caught up in his external appearance that he came off as cold toward others. I wondered how we could penetrate the thick, defensive shields he'd raised against further hurt. But, for some reason, Mike developed a strong trust in me during the early months of the program. Ironically, that may have been because I myself had lost the ideal look for a gay man; I was getting older, I'd put on some weight, and I wasn't dressing fashionably anymore.

Still, I think more than just my nonthreatening appearance inspired his confidence. Mike observed the way I related to the other men in the house, and he gradually began to believe he could really trust me. (Later, Mike told me that I had been the first person in his whole life whose love he hadn't felt a need to test.) He sensed deep inside that I loved him unconditionally. And that love helped to carry Mike successfully through the entire program and into leadership training.

Ross, on the other hand, came to LIA very young—and also trapped in severe sexual addiction. He became like the little brother I'd never had. We both affirmed each other's masculinity as we continued to mature and grow together through that year. I began to feel like a father toward Ross and the other men in my house. I felt deeply fulfilled, helping these men face the same battles I'd faced a few years previous. It was a joy to offer them the same strong leadership and direction that had been provided to me by my role models: Pastor Mike Riley, John Smid, and Frank Worthen.

I continued to put into practice the lessons I'd learned during the Steps Out program. One night Frank had talked about the mystique many gay men feel toward straight men, and I remembered his practical advice: "One way to press through that straight-male mystique is by seeking out real relationships. If you find a straight man attractive, become friends with him. When you get to know him, the mystique will fade away as you get to know him as a real human being with failings and problems like anyone else."

His advice was helpful. For example, one day when I was invited to be a guest on a Christian talk-radio show, I found myself attracted to the man who was screening the incoming calls. At first I was afraid that this man would somehow look down on me because I had once been involved in homosexuality. But I could tell from his enthusiastic hand-signals during the show that he approved of the way I was handling myself with the callers and difficult questions.

After the show I went up to him and began a conversation; I asked him about his job and found out more about him as a person. I noticed he was wearing a wedding ring and thought, *This man is heterosexual and married. He doesn't want sex with you. And would you want to tempt him into something that might possibly destroy his marriage? You know what you really desire from him: acceptance. And he's obviously giving you that!* As we talked and I let myself feel his sincere affirmation and interest, I found the mystique was indeed shattering. He became a real individual to me. Yes, he was physically attractive, but he wasn't a potential sex partner.

Meanwhile, at church, I continued to reach out in friendship to straight men without passively waiting for them to come to me. Previously I had waited for potential male friends to walk into my world. I wanted them to understand me, to accept me in spite of my past and my failings.

Now I began to turn that around. I could reach out to them with interest and acceptance. When I tried this, like that day in the radio studio, I found that straight men treated me with respect—as they had when I first switched jobs from the candymaker to the computer firm. I was not as different from straight men as I'd once believed. My ultimate goal, of course, was not just friendship with straight men; I wanted to *be* a straight man. Inside I felt masculine. Increasingly, I was looking outward at the opposite sex with the eyes of a straight man. But I wanted to walk right into the world of straight men at any time and feel like I belonged there, was welcome, and right at home. And I knew that would never happen if I sat in Love in Action and waited for other men to come to me.

So I forced myself to move beyond my self-imposed fears and insecurities and walk into the world I wanted to inhabit. I had to face the most blatant symbols of straight masculinity in our culture. And I decided what signified those symbols most flagrantly to me was the whole area of sports. Like many gay men, I had never had any real interest in sports. I had avoided that whole area of life as much as possible. It only represented awkwardness and failure to me, rather than a source of bonding and identification with other men.

But during my year as a house leader, I decided to wade right into the cyclone of my fears and see what happened. The perfect opportunity came when I was invited to attend a Super Bowl party with some guys from the church. That afternoon I sat in a living room full of Christian men as we glued our attention to the action happening on the TV screen.

I made a discovery that day that was confirmed through numerous similar occasions. That day's event wasn't really focused on football; it was simply an excuse for us as men to get together. It was really about us sharing an event as men, building relationships through common experiences, and getting to know one another. We talked about our lives, our jobs, our spiritual struggles and victories. Football wasn't really what our afternoon was about at all. As men, we were simply using sports as a vehicle to come together and enjoy each other's fellowship.

I had always been highly relational as a person. When I realized the underlying relational aspects of these gatherings, I found myself gaining a whole new interest in sports. As I got to know these men, I saw beneath the superficial aspects of how I had thought we might be different. I began to glimpse their fears, insecurities, frustrations, and emotions. I realized that even straight men had been afraid when they first began dating girls. They had also faced insecurities when starting new jobs. Like me, they had also felt rejected by other men and inferior in some ways to men who seemed superior. Under the skin, I was really not that much different from these guys.

Slowly I came to feel that I truly did belong in this world of masculinity. And I enjoyed belonging. I was identifying with other men in a way I had missed as a boy, and more deeply than when I had assumed the pseudofemininity known as Candi. By increments, I was filling myself with masculinity and becoming more secure in it. I was discovering my own masculinity by forming deep, meaningful, and fulfilling relationships with other men that had nothing to do with homosexuality.

Besides my leadership role in Love in Action's program, I continued to grow in my responsibilities at church. I joined the praise and worship team that led the musical portion of services each Sunday. Here, for the first time, I used my singing talent for the Lord. And I discovered a new reason to sing that I'd never had before. In gay life I'd sung to sound good and make an impression on other men. Now I sang with all my heart to express the depth of my joy in God and what He was doing in my life.

I also became an official member of the church. This was a meaningful step for me. By the time I joined Open Door, the people had truly become my family. People in that congregation deeply loved and supported me, and becoming a member there signified that I belonged to them and they to me—permanently.

During this time in my life, I often thought back to an event that occurred near the end of my first year at Love in Action. Frank had been teaching one evening on the subject of marriage. "God created women to complement you," he had told us. "Of course, this doesn't mean all of you will get married. But . . ." he paused to look around at the group of men sitting before him, "I firmly believe that some of you in this very room will be married one day."

Little did I know why Frank's words were coming back to my mind. I knew that marriage was certainly a future dream for me. And I knew my life had undergone a radical transformation from the inside out. But I couldn't peer into the future to see what was just ahead. Unknown to me, my life was about to take a radical turn that would propel it beyond my wildest hopes and dreams.

NINETEEN

L IFE AT LOVE IN ACTION rolled on, along with my involvement in Church of the Open Door. As I felt my true masculinity emerging, I became even more certain that I wanted to get married. I found women attractive, and I was beginning to greatly appreciate their qualities and gifts.

Several of us from Love in Action were active in the church singles' group. We'd play volleyball, go on picnics and hikes, or attend Christian concerts together.

My involvement in the singles' group helped me learn how to relate to women in a safe, nonthreatening environment. I could test the waters to see how women reacted to me as a person. I didn't have to worry about the pressure of dating; we could relate to each other as if we were brothers and sisters and pray for each other as personal challenges arose.

After some months I put my toes in the dating waters by asking some of my female friends to go out for coffee or for a drive. Nothing serious, no sweaty palms or big lumps in the throat—just learning to relate with women in ways I had never experienced. By now, I had also been part of Open Door's worship team for three years, and I was pleased when Anne Edward joined the group to sing and play guitar. She did both very well.

Now that I was on staff at Love in Action, I had my own car and no longer needed to carpool with Anne. But I missed some of the conversations we'd had, so we started talking again during breaks at music practice. Gradually Anne began to open up and tell me about herself and about the events that had brought her, like me, to the ministry of Love in Action.

Born to a middle-class family, Anne's inner security was profoundly shaken when, at four years of age, a teenage boy made sexual advances. She never told anyone, fearing they'd both get into serious trouble. During her childhood, Anne developed into a classic tomboy, mostly playing boys' games. She craved special affirmation from her father but never felt that she got it. "For years," Anne told me, "I believed lies about myself and about men. I couldn't embrace my femininity, because my early sexual experience had taught me that being female meant being weak and vulnerable. I couldn't trust males, either, because they all seemed distant and emotionally absent."

In high school Anne was experiencing crushes on some of her female friends. She felt disillusioned with her church's youth group; they didn't behave any different from unchurched kids at school. She stopped going to church as soon as her parents no longer forced her, then started drinking and hanging out with several boys at once to prove her femininity. Eventually she started exploring lesbian relationships.

In college Anne met Sara, a strong, confident young woman. Anne felt sexual feelings toward Sara; at a gay counselor's suggestion, Anne joined her college's gay/lesbian solidarity group.

"But at one of their meetings," Anne said, "I had a piercing thought: *There really is something wrong with being gay.*" She knew somehow that those words—which made her feel very sad—were true. They shattered her dreams of finding happiness with a female life partner. After the meeting, Anne went home in tears. "God," she prayed, "please show me who You are and fill this void in my heart."

Almost immediately, she began to experience a strong hunger to know Jesus Christ. "It struck me one night that I wanted to follow whatever is true, whatever the cost," she continued. "I didn't want to go just by my feelings." Anne sensed that something much more profound than her feelings had to guide her life—that there was a right way to live and she could find it. Six months later, she decided to leave homosexuality.

However, Anne's decision led to frustration. No leaders on campus or at church seemed to know how to give her hope that her attraction to women could change. Then, after college, Anne fell into a sexual relationship with a Christian girlfriend who also struggled with lesbianism. After three months, Anne prayed, "Lord, You know I really enjoy this lifestyle. But I want You to be my first love. I need Your help. I need You to somehow change my heart." This prayer marked a major turning point in Anne's life. A few days later, Anne and her lover had dinner with a Christian woman who had left lesbianism. Through her, Anne and her friend made contact with Love in Action. That's when Anne started becoming a regular at the ministry's weekly meetings.

At Love in Action, Anne felt loved and cared for, which led her to sever all contact with her lover. She attended meetings for the next eighteen months. "I gained insights," she said, "like how to look for patterns in my same-sex attractions, so I could see the underlying needs that led to temptation in the first place. My relationship with God really started growing, and eventually I decided to join the live-in program at Love in Action."

I told Anne that I admired her determination to seek the truth at all costs. I also greatly admired the evidence of her growing devotion to the Lord.

I was drawn to Anne, but other women at church also attracted my attention. One Sunday, as I stood singing on the platform with the praise and worship team, I noticed a stunning-looking woman in the congregation: gleaming auburn hair, attractive smile, high-fashion clothes.

After the church service, I found Pastor Mike. I described the girl I'd seen and asked him if he knew who she was. "That's Renee," he said.

"Is she a Christian?"

"Yes, but she's a new believer."

"What's her phone number?" My masculine assertiveness was kicking into high gear by this time.

After Mike gave me the information, I went back home and dialed the number. Renee answered and I said, "Hi, I'm John Paulk, from Open Door. I've seen you in church." I described myself and where I stood on the platform with the worship team. She remembered me, and we had the first of several phone conversations. Renee was a new Christian—and a needy one. She had been badly used by men in the past, but she was sweet and pleasant—and very attractive. Soon I asked her to go out, and she said yes. We went on several dates and started to develop a relationship, even talking vaguely about whether we should get married someday.

But it quickly became clear to me that Renee and I really didn't have that much in common. Future ministry was a major focus in my life, and she wasn't particularly excited about that possibility. I was already trying to find a graceful way to ease out of the relationship when something unexpected came up: I was asked to go as a missionary to Singapore to assist with a Christian ministry similar to Love in Action.

The idea of being some kind of missionary appealed to me, and I began praying for guidance. I told Renee what was on my mind, and she responded,

"I don't know how I feel about going to Singapore." I was shocked by her presumption that she would be going with me. I decided I would have to let her know that the time had come for us to break off our dating. I knew I had to let Renee know how I felt.

Later in church, my face must have betrayed the concern I felt over Renee. Afterward, Anne saw me and asked, "Is anything wrong?"

"Yeah, I guess so."

"Mind sharing what it is?"

"I'm not doing too well with Renee. We just don't see eye to eye on God's direction for my life. I feel called to minister, but she doesn't share that vision. I think we're going to have to call it quits." I let out a big sigh.

"John, if that's the way you feel, you'd better tell her soon."

"Yeah, I guess so."

"Would you like me to pray with you about it?" I readily agreed.

We sat down on the edge of the platform. She put her hand on my shoulder, and we bowed our heads. "Lord God," she said, "I pray that You would give John the courage to talk to Renee. And Lord, I pray that You would show him who the right woman is for him. . . ."

At that very second, I sensed an inner voice saying, *"John, she's sitting right beside you. It's Anne."*

I didn't say a word. But I opened my eyes and watched Anne pray. And the voice repeated, *"John, this is the right woman for you."* As Anne finished praying, I felt tears stinging my eyes. I quickly rubbed them dry and thanked Anne for her concern. As we parted, I watched her carry her guitar case toward the back of the church.

What just happened? I wondered. *Was that the Lord speaking to my heart? Or was it just me talking to myself in an emotionally vulnerable moment?* I was perplexed and decided it would be better to shrug the whole thing off for the moment.

God answered Anne's prayer; Renee and I did break up peaceably. She agreed with me that we would be better off as "just friends." Then, of all things, she said, "Why haven't you asked Anne out? You talk so much about her all the time."

I did? I hadn't noticed. But I had to admit I did admire many of her qualities. She was quiet and gentle, and her love for God was more than just words. She seemed concerned for other people and quick to serve. She was always ready to pray for someone who was hurting or needing encouragement.

Her whole demeanor reflected an unselfish and caring spirit. Also, she wasn't silly or giggly or gossipy like so many women I had known. She didn't delight in evil things or in other people's misfortunes. Nor did she seem judgmental or critical of people; she always seemed willing to think the best of others. I also noticed that Anne had become increasingly feminine over the time I'd known her. She let her hair grow out, made herself up attractively, and always dressed modestly in pretty outfits.

Yes, I had to admit it: I found Anne lovely. But far more than Anne's mere outward appearance attracted me. She reflected the deep changes that had happened inside her. Her new exterior wasn't a costume she was wearing; it was vibrant new life, radiating out from deep inside.

One day in early June, I was packing to leave the next morning for the 1991 Exodus conference. My friend, Sandra, asked Anne and me if we would like to join her for a hamburger. After lunch, as we strolled back toward the Love in Action residence, Sandra suddenly interrupted our innocent bantering: "Would you two just come off it? I know you both like each other, so just admit it and get it over with!"

I felt like the pit of my stomach dropped into the Grand Canyon. I glanced at Anne and saw that she was blushing ruby red. My own face felt very hot. I couldn't look her in the eye.

I swallowed hard and gulped, "OK, I admit it. I do like you."

Anne caught my eye and smiled coyly. "I guess I like you, too." Neither of us could say another word. Sandra strode a couple of steps ahead of us, humming merrily to herself. I felt like a young schoolboy who had clumsily gushed out his heart. I also felt incredibly giddy and very happy.

During the next week at the conference, the Exodus board of directors considered my application for their Singapore ministry, then turned it down. They said I had no cross-cultural training and going to Singapore would interfere with other goals I'd written in my application, including my desire to get married.

I returned from the conference in a major funk. I phoned Anne right away. Could she take a walk with me and help me sort through a problem? I didn't give her any details, but she agreed to come right over. Soon we were strolling around the pond in a nearby park. "I won't be going to Singapore," I told her and explained why. She was silent, but suddenly I had an encouraging thought: *Hey, now Anne and I will actually have a chance to build a relationship.* Suddenly I felt quite a bit better!

After that day, every time I was close to Anne I felt something weird coming from inside me: an overwhelming urge to nurture and protect her. It felt strange. If anyone said the slightest critical thing, I quickly defended her.

When we'd walk together, I'd reflexively find myself moving toward the outside, nearer to the street. When we'd enter a building or a restaurant, I would automatically stride a step or two ahead and open the door for her. Being with Anne was bringing out things in me that no one had ever touched before. I had learned to identify with heterosexual men. Now being near Anne was bringing out a sense of security in my masculinity that I'd never experienced.

In July, our church held a men's retreat near the foothills of Mt. Tamalpais, a lush, forested peak overlooking the Golden Gate Bridge. During the retreat I was sitting next to my pastor and asked him, "Mike, how will it ever be possible for me to be completely changed and married? How is God ever going to do that?"

This kind, gentle-hearted man put his arm around me. "John, God has a wonderful way of catching you up to just where you need to be. Don't worry, when His time comes, you'll be ready."

Anne and I were discovering that we wanted to spend more time with each other. But we were nervous about being alone together. We had never even held hands, much less kissed. So I came up with a scheme. I would call my friend Arnie, and Anne would call her friend Sandra, and we'd get together at the live-in program house and play team chess. Anne and I would be partners against Arnie and Sandra.

I'll never forget the first time Anne's and my knees "accidentally" touched under the chess table. I had been consciously scooting my leg closer and closer, hoping it might touch hers. When our knees finally made contact, I could have sworn electric shock waves throbbed through my body. Neither of us said a word, but I must have looked surprised because I caught Arnie shooting me a look that said, "What in the world is wrong with you?"

I *was* startled. I had never felt anything physically comparable in my entire life. Anne's touch made me feel tingly, like my whole body had suddenly gone to sleep and then awakened.

Several weeks later, Anne and I were sitting by ourselves, enjoying chili, Sprites, and fries at Wendy's. I looked over the table at her. "It's clear—at least to me—there's something about our relationship that's moved us out of friendship into a new thing."

She smiled and nodded slightly. "What do we call it?"

"W-well, I think I'd call it—you're my girlfriend." My lips felt dry, and I had to unstick them with my tongue before I could finally say, "How does that sound?"

Her eyes glowed warmly. "I really like it, John." Her eyes lowered to her right hand, which was twirling soda-straw paper. Then she looked up at me again. "I guess that makes you my boyfriend, right?"

Instinctively, I reached out for her hand, but I only touched the straw paper before nervously yanking my fingers back. She blushed, smiled and looked flustered. "Gosh," she said, "suddenly I'm not even hungry! I don't think I'll be able to finish my lunch."

"I–I can't eat my lunch, either. What's the matter with me? As long as you've known me, have you ever seen me refuse food?"

"No, I sure haven't!" We hardly took our eyes off each other as we trashed the remains of our unfinished lunches and walked out the door together.

Obviously, the time had come for me to screw up my courage and ask Anne out on a real date. One Saturday morning, I phoned her and asked if she would like to spend a whole day with me. I suggested we go and see the wine country—a valley of lush vineyards about two hours north. She agreed, and we set a departure time for later that morning. A couple of hours later, Anne walked into the house where I lived. The moment I saw her in the hallway, I was terrified. She started talking with a couple of the other guys in the house, and I ducked downstairs to use the bathroom.

I stood at the mirror, trying to calm my nervous stomach. "Lord, I can't go through with this," I prayed. "I'm scared—I just can't do it." I felt so cold that my teeth were nearly chattering.

Then I sensed that familiar inner voice. *Yes, you can, John. You can do it. I have every confidence in you.* With the Lord's assurance as my backbone, I straightened myself up, smoothed my hair, put on my bravest face, and walked out the door to my waiting girlfriend.

Our journey through the Napa Valley vineyards that day seemed like a dazed hallucination to me. It was really Anne's presence I was exploring, and her nearness seemed at once both exhilarating and much too close for comfort.

We drove back toward home as dusk fell. I had no idea from where I would summon the courage, but I knew I wanted to take Anne's hand in mine. Without turning my head in her direction, I glanced out of the corner of my eye to see just where her left hand was located. *If you miss it when you reach out, maybe you can pretend you were trying to turn on the radio,* I thought.

My aim securely fixed, my heart beating fast, I reached over slowly, found her hand perfectly, and curled it into mine. At that moment, I felt more ecstatic than if I'd won an international drag contest.

By this time, our pastor knew something was up with Anne and me. He had seen us sitting together in church, and John Smid had told him that we were dating.

"I understand," Mike told me during a phone call, "that you and Miss Edward are, uh, . . . seeing each other."

"Yes," I agreed, giggling.

"I also realize that you and Anne are something of an unusual couple, having both come from a gay background." Then he asked if we would get together to talk about it.

Anne and I met with Mike for a picnic lunch at a local park. But the two of us could do nothing but giggle, glance at each other, blush and turn away, giggling some more. Here we were, both twenty-eight years old and acting like silly teenagers. Mike just smiled at our antics, then launched the discussion. "So I understand you two are interested in each other. I'm curious. What does this mean?"

"I don't know," I said grinning. "We really like each other, though."

Anne added, "There's something special about how we feel together."

Mike nodded and stroked his jaw. "I feel really protective of you two," he said at last. "If it's OK, I'd like to meet with both of you every three weeks, just to see how it's going."

Soon after, Anne came to my office to show me a new dress she had bought. I felt immensely flattered that she would ask my opinion. She said later that she felt foolish about doing this, but I told her what she did was sweet. I sensed I might really be in love with Anne at this point, but I wasn't sure what this type of love should be like. I'd never felt it before.

I invited Anne over to my house to watch some skits the guys had thrown together to dramatize the lessons in a book we'd been reading. After the skits were done, I walked her down to her car. Before she opened the door, I took her in my arms and hugged her goodbye. Into her ear, which I could feel beneath her hair, I breathed softly, "I love you, Anne."

I held her at arms' length, and we looked at each other in silence for what seemed like a long time. Then I said, "You don't need to say anything; I just wanted you to know how I felt."

Her eyes lingered on mine as she slowly drove away. What had I just said? I had certainly told enough men I loved them, but never had I expressed those words to any adult woman, except my mom.

August 29th was Anne's birthday, and I bought Amy Grant concert tickets for us. I also found her a little book that told the fairy tale *The Princess and the Pea*. I wrote on the title page, "To my princess. Love, John." I took her to the concert and treated her like a princess; I wanted to honor her in every way I possibly could.

I determined not to leave anything about our relationship to chance. So I went to my favorite Christian bookstore to buy every book about dating I could find. Anne was immeasurably precious to me, and I knew in my heart that I needed her more than I'd ever needed anyone.

At this point, Anne had never worn much in the way of makeup. And that hadn't made any appreciable difference to me. But one day, when we were shopping in a local department store, I spied the cosmetics counter. I knew the clerk, Beverly, and hailed her as we approached the counter. "Oh, Jo-hun!" she squealed in her native South Carolina lilt. "C'mere, hon—and who is this lovely gal with you?" I introduced Anne as my girlfriend. Bev knew about Love in Action and some of my history, so she was delighted. She was also quick to make an intriguing suggestion: "We're doing free makeovers tonight. Anne, would you like me to give you one?"

Blushing shyly, Anne nodded and said she'd give it a try. I joyously agreed, so Anne sat down on a stool and Beverly went to work. When the makeover was done, I could hardly take my eyes off Anne's face. I had never seen her look like this; the full, but not lavish makeup brought out her features even more strikingly. She was absolutely stunning.

Afterward, Anne had to go home to take care of some chores, but we agreed to meet later that night at our favorite coffee shop. I ran home, rifled through a box of odds and ends and discovered a fourteen-carat gold ring some old boyfriend had given me. I put it into a small velvet box, then slipped to my knees and began praying. "Lord, You know this ring has long ago stopped meaning anything gay to me. I want to give it to Anne, as something special from me. Please bless it, and let her love it."

Later, we chatted as we enjoyed our coffee and pie. After we finished eating, Anne drove me back to the Love in Action house. Before either of us could open our car doors, I reached into my pocket and found the little velvet box. I held it out to her. "This is something I want to give you, to show you how much you mean to me." I opened the box, plucked out the ring, took Anne's hand, and unerringly slipped it onto her pinky. Anne's eyes half-closed, and I took that as a signal to lean over and press my lips to hers.

What passed between us in the moments that followed was anything but a quick peck. We did nothing inappropriate, but I felt a sense of delight and pleasure surge through me. And, since nothing thrilling like this had ever happened to me with a woman before, I was also totally shocked.

I was similarly shocked more than once in the coming weeks. As Anne and I embraced and kissed more often, a powerful force seemed to be trying to drive our bodies together. As this happened, I can only describe my feelings as ecstatically strange. *Why does my body want to unite with hers so badly?*

Of course, this feeling was common to most men my age, but I had never felt anything like it for a woman. To my delight, Anne confessed similar desires for me.

Anne pointed out to me one night that I had a tendency to attack everything I did—even the physical affection I bestowed on her—"with a vengeance." Wouldn't it be better, she asked, if we took things a bit more slowly? I was depressed when we parted that night. Had I let my overeagerness foul things up? I didn't know how to take love "more slowly."

"Lord Jesus," I prayed that night, "I bring to you these feelings of joy, sexuality, and affirmation of my maleness. Please guard Anne's heart with Your cloak of protection and build in us a love that will stand the test of time." Then I prayed for a miracle: That God would unite Anne—a former lesbian—and myself in marriage.

I phoned my dad and told him I had a girlfriend. He seemed a bit startled, but he was delighted when I told him how much I cared for Anne. When my mother heard the news, she thought this turn of events was wonderful. She was excited—but I could tell she didn't have the slightest idea what to make of it. Neither did my sister, Vicky, or the rest of my family. But their unanimous attitude seemed to be, "OK, whatever you say, John—and we wish you the very best!"

In late October, at one of our regular get-togethers, Mike Riley asked Anne and me, "If all keeps going well with the two of you, when do you think you might get engaged?"

I blurted out, "By Thanksgiving!"

Anne looked at me incredulously, as if to say, "Hey, wait a minute!" She actually said, "Before you ask me to marry you, you'll have to ask my dad."

I was astounded. "You can't really mean that. This is the last decade of the twentieth century, for Pete's sake!" Anne's unflinching gaze told me she wasn't joking. I persisted. "You really want me to go through that archaic ritual of asking your dad for your hand in marriage? I mean, both of us are pushing thirty!"

She continued to look serious. "I mean every word, John."

Later I pondered Anne's demand. If I had to, I certainly would ask her father for permission to marry her. I knew that I wanted to marry Anne. I had known it since we had first started dating, and I hoped that she felt the same way about me.

As Thanksgiving neared, Anne and I decided to drive up to Oregon so she could meet some of my family. Then we would go to Seattle to meet Anne's parents and the rest of her family. But even while we made our plans, some things began happening that weren't so blissful. From somewhere buried deep in my memories, Candi began rearing her seductive head. It was subtle at first. I had slaved over the role and image of Candi for years. Now, after giving up a preoccupation with my own appearance, I subconsciously began trying to re-create Candi through Anne's appearance.

During our trip to Oregon, Anne started resisting my "helpful" suggestions. One day we decided to visit Multnomah Falls, and Anne didn't bother to put on any makeup. Despite my efforts to remain cool, I was upset that she would appear in public with me this way. A stony silence hung between us, until Anne finally asked me what was wrong.

I told her that, by not wearing any makeup, she was telling me that she didn't care about me enough to look good for me. She said, "Hold on—this is ridiculous! We had a late night last night, we got up early, we're not seeing family today, we're just spending time together. So I thought I'd be casual, and we'd both be more comfortable. What's the big deal?" I couldn't answer her question, but over the next few days I kept putting subtle and not-so-subtle pressure on Anne, trying to manipulate her into acting, making up, and dressing in ways that fit my still-alive, warped aesthetic.

After a while, my comments were making her cringe. Soon Anne got sufficiently fed up with my niggling remarks to say, "John, you have to trust that God is developing me as a woman. I *do* have a desire to look nice, but I can't do everything on your time schedule. I'm not a little windup doll you can program; I'm a human being."

But I just didn't get it. At Anne's folks', we broke out in a constant stream of mutual snitting. At last, sitting in her car outside her parents' house, Anne broke into tears and told me she didn't think we should become engaged. "You make me feel like I'm just not good enough for you. I can't dress or do makeup or act the way you want. It's not going to work. I feel like you're comparing me to your mother." Then she gave it to me straight: "If you can't handle me the way I am, I know God can bring me a man who will. I'll even help you find someone perfect for you if you like—I love you that much."

With her eyes glistening with tears, Anne added, "I really care for you, John, and I wish things could work for us. But I can't be this . . . this person you want me to be. I am who I am, and you'll have to love me as I am or go find someone else you can love."

I broke into tears, utterly torn apart inside. I knew Anne was everything I wanted in a wife. But, in a terrible paradox, everything I wanted was all so unfamiliar. I was only familiar with one kind of female image—a chic, sophisticated one.

When I could speak again, I said hoarsely, "I'm so sorry, Anne. Can you ever forgive me? I see what I've done, and I know I've hurt you deeply. Please try to believe me. I do love you for who you are, and God will continue to mold my character." These differences weren't completely resolved right then, but from that moment on they began to mend.

Somehow we got through the remainder of the trip and back to San Rafael without our relationship being totally shredded. But though I repeatedly asked Anne to forgive me, it seemed to be a total impasse. As soon as possible, we made an appointment with our pastor. By the time we got together, I was ready to break. I loved Anne so much that I couldn't imagine her not being in my life. At the start of the meeting I collapsed in tears. I knew that I needed to ask Anne's forgiveness again for trying to recast her in a mold that wasn't her. And I needed to throw away the molds of Candi and my mother, once and for all, tossing out all my "old tapes" about womanhood: the glittery ones about appearance, the fearful ones that said women would only take from me or make me vanish—the whole batch.

I prayed in front of Anne, "Lord, I cherish this woman and accept her for who she is. Forgive me for trying to turn her into something she's not. Please help me to see her as the woman she is, not the woman I'm trying to create her to be. I know that artificial image is not the woman I really love." Afterward, Anne was able to totally forgive me, and we embraced in a tearful hug.

Weeks passed. I met alone with Mike and asked him if he felt now was the right time for me to propose to Anne. He sensed that it was. After I left his office, I went home and made a long-distance phone call to Anne's father in Seattle. . . .

Then I went shopping for a ring. A friend of mine owned a jewelry store in San Rafael. Dan had come out of homosexuality nearly twenty years before, married, and had several children. He had a special heart for men like me who were doing what he'd done, and he showed this affection by making engagement and wedding rings available to us at greatly reduced prices.

At his store I asked Dan if he had a truly unique engagement ring that I might give Anne. He told me he'd recently been to an estate sale and found just the thing: a gold ring with a one-third-carat diamond solitaire and twenty-four little diamonds surrounding the band.

When I saw it, I was delighted with the ring's perfect, delicate design. I bought it, then began to make plans to propose on New Year's Eve.

I collared Ross, a fellow Love in Action grad, and together we drove around San Francisco, searching for the perfect place where I would ask Anne to marry me. We looked at all the well-known landmarks, but I wasn't happy with any of them. We decided to quit and go home. We were approaching the Golden Gate Bridge when I spied the Palace of Fine Arts to my right.

Eureka! It had always been one of our favorite spots. Anne and I had walked here often, enjoying the lovely pond with its stately fountain and noisy, resident ducks. Built for an international exposition in the 1920s, the Palace also featured a classic, Greek-columned, open-air dome. And every New Year's Eve, a fireworks display over San Francisco Bay was launched precisely at midnight—and visible from the Palace.

Anne and I both loved big band music, so Ross drove me to the Curran Theatre in San Francisco to buy tickets so Anne and I could hear Rosemary Clooney's New Year's Eve concert. When we arrived, the box office sign said SOLD OUT. But we just happened to pick up two recent cancellations, front row center. Then I made reservations for dinner at Il Fornio, a wonderfully romantic San Francisco restaurant.

The engagement ring went with me to Ohio for Christmas at my grandmother's. I showed the ring to Parker. He looked stunned and said little. I also showed it to Grandma and to Mom and her husband, Tom. My whole family was thrilled.

Anne spent Christmas with her family, completely unaware that I was going to pop the question on New Year's Eve. I called a florist back home in San Rafael and reserved a dozen champagne roses, to be picked up on New Year's Eve. At last, everything was set.

I returned home the morning of December 31. The afternoon crawled by as I nervously dressed up in my best suit and tie. I picked up the roses at the florist's and placed them carefully in the trunk of my car. I double-checked to make sure the ring box was secure in my outer jacket pocket. Then I went to pick up Anne, whom I hadn't seen since before Christmas.

She looked beautiful in a lovely royal blue silk dress. As we drove across the Golden Gate Bridge, San Francisco was a sea of glimmering lights spread before us. Dinner was delicious—candlelit—and we were mutually dazzle-eyed. Afterward, we made our way to the theater. "Sold Out" didn't begin to describe the standing-room-only status of the Curran that night. I escorted Anne down past the throngs to the front row seats waiting for us. Backed by her big band, Rosemary Clooney was the essence of glamour and class.

The concert ended before eleven; I glanced at my watch and realized my timing was a bit off. I had expected Rosemary and the band to finish a little later. Anne and I still had some time to kill before I could realize my perfect moment. I tried to use up a few minutes by strolling around the area by the Theatre, looking in shop windows. Finally I asked Anne, "What would you like to do now? Maybe grab a cup of coffee somewhere?"

"John, we don't have to do anything special," she said. "Just being with you is all the special I need."

We took off in the car toward the Golden Gate Bridge. Before we got there, I said casually, "There's the Palace of Fine Arts. Why don't we drive down and just take a little walk around?"

Anne's eyes lit up. "Yes, let's!" We descended to the Palace, and I parked.

Then, as I stepped around to open Anne's door, I glanced at my watch. 11:17. *Still time to burn.* I led Anne to the path circling the Palace, and we walked around it, arm in arm, as slowly as I could manage.

We chatted casually as I kept trying to glimpse my watch. Suddenly I felt butterflies begin to flail in my stomach. I wasn't frightened, but I was eager and dizzy—and growing more so by the minute.

My throat grew sandy-parched, and I knew we were walking too long to keep my ruse credible. As many times as I'd mentally rehearsed this whole scene, I hadn't counted on feeling the way I did right now. I tried to say something but discovered my mouth totally clammed up. Now that we were actually here, how was I ever going to make the big moment actually happen?

Finally I eased Anne off the path, and we tripped along until we were under the big, columned dome where I was determined to spring the Question.

It was still a bit early, but, fireworks or not, there was no more delaying the moment. I stood at arm's length from Anne. I cleared my throat, tried to adjust my face to its most tender, romantic configuration—and started to nervously giggle. First faintly. Then loudly. Then uncontrollably.

Anne looked very perplexed. "What's wrong?"

"Anne, I-I-I-I (giggle, giggle) I j-j-just want to let you know (burst of giggles) I h-h-had a phone conversation (more giggles) with y-your dad the other day (explosion of giggles)."

"Oh? About what?"

"Well (giggles), I asked him what he thought (more giggles) about our getting married. . . ."

"You did? W-well, what did he say?"

"I . . ." I was enveloped in a fit of giggles so profuse, my knees turned to jelly and I found myself sinking to the concrete. As I sank, Anne started to giggle, too.

"John! What did my dad say?"

"Well . . ." On my knees now, with a superhuman effort I stifled my laughing fit just long enough to rattle out, "He said it would be fine with him if we got married." Then I flew into giggles so violent I fell backward, hugged my sides, and began rolling from side to side.

"John!" Anne sounded worried and amused at the same time. "Are you sure you're going to be all right?"

"Yeah." I giggled. "Give me a minute." At last I recovered enough presence of mind to ask Anne to help me up. I got my feet under me, and with her assistance, regained a shaky standing position. Without further delay, I reached my hand into my pocket and grabbed the velvet box that held our engagement ring.

Before the giggles could overwhelm me again I blurted, "So, what I was wondering was . . . W-would you marry me?" With that, I thrust the ring box straight in front of me—just as Anne leaped forward and threw her arms around my neck, ignoring my outstretched arm. I tried to keep my balance as I said, "Don't you want to see what's in the box?"

"Box? What box? Not right now. I'm too happy—I just want to hold on to you." Which she did, until I couldn't stand it anymore. "Anne, please look in the box!"

"Box? Where is it?"

"Here." I stepped back. She let go of my neck, and I moved the box near her face. Leaving it in my hand, she slowly opened its lid and stared, motionless and wide-eyed, at the ring on its velvet mound. Finally she found her voice. "Wow! Wow, John. I can't believe this. Wow. I don't know what . . . Wow! . . ."

I blurted out, "Uh, Anne—I suppose the answer is yes?" I started to giggle again.

"Yes! Of course, it's yes!"

"Here, let me put the ring on you." My fingers trembling, I fumbled the ring onto Anne's finger. At that very instant, all of the lights went out in the dome and park. Box still in hand, I reached to where I knew Anne's shoulder must be and drew her to me. Instantly three bright rockets screamed over San Francisco Bay, scattering multihued sparkles across the water. Then a veritable pandemonium of sight and sound broke out: booms mixed with distant sounds of party favors, car horns, whistles, the works.

Anne and I embraced and kissed until the last *boom* had exploded and the lights came back on. Then I took Anne's hand, and we walked silently back to the car. I opened the trunk, got out the bouquet of roses, and presented them to her. She was overwhelmed.

As we headed back toward San Rafael, I thought, *Our big moment turned out almost perfect after all!* It had been a wonderful evening I would never forget.

The next Sunday at church, right after the opening hymn, Pastor Mike said, "I have a wonderful announcement to make. Anne and John, would you please stand?" We did, and Mike continued, "Friends, I am delighted to tell you that Anne Edward and John Paulk are engaged to be married." If Mike had more to say, no one heard it. The congregation burst into cheers and prolonged applause.

After the service ended, I didn't think we'd ever get out of the building, nor did I think my cheeks or ribs would ever recover from the seemingly endless kisses and bear hugs I absorbed before Anne and I finally walked out and breathed in the cool January air, looking into each other's eyes . . . amazed.

TWENTY

A LMOST AS SOON as we were engaged, Anne and I picked a summer wedding date: Sunday afternoon, July 19. Her parents let us know we could have any kind of wedding we wanted. Both of us decided that we wanted the ultimate storybook wedding ceremony. No small, private garden party for us; we would pull out all the stops and whistles and go for it!

In January, I retired from being a house leader at the Love in Action live-in program. I remained in the LIA office as administrator for incoming live-in program applicants. I began taking more time to prepare myself for my coming marriage and also assumed a wider-ranging role in promoting the work of Love in Action and Exodus International's expanding worldwide network of ministries to people seeking freedom from homosexuality.

From January until July, I lived with a couple from my church. Years before, Marty and Nanette had purchased a house large enough to have several bedrooms available for people coming out of homosexuality. Marty couldn't have been a better role model of a Christian husband and father; he and I enjoyed many conversations about marriage. I closely observed his love and patience in action, seeing how gently he treated his wife and baby daughter.

Anne and I searched for the perfect place to be married and found a quaint fairy-tale setting at a nearby Presbyterian seminary. The century-old stone chapel was set in a lush, forested campus near the base of Mt. Tamalpais. In fact, Stewart Chapel looked so much like an ancient castle that its rustic setting had been used to film numerous Irish Spring soap commercials.

We stepped into the chapel's sanctuary and decided it was perfect: a long central aisle, stained-glass windows, mahogany pews, and a front marble-terraced altar faced by a hand-carved depiction of the Last Supper. In the loft sat an enormous pipe organ; beyond the altar spread a fabulous rose window. As we exited, we noticed a rack of gay-affirmative literature in the narthex. Anne and I just looked at each other and winked. In fact, it was that rack of literature that clinched our choice! We decided to tell no one at the seminary about our background. After all, we weren't gay or ex-gay, just another happy couple wanting to get married on their lovely grounds.

Once we were engaged, it seemed like a multitude of attacks and hardships came thick and fast. I wondered if I had sufficiently changed to be a good husband, and I questioned whether I would be sexually compatible in a heterosexual relationship. Both Anne and I were sensitive, and got easily hurt by something the other person did or said.

We entered more in-depth premarital counseling with Mike to learn better patterns of communication with each other. As we clung to the commitment we made when I put the engagement ring on Anne's finger, the conflicts eased off.

About three months after our engagement began, I told Anne, "When the world finds out about us, they are going to want to know what happened. They won't know what to do with us, but I hope they will want to find out what God has done in our lives."

I sent my former therapist, Howard Bryant, a letter about our wedding, together with an invitation. He wrote back a beautiful note saying prior commitments would prevent his attendance, but he was rejoicing that I'd found such happiness. And he wished us all his love, support, and encouragement. His note made me feel great.

The last few months before the wedding were a blur of preparatory details. Anne and I leafed through magazines, comparing notes on our respective taste in china, furniture, and one thousand other details of combining two lives on a practical level. Then there were wedding-related decisions to make—stationery, invitations, wording of vows, selection of the bridal party and groomsmen. We mailed out wedding invitations to three hundred potential guests. With our mutual penchant for organization, all the details were taken care of ahead of schedule.

I enjoyed private conversations with several former homosexuals, now married, who told me more details of life on the other side of the wedding ceremony. Each one reassured me that I would do just fine. They also confided that, on their respective wedding nights, all the sexual "mechanics" had worked fine, physical attraction was not a problem, and their sexual experiences with the brides had been exciting and fulfilling.

In fact, two days before my wedding, Frank Worthen—now married for over seven years—took me aside and gave me a warm and wise father-son chat about sex. "What you're doing is a wonderful thing," he said. "God has ordained it, and don't worry: He's not going to leave you in the moment when you need Him the most." Frank gave me some details about female anatomy, what the sexual act entails for a woman, and the things I could do to make our intimacy pleasurable for my wife. It was a talk that I'd never had as a teen with my own father. I saw it as a beautiful provision from a loving God Who knew I still had so much to learn.

It was special to receive a response to my wedding invitation from Greg, offering congratulations and a gift from him and his partner in Hawaii. He told me he had been living there in a long-term relationship since about 1989. I also received an encouraging telegram from the Exodus International Europe office in London, England.

Finally the big day itself arrived. I woke up and lay in bed with my eyes barely open, listening to the robins chirping outside my apartment window. A sense of God's love surrounded me. I had faced so many years of loneliness, anger, alienation, hurt, and grief—all trying to destroy this wonderful day before it could happen. But God had triumphed over them all, and I was filled with thanksgiving.

I thought back to the previous evening, when the wedding rehearsal had made me cry so hard that I couldn't get the vows out, which started everyone crying.

Finally, after a leisurely cup of coffee to jump-start me into a frenzy-filled day, I showered and shaved, then slipped into my stately black tux-with-tails. After a final check in the mirror, I was ready to stride out the door.

It was a short drive to the neighboring town of San Anselmo. I pulled into the driveway at San Francisco Theological Seminary. As I drove up the curving roadway, the steeple of Stewart Chapel was visible above the trees. Walking up the steps, I opened the massive chapel door, entered the narthex, and pushed the French doors open into the sanctuary. It was empty and still; no one else had arrived yet.

I stood at the back. My eyes roamed down the seventy-five-foot aisle as I tried to imagine how my beautiful bride would look as she walked toward me. The high, gothic ceiling arches and stained-glass colors from the side windows melded into a magnificent setting for our service.

Soon, people began arriving—the florist, photographer, organist, and wedding coordinator, as well as my wedding party and other guests. Suddenly Mike strode in from a side room by the altar, breaking into a huge grin when he saw me. He pulled me to my feet, punched me gently on the arm, then threw his arms around me in a big bear hug. "How goes it, Mr. Groom?"

Gasping for breath, I stammered, "G-great, Mike, I think!" As the organ prelude began, I felt reassured by Mike's confidence and love. Glancing toward the back, I saw my family preparing to enter the sanctuary and take their places. With a hand under my elbow, Mike guided me toward the side room, where he put his arms around me again and prayed for me. I felt God's presence wash over me as butterflies erupted in my stomach.

Then my five groomsmen squeezed into the tiny room, tugging at their ties and squeezing my shoulders as they reassured me. "Hang in there."

"We're right here with you, John."

"You're not going through this alone."

All five of them had left the gay life like I had, and I appreciated their friendship and support at this special moment.

I heard the organ begin "His Sheep May Safely Graze." I couldn't see them, but I knew my mom and Anne's mother had been seated. It was almost time for the groom's party to make their entrance. I turned and smiled at my best man, John Smid, who had walked beside me since my first day at Love in Action five years before.

Suddenly Mike turned to us. "It's time to go, gentlemen." As we stepped through the doorway into the main chapel, I said over my shoulder to John, "You're gonna have to hold me up. I feel like my legs are about to collapse."

"Don't worry," John said with a final pat on my back. "I'm right behind you. You'll make it just fine."

As we took our places, my eyes took in the beautiful sight: a sea of hundreds of faces in the sanctuary mingled with the perfect whiteness of multitudes of blossoms. Down the full length of the aisle hung candles; hurricane lamps; and sprays of cascading white roses, tulips, gardenias, jasmine, and lilies. It looked like someone had draped a tender, pure white canopy over the entire sanctuary. An intensely fresh fragrance saturated the air.

My family members were all smiling. As I waited for the service to begin, I silently prayed, "Lord, please help me never forget this day. Help me recall each scent and blossom, each color and face. Please let me remember the details of today for the rest of my life!"

Suddenly there was a quick movement to my right. *Oh no, they didn't!* The LIA guys—about fifty of them—in unison slipped on fifty pairs of hot-pink sunglasses—triangle-shaped, no less. *Didn't I tell those bozos there would be no shenanigans? I should have known better.* I totally lost my composure and roared while a wave of laughter rippled through the audience.

The laughter died away as the organist played the opening notes of Purcell's "Trumpet Voluntary." Two groomsmen walked to the base of the altar and rolled out a gleaming white aisle runner, down which the bridesmaids and my bride were about to proceed. Then the French doors opened into the sanctuary, and bridesmaids came down the aisle in their floor-length, royal-blue satin evening gowns.

The last bridesmaid up the aisle was Carol, Anne's sister and matron of honor, looking lovely in a shimmering violet-purple gown. She was crying so hard that I feared she would stumble. I put out my hand to touch her arm comfortingly as she passed me to take her place.

Now everyone was in place, and the music stopped. Slowly the French doors at the back of the chapel closed and total silence hung over the sanctuary. My knees began to shake a bit, and I leaned against the grand piano to steady myself. From the steeple outside, a single bell softly chimed five times, tolling the hour. The organ began Wagner's "Bridal March" as the French doors slowly reopened.

Anne was leaning on her father's arm, and they began their stately walk down the long aisle. Her dress was purest white; its bodice covered with a sparkling layer of beads, pearls, and sequins. Anne seemed to float down the aisle, her six-foot train flowing behind her. I had to bite my bottom lip to keep it from quivering. *If I don't maintain some sense of control, I'll completely crumble.* She carried an enormous bouquet of white flowers. She approached me, and our eyes finally met. As the fragrance of her flowers and her perfume wafted my way, I felt a strange peace settle over me.

The music stopped and Mike began, "Dearly beloved, we are gathered today in the sight of God and this company to join together these two people in holy matrimony. . . ."

I took Anne's arm in mine and led her up the steps to the main altar. Mike nodded to Anne, and she passed her bouquet to Carol. Anne and I turned to face each other and held hands as we repeated our first vows of lifelong love and commitment.

"John, repeat after me," Mike said. "I, John, take you, Anne. . . ." I looked into Anne's eyes, and my lips began to form the words. Suddenly it seemed as if I had no voice and time was standing still. Startlingly, my past careened through my mind from the beginning, in images as clear as a series of movie jump-cuts.

I'm seven years old. My dad is kneeling in the Park of Roses to tell Vicky and me that he and Mom are divorcing. . . . I'm age ten, lonely and confused, looking up at the handsome psychologist I desperately hope will help me and take care of me. . . .

I'm fourteen, choking down my first gulp of Scotch. . . . I'm eighteen, walking into the K for the first time. . . . I'm at Parker's house the night we first enter into sexual intimacy. . . . I'm nineteen, in the middle of my first "assignment" for Dulcet Escort Service. . . .

I'm with Lauren, submitting to my first drag "do.". . . I'm Candi, on stage and in my last Gay Pride parade. . . . I'm twenty-three, waking up the morning after being raped, and I'm asking, "Is this all my life will ever be?"

The memories stopped abruptly, and I was back to the present. I heard myself say, "I, John, take you, Anne, to be my lawfully wedded wife. . . ." Then the memories began hurtling again.

I'm twenty-four, kneeling beside my waterbed, asking God to re-enter my life. . . . I'm writing all my gay friends, telling them that Jesus Christ could change their lives, just as He was changing mine. . . . I'm kneeling on my bathroom floor, begging God to help me resist the temptation to go out to the gay bars that night. . . .

I'm twenty-five, walking toward the outstretched arms of Frank Worthen, who has come to meet me at the San Rafael bus station. . . . I'm walking into Church of the Open Door for the first time and feeling overwhelmed by the people's love and acceptance . . . I'm crying in my bedroom, grieved that I have fallen into an emotionally-dependent relationship with Randy . . . I'm twenty-eight, praying that God will lead me into a happy marriage with a godly woman . . . I'm twenty-nine, kissing Anne as the fireworks burst over our heads at the Palace of Fine Arts near the San Francisco waterfront. . . .

The memories faded, and I was back in the present, gazing at Anne in her bridal splendor as she listened to my halting vows. As a sense of joyful awe flooded my heart and tears began to flow, I struggled to get the remaining words out: ". . . to love and to cherish, till death do us part, according to God's holy ordinance, and thereto do I give thee my pledge. . . ." Somehow I made it through the vows, and my tears continued to flow as I listened to Anne's.

As Mike began his brief sermon, his eyes welled with tears, and he had to stop to compose himself. He resumed, then looked from Anne's face to mine a few minutes later as he concluded: "Anne and John, your marriage will only be as strong as your personal relationship with Jesus Christ. As long as each of you keep Him as the center of your life, you will be able to weather any storm." He smiled and looked out over the audience. "And now, by the power invested in me, I pronounce you husband and wife. And what God has joined together, let no man put asunder." He looked down at me. "John, you may kiss your bride!"

I felt an enormous smile stretch across my face as I seized the lower hem of Anne's veil. I couldn't quite reach far enough to lower it completely over her hair, so I tossed it back, to peals of laughter. Then I reached out and gently pulled her toward me. Our lips met and loud applause filled my ears. When the clapping ebbed, Anne and I released our embrace and turned, hand in hand, to face the congregation. Behind us, Mike said, "Ladies and gentlemen, I now have the extreme pleasure of introducing to you . . . Mr. and Mrs. John Paulk!"

Applause burst forth again as the organ roared into the recessional. Impulsively, I raised my fist and exulted, "We did it! We did it!" Laughter and weeping were swept together as the congregation broke into more applause.

After we descended the altar steps to the main floor, Anne and I hugged our respective mothers. Mom threw her arms around me and whispered through her tears, "I love you so much, John. I can't tell you how proud I am of you."

After a multitude of handshakes, well-wishes, and photo flashes, we found ourselves sitting in a stretch limousine, ready to head to the reception at the San Rafael Embassy Suites Hotel. The huge ballroom was set for a massive, candlelit wedding dinner, and our three hundred guests enjoyed a sumptuous meal.

Following dessert, the music began for the first dance: a recording of Rosemary Clooney singing "Our Love Is Here to Stay." After Anne and I held each other close for the first dance, we changed partners, and I went cheek to cheek with my mother, and Anne with her father. "I'm so happy," my mother whispered, "just so happy for you!" After the dance, my father approached me with a big smile, kissed me on the cheek and forehead, then turned away, shaking his head with wonderment as I felt the tingle of his tears on my nose.

Soon it was 10:00 P.M., time for our departure. Suddenly I felt jitters, and I looked around for any remaining guests I hadn't talked with. Anne glanced sideways at me. "Don't you think we ought to be going?"

"Let's stay a little longer. Tonight is the only time we'll ever get to do this." But finally, people began filing out in large numbers, and I was out of excuses. I said goodbye to my family and thanked Dad for booking us into the bridal suite at the gorgeous, turn-of-the-century Sheraton Palace in San Francisco.

The city's sparking skyline beckoned us as we drove across the Golden Gate Bridge. We checked into the Sheraton Palace, and I carried our two suitcases to the hotel room door. I carried Anne over the threshold (how light she felt!) and into the room. Lush, wood trim stretched everywhere; the bedroom featured a huge, four-poster bed and mahogany wardrobe. Anne unpacked and slipped into the bathroom to change while I lit candles, started some music, and then sprawled on the couch. Anne emerged in a sumptuous, floor-length, white silk nightgown and floor-length robe—gifts from my mother. She curled into my lap as we embraced and kissed leisurely.

At last we fell to our knees at the foot of our wedding bed, joined hands, and prayed. We thanked the Lord for everything He had made possible in our lives. We thanked Him for this most lovely day and evening. Then we invited Him to be with us as we made love together for the first time. After our prayer, I told Anne what one bridesmaid had told me at the reception. "'During the wedding, I could swear I saw swarms of angels flying over the altar, enfolding it in a blaze of golden light. Each one held a drawn sword, pointed up toward heaven, and together they cried, "Victory, victory!"'"

With that last word of encouragement, Anne and I climbed into bed together. We clung to each other as our marriage was joined—two becoming one. At that moment, all my fears and insecurities melted away. I could sense God's pleasure with us as we enjoyed the bliss of full marital intimacy.

The next morning, after a leisurely breakfast in our room and a late checkout, we drove to our apartment, where we'd arranged for our wedding presents to be deposited. As a gift for this morning, I handed Anne a delicate Queen Anne-style jewelry box. Inside was an engraving on the brass plate: "To my beautiful bride on our wedding day, July 19, 1992."

As Anne was admiring the gift, my brother-in-law called. "Are you ready for the most spectacular wedding present of all?" he asked breathlessly.

My pulse quickened. "Sure."

"After the wedding reception, Vicky and I were up in the hotel room with your mother and her husband, Tom. They were so taken with everything that had occurred at the wedding. I told them that the source of the joy they had experienced was Jesus Christ. I explained God's plan of salvation to them, and asked them if they wanted to accept Christ into their hearts. And they did—they prayed with me to receive the Lord!" After I put down the phone, Anne and I were literally jumping up and down, hand in hand, for joy. No wedding present could have been more precious than this.

The next morning we flew to Hawaii for the honeymoon of our dreams. The next day, at our oceanside condominium in Maui, Anne wrote these words in our honeymoon journal:

> "John and I were sitting in lawn chairs, watching the sunset, and he fell asleep on my lap. My heart was so full of thankfulness. And I asked God to strengthen me in my weak areas: believing that God and John love me. When John woke up, he was so happy that he had married me and God had finally given him his other half. Wow, what a wonderful and fast answer to prayer! I love being married to John!"

Our honeymoon was marvelous in every way, and we enjoyed every moment we spent together.

No sooner had our married life begun than major media opportunities began opening up for us. We were still newlyweds when, in September, Anne and I were interviewed in our own apartment for *Good Morning, America*. It made me feel proud to tell America what God had done for us. We knew He would use our testimony to give hope and encouragement to other men and women who shared our past struggles. The producer seemed open to us, and Anne was especially good in answering the questions with charming self-control.

But our newly formed union wasn't all smooth sailing. After several months, Anne and I found ourselves starting to bicker at each other about minor matters. We argued over where to hang pictures, how to squeeze the toothpaste tube, where to place our furniture. We wondered if some deep-seated issues stemming from our gay lives could be the root of these quarrels. So we sought out a Christian marriage counselor. "I know these conflicts are because we both come from a gay background," I said, "and we must have an unusual number of issues to work through."

He started chuckling at us. "Please forgive me for laughing, but if you could only know how normal you two are! Your problems are so minimal for newlyweds. What you're working through are the normal dynamics of male-female relating. The two of you are so compatible and well matched, it's almost ridiculous!"

Over time, Anne and I realized that our differences could add up to major assets if we put them to work on our behalf. One's individual strengths balanced weaknesses in the other. For example, I saw on many occasions where Anne's patience and deliberation counterbalanced my impulsiveness and tendency to boldly rush ahead. As time went by, our life together smoothed out and our identity as a married couple became sure. And something wonderful began to happen to Anne. Out of her deep sense of security in being married, she blossomed: Her inner strength grew, and her outer presentation softened even more. As her confidence grew, so did her outward femininity.

For my part, I felt terrific the more I embraced my responsibility to love Anne and to nurture her. If I said anything that might hurt her, I could pray about it, tell God how sorry I was, then go to Anne and ask her forgiveness. We were learning that, with our commitment, nothing would be impossible for us to work through.

During the latter part of 1993, it became apparent to us that we needed to move away from San Rafael. Our identities had been so absorbed with homosexuality for so long. Our friends in church and our family members encouraged us to take a break so our identities could mold together as husband and wife. Also, as Anne and I appeared on such shows as *Oprah* and *The 700 Club*, plus numerous local programs, we began to feel like hometown celebrities. It would be nice, we decided, to start again somewhere we wouldn't be well known. We weren't running from anything; it was just time to move forward into the next step for our lives.

We wanted to live near our families in the northwestern United States. My dad told me that he would do anything in his power to help us get established in Portland, Oregon, where he and my brother and sisters lived. He even asked us to come and live with him and his wife, Vicki, while we adjusted to this new locale. "You've never been able to live with me," he told me, "but now is the time I can give you this." It was a gesture that I would cherish deeply.

In mid-December we packed our belongings into a U-Haul truck and all our friends gathered around us for a bittersweet sendoff. After rounds of hugs and tears we headed for Portland, excited about the future but saddened to leave San Rafael, the site of much growth and wonderful friendships. But we knew that we didn't need Love in Action any longer. Anne and I could walk on our own now. Wherever we might go, we would be taking our family with us—in each other.

The next three months with my dad and his wife, Vicki, were rich and beautiful. Dad and I didn't have a cross word the whole time. We worked in the yard and hung out together, enjoying a growing friendship between father and adult son. Before long, I landed a job with a local Christian company that shared humanitarian aid around the world. By Valentine's Day, Anne and I had been at my dad and step-mom's for two months. My step-mother told me, "You have no idea how much this time means to your dad; he knows that he didn't give it to you when you were young. Now he's able to give you something you really need, and it's wonderful."

That same morning, while we were sharing cards and gifts, Anne told me that her period was a week late. At first we tried to blame it on nerves and the stress of moving. But Anne bought a pregnancy test, just to be sure. Not five minutes after we applied it, the PREGNANT button was bright pink. We were ecstatic. I ran around the house whooping and hollering. As I drove to work the next day, I kept thinking, *How tremendous—I'm going to be a father!* What a glorious feeling!

But then came a devastating tragedy. Anne began bleeding over a five-day period. Then terrible cramps woke her out of a sound sleep. I called the nurse, who immediately scheduled an appointment at the hospital for the next afternoon.

Although we were worried that something was wrong, somehow we believed that the baby would be OK. An ultrasound was taken, then we walked down to the emergency room for the results. The physician called us into a private room and rather abruptly gave us the terrible news: There was no heartbeat; the baby was dead. We went into stunned shock. She told us that its life had probably ceased two weeks ago, just about the time we discovered we were pregnant. The death was probably chromosomal, she said, and nothing we could have done would have saved it.

Anne started to cry. As the nurse put the blood-pressure cuff on her, I went from light weeping to deep sobbing. We held each other and cried. Later, we both sat on a table in the emergency room and said a few words to each other. Yes, it was good to know we'd had a baby. It was also incredibly sad and disappointing to know there was a problem with the developing fetus. No blame for anyone. *The Lord is much wiser than we are, but this really hurts,* I thought.

By the next morning, we felt ready to have the baby removed. Anne underwent a D&C procedure. The sac containing the fetus had already come out, and that helped her feel more like the baby had been placed directly into God's hand. She shared with me the comfort that Christ's presence was with her; I told her that I felt it, too.

When we'd put enough money away, we moved from my dad's house into our own apartment and lived there for a few months. Then we decided we'd like to find a house of our own, preferably an old place that we could fix up. Portland had an Exodus-affiliated ministry, The Portland Fellowship. Anne and I had been in contact with the ministry, but we didn't feel ready to become involved yet. We still felt the need for a break from that type of outreach. But Phil Hobizal, the ministry's director who was also a contractor, heard that we were looking for a home and suggested we look at a house he was remodeling. It was an old farmhouse, built in 1909, that Phil had recently moved to a suburb of Portland.

We drove to the address, parked in front of the house, and walked through it. Immediately we fell in love with its nine-foot ceilings; hardwood floors; and beautiful, built-in china cabinet. There were four bedrooms upstairs, with lots of space for guests, and a sewing room for Anne. We told Phil how badly we wanted it, and he said he'd been praying that someone would buy it who had been in the gay life and was now ministering to people struggling with homosexuality.

In October 1994 Anne and I moved into our home—and then the work began. We painted, plastered, wallpapered, and repaired for weeks, until the house was completely finished—a cozy retreat for ourselves and the frequent guests who came to visit.

Then in May 1995, John Smid called me from California and wondered if I might like to run for election to the Exodus board of directors. It had been two years since I was actively involved in ex-gay ministry, and I felt ready to once again immerse myself. I attended the Exodus conference in San Diego and, much to my delight, was elected to a board position for the next three years.

A few months later, two Portland-area businessmen approached me with a proposal to enter into full-time ministry, publicizing the truth that homosexuals could be set free. This overwhelmed me with joy. Over time, one of these men, Wayne, became a father figure to me. He was so supportive to Anne and me, in giving me the chance of a lifetime to use my experience on a much grander scale to make a difference. I felt so honored by his gesture to financially fund my position. I began working under the covering of the Portland Fellowship.

While at the Portland Fellowship, media and speaking opportunities began to inundate Anne and me. God had prepared our marriage for the visibility and was clearly opening national doors of opportunity.

In August 1995, Anne discovered she was pregnant again, and we were thrilled. But five days passed, and she again started bleeding. Like a recurring nightmare, we went through the whole awful ordeal again. Ten days later, there was no heartbeat. Our pain was inconsolable; we grieved for months.

As New Year's of 1996 dawned, I found myself wrestling in my relationship with God. I felt He had rejected and betrayed us because He had allowed our two babies to die. Was He never to give us the desire of our hearts, to share our love with a child of our own?

I sat in church one Sunday while the pastor performed a baby dedication. I bowed my head and prayed again. "Why, Lord? Why did You take our babies? Will I never get to be a father? Won't Anne and I ever have our own family?"

Then, in His tender way, I felt God impress upon me that we did have a family—we were already a family of four. Two of our children were already in heaven, for reasons we couldn't understand. I was to trust God in this matter. And I was thankful. Our two children would never have to face the sorrow of loss, the pain of sin, or the agony of broken relationships, because they were being raised close to our Heavenly Father. Someday we would see them face to face, when we were reunited as a family in God's presence.

As I let those insights sink deep into my heart, I was finally able to let my unborn children go, and I felt a new level of peace. I knew that we would be reunited as a family in heaven.

TWENTY-ONE

S EVERAL MONTHS PASSED after Anne's second miscarriage. My work with
Exodus and the Portland Fellowship continued. I had a letter to the
editor about my marriage to Anne appear in the *Wall Street Journal*, and we
made television appearances on *ABC Evening News* with Peter Jennings, *60
Minutes*, and others.

Then, in February, Anne and I went to our church Bible study group.
After the evening's discussion a friend asked, "How are you two doing with
the pregnancy issue? I guess I ask because you both seem so . . . peaceful and
unpreoccupied about it now, like the Lord has really healed the emotional
pain of the miscarriages."

Anne and I looked at each other and smiled. "Yes," I responded, "we do
feel pretty good about it. We've just decided to leave it all in the Lord's hands,
go on with life as usual, and not really think about getting pregnant anymore." The peace was a welcome relief. After two years of Anne taking her
temperature day after day, and both of us working so diligently to get pregnant, it was nice to let it go and see what happened apart from our efforts.

"Only a couple of weeks ago," I told our friend, "we mutually decided to
stop trying to make it happen." Pregnancy had meant nothing but heartache
for us anyway.

Less than two weeks later, on a sunny Saturday morning, Anne and I
were out in the back yard gardening when she looked my way. "John, my
period's late about five or six days."

"Why didn't you let me know before now?"

"I guess this time I didn't pay much attention."

I leaned on my shovel and looked at her. "What would you think about
taking a home pregnancy test? We've still got some in the medicine chest."

"Hmm . . ." Anne mused. A moment later, she put down her garden tools and walked into the house. This time I didn't get all excited about what the test might show. When Anne came out a few minutes later, she seemed pretty calm. She held the pregnancy stick close to my nose, and we looked at it together. Both windows registered bright POSITIVE.

"Whaddya know?" I said. "You're pregnant." Neither of us started jumping up and down or hollering. It was wonderful to see that glowing pink, but all I did was take Anne's hand and silently lead her inside the house.

I sat down at our antique oak kitchen table, and Anne cuddled into my lap. She put her arms around me and buried her head in the crook of my neck. I stroked her hair tenderly and prayed, "Lord, we thank You for this pregnancy. But You know pregnancy has meant only grief and pain for us. So right here and now, we give You this child, and we lay no claims to it. This baby belongs to You, and we trust You to help us care for it as long as You want, whether that's four weeks or twenty years." I also prayed that God would protect our baby from all harm.

The next few days crawled slowly by like lazy turtles. *So far, so good,* I'd think every night. On Monday, Anne called our Christian fertility gynecologist, Dr. Timothy Stewart, who knew our history. Dr. Stewart had recently put Anne on a drug to strengthen her ovulation cycle, so he wasn't surprised to learn she might be pregnant. He told us to come in the next day for an ultrasound.

I was terrified that Tuesday morning as we rode the elevator up to Dr. Stewart's seventh floor clinic. Could our baby have died already, yet still have given a positive test result? Anne lay down on the ultrasound table, and Dr. Stewart's nurse squeezed the ultrasonic gel onto her flat stomach. On the screen we saw a tiny egg shape with a little round spherical mass in its middle going *blip-blip-blip.* . . .

"Wow, the baby's heartbeat!" I blurted out. It was alive! At that moment, I felt tremendous relief—but also colossal butterflies. Anne's face was beaming.

Then the doctor measured the fetus and the yoke sac. "Congratulations!" he exclaimed. "You're about four weeks along—barely, but most definitely, pregnant." He prescribed progesterone immediately to strengthen the pregnancy. Then he added, "Ah, you'll want a due date!" He got out a little chart and asked us when we conceived. We knew exactly because Anne had been taking her temperature every day until a few weeks ago and we had carefully charted when we had had sexual relations. After he got the information, Dr. Stewart announced his conclusion: "Your baby should arrive exactly on Christmas Day!"

Anne and I walked out of that office thrilled. Yet I couldn't help thinking, *It's only March. Christmas is such a long way off, and I can't let myself think that far into the future. I can't let myself hope too hard that this baby will even be alive tomorrow!* Later that day we went to a bookstore and bought a book called *Pregnancy, Week by Week.* From then on, we took this book out almost daily, looking at the pictures and reading the explanations of exactly what our baby must look like.

Anne and I had agreed not to tell anyone about her pregnancy. We kept the secret just between ourselves as the days crept by. But almost every hour, both of us wondered if our baby would die that day. Each morning I would ask Anne if she had bled at all during the night. But each time, her answer was no.

As the eighth week began, we found ourselves getting anxious. We called the doctor's office and asked if we could come in for another ultrasound. Much to our relief, the baby's tiny heart was still beating strong.

Dr. Stewart measured the baby. "It's just where it should be and doing great." He told Anne to keep taking the progesterone until the eleventh week, then stop.

The worst time in terms of our anxiety came during the tenth week, about the time we had lost our first two children. But as week ten went by without incident, we decided to tell our families. They were thrilled for us but also cautious.

At the end of week twelve, we breathed sighs of relief to hear Dr. Stewart say, "Your chances for a miscarriage are now down to just 5 percent. From here on, there is minimal risk." On the exact day the twelfth week ended, my mother and stepfather sent us a beautiful flower arrangement with a card, "Congratulations—we all made it through the 12th week!" Their gift and note made us feel wonderful.

From that time on we had a great time. Anne and I began allowing ourselves to get really excited and start imagining the future. Now and then, Anne would weep for sheer joy in my arms. She would put her hands on her still-flat stomach and give God thanks for giving her the blessing of being a mother.

Time started moving even faster for us. Before long we neared week twenty, the midpoint in Anne's pregnancy. By this time, Anne was definitely starting to show. We let loose and told everyone that she was pregnant. Finally we decided to start working on the nursery. During the first two pregnancies we had bought some items to decorate the baby's room in a Winnie-the-Pooh motif. So I went up into the attic and brought down the box filled with the things we had hidden away after we lost our second baby. Then I opened the door to the bedroom we'd set aside for our baby and took a stuffed Winnie-the-Pooh out of the box. It was time to decorate the room and prepare for our baby's arrival.

My father and stepmother came over one Saturday and helped us paste Pooh wallpaper around the room. Then we hung molding up, painted the room, and hung Winnie-the-Pooh drapes.

Time came again for the annual Exodus International conference, and Anne and I flew to Boston to take part. Many people in Exodus knew Anne was pregnant by now. Several women came and congratulated Anne, making it a wonderful time for her. It was almost like the blossoming of still another brand-new identity. Beyond merely coming out of lesbianism, Anne was coming into the full reality of womanhood that God had always intended for her to enjoy.

During the conference, Anne felt the baby kick for the first time. I'll never forget that day and its tangible sign to us that our baby was moving and thriving. Anne and I felt so close to each other as we worshiped God together in the chapel on the last night of the conference.

At twenty-two weeks, we returned to Dr. Stewart for our midpoint ultrasound. "The baby's so big!" I exclaimed.

"Everything looks perfect," Dr. Stewart said with a grin. "Fingers, toes, eyes, nose—everything in place!"

"Look, its mouth is moving," Anne said, "and you can see the little fingers bend." As we watched in wonder, the baby wiggled and bounced and flipped. Anne couldn't feel all these movements, but the screen left no doubt that they were occurring.

"My gosh," I chuckled, "that baby is all over the place."

Moments later, we asked if the ultrasound could tell us the baby's sex. My heart leaped wildly as Dr. Stewart calmly said, "You have a little boy."

My heart palpitations were fraught with a bit of anxiety as well as floods of glee. I was delighted to be fathering a son, but I also had qualms. Would my son grow up to be a teenager who'd be the brunt of taunts and ridicule like I'd been? And, because of the pain he'd suffer, would he be tempted to withdraw from me as I had abandoned my own father? I wondered if a girl might be easier for me to raise.

In the days following, I battled other anxieties, like the fear that my son wouldn't be able to bond with me, that something in my past would make it more difficult for him to love me. I knew in my calmer moments that these fears were irrational. It was comforting to talk with other former gay men who now had children; they could totally relate to my feelings. It was reassuring to hear that they had conquered their fears with God's help.

One night after the ultrasound, Anne and I went with my dad and Vicki to see a play. When we told them the baby was a boy, they were absolutely delighted.

"Why are you so thrilled it's a boy? Vicky has two boys already," I said, referring to my sister.

Dad looked thoughtful for a moment, then smiled. "John, I've got this feeling that having a boy is going to be one of the best things that's ever happened *to* you and *for* you." Then he added, "And your baby will be the first child in his generation to carry on our name." I pondered his words with deep satisfaction as we drove home that night.

When I met with my pastor and told him the baby was a boy, he encouraged me, "I think it's fantastic! I've seen you with little boys, and you're wonderful. I can't imagine anyone being a better father for a boy."

You know, he's right, I thought. *I love my nephews all to pieces. It's gonna be all right!* After that conversation, my fears disappeared, and I became 100 percent thrilled about having a son.

Soon afterward, I felt the Lord nudging me to go out and buy a basketball, a football, and a soccer ball. At first the idea made me feel quite uncomfortable because it meant I'd have to shop in a sporting goods store, which could arouse painful old memories of my failures in the whole area of sports. But I knew I needed to do it, to purchase for my son the very symbols of masculinity that I had feared in my own past. And, although I had experienced vast amounts of growth, I knew buying those three balls would also mean more healing for me.

I was now on the threshold of a new plateau in my life: shouldering the awesome responsibility of raising a young boy. And all I had learned about healthy emotional development by this time made me take this responsibility with utmost seriousness.

Suddenly I thought, *I'm so glad God gives us nine months of pregnancy so we can contemplate this great responsibility of raising a child.* Then I went out and joyfully bought that football, soccer ball, and basketball and put them all on display in our son's room.

During late August, Mom and her husband, Tom, came from Ohio to visit. For one weekend they took Anne, me, my sister, and brother-in-law three hours north to Seattle for a fun getaway. They drove us to one of the most expensive maternity shops in the area, then told Anne to look for a maternity outfit.

"I can only buy one," Tom said, "but keep trying them on until you find one perfect for you."

Anne modeled gracefully for us, and we all cheered her on as she emerged from the dressing room in one gorgeous maternity outfit after another. We couldn't decide which one we liked the best. "You'll have to choose, Anne," I told her with a grin.

Finally she narrowed her selection down to fifteen outfits. Then Tom directed, "Now pick the ten you like best and rate them in order." Anne made her selection, and Tom shoved us out the door while he paid the clerk. Later in the day when we opened the car trunk, we got a shock: Tom had bought Anne all ten fabulous maternity outfits! Anne was overwhelmed with this expression of my stepfather's love.

We spent hours thinking about potential names for our son. We wanted to honor Anne's parents by using *Edward*, Anne's maiden name. We also wanted to express deep gratitude to our wonderful Christian doctor, Timothy Stewart, who had done so much over the years to help us have a healthy baby. We loved the name *Timothy* because it meant "one who honors God," and we thought *Timmy* was a cute nickname. Finally we decided on the perfect name: Timothy Edward Paulk.

I went on a buying binge of children's books and then wrote little messages to Timothy in all the books I bought. Inside the cover of one entitled *Guess How Much I Love You,* I wrote: "To my beloved son, Timothy. You won't be born for three more months, but I love you already. I felt you move in Mommy's tummy yesterday, and I can't wait to see you. Remember, I will always love you. Your daddy. September 8, 1996."

Now we had just three more months to go, and Anne was soaring along without a problem. She hadn't even had a bout of morning sickness. Her blood pressure was normal, and she stayed perfectly healthy for an expectant mother. Nearly every night after Anne went to bed, I went into Timmy's room and sat on the nursery rocker. I turned on his little Winnie-the-Pooh night-light and stayed there for a while, looking around the beautiful nursery and dreaming what it would be like when our son finally arrived.

Timmy would be someone like me, a male I could relate with in the most special way. I had learned so much about how to nurture and love men in healthy and noncontrolling ways. I prayed fervently for Timothy, that God would help Anne and me be good parents.

Still, even through this happy time, fear would sometimes try to creep into my thoughts again. *What if things go wrong at the delivery? What if some problem occurs? What if Timmy comes out stillborn?* But from talking to other parents I learned that my fears were common during the last months of a pregnancy. As the time drew close, Dr. Stewart convinced us that even if Timmy was born early he'd have a good chance of surviving.

Six weeks before our due date, Anne and I started attending childbirth classes. Those four weeks were precious for us; just another expectant mom and dad sitting in an auditorium along with dozens of others. By this time, Anne's size made waddling her primary means of locomotion, and once seated, she had a hard time getting back up. But it all made us feel even more like normal parents-to-be.

As these weeks unfolded, God lovingly used each event to reinforce our growing identities as heterosexuals and as a married couple. We didn't need Timmy as some sort of advertisement, to prove that our lives had changed, but he did offer living confirmation of all that God has done for us.

After work I enjoyed hearing Anne's stories of how women would approach her on the street or in the supermarket for some spontaneous discussion about babies. "When are you due?" they'd ask, then launch into their own tales of being pregnant. She enjoyed these impromptu conversations with other women at work, church, and everywhere she went.

The day after Thanksgiving, Dr. Stewart called to tell us he'd determined that Timmy was sitting breach, in a position that would prevent his being turned in utero. So he would have to be delivered via C-section. "That means you can pick out Timmy's birthday," he said, "any time up to nine days before the due date." We picked December 17, so Timmy would always have a birthday all to himself, separate from Christmas.

On the evening of December 16, Anne and I sat on our bed together before trying to sleep. We held each other and prayed, placing everything in

God's hands and asking that all would go well the next day. We thanked God that we would finally meet our son the next morning and find out what he looked like. Then we drifted in and out of sleep until 4:30 A.M.

December 17, 1996. We awoke before daylight, instantly alert with excitement. We got up, dressed quickly, grabbed our bags, and drove to St. Vincent's Hospital. We were ushered into a birthing suite as lavish as a fine hotel room, decked with luxurious furniture, including a sofa, wingback chairs, and tasteful wallpaper. A few hours went by; nurses strolled in and out to prepare for the birth. After they gave Anne an epidural, we prayed together one last time. Then my family arrived, and everyone donned surgical masks, hats, and outfits.

About 7:30 A.M., they wheeled Anne into surgery. I walked alongside her gurney to watch them bring Timmy into the world. Within thirty minutes, our son began emerging—completely free of complications! He was still only partially born when we heard his first cry. Anne and I instantly dissolved into tears.

Timmy looked like a perfect cross between me and Anne's mother. He yelled ferociously while a nurse took him, wiped him off, then put him on the cold baby scale. "Eight pounds, one ounce," she announced, then determined his length: twenty inches. As I bent down to kiss Anne, I had never felt more excited in my life.

We spent the next three days in the hospital while Anne recuperated from her surgery. We cuddled Timmy and thanked God for him as we entertained a steady stream of family members and well-wishers. Now, at last, Anne and I had one child we could see and hold.

Soon we brought Timmy home, and the first few weeks flew by in a sleep-deprived haze. Then, when Timmy was six weeks old, I was sitting in his room one night, rocking him in his chair after feeding him a bottle. He was snuggled in a blanket, and I could feel the soft puffs of his breath on my neck.

I let my eyes drift toward the ceiling and felt them ease shut. I may have dozed for a few moments. Even if I did, I felt strangely alert, as if I had entered some other level of consciousness. And while in that muse, I witnessed a vision so vivid that I can see it again almost as clearly as I saw it that night.

Anne and I were backstage in the wings of what seemed to be a darkened theater. Beyond the folds of heavy velvet curtains, I could see beat-up, hardwood planks roughly reflecting bright stage lights. I smiled at Anne and was shocked to see at second glance that her hair had turned gray. I looked down at my hands and saw that their backs seemed wizened and liver spotted. *How strange,* I thought. *We look like we're at least in our sixties!*

I leaned toward Anne and whispered, "What are we doing here?" Just then we heard footsteps cross the wooden stage. Anne and I peeked around the curtain and saw a tall, thin young man in a dark brown suit stride to a podium. We couldn't see his face clearly, but his appearance reminded me of a younger version of Billy Graham. We heard the audience stirring beyond the stage, and I could see that the houselights were up about halfway. It seemed like at least a thousand people were packed into the theater's main floor and balcony.

The young man began to speak, and I heard him say, "Ladies and gentlemen, I'm here tonight to share a miracle with you, to share the good news that, regardless of what you may have heard, sexual orientation can change. Homosexuality can be forsaken."

He paused to look up into the balcony, then continued. "I know of thousands of people across this country who have changed their sexual orientation through a dynamic relationship with Jesus Christ. And the reason I'm able to stand here today to bear witness to this miracle—the only reason I have life and breath today—is this: Both my mother and father changed their sexual orientations and came out of homosexuality. Then, after God transformed their lives, they married one another and gave me life. I'm here today as living proof that everything I'm saying is true!"

Suddenly the little puffs and smacks from Timmy's lips against my neck brought me back to the present. He squirmed slightly in my arms, and again I was staring at the ceiling of his little room. I gazed at his sleeping form and wondered, *Have I been somewhere else in time? What just rushed through my mind like a movie preview?* Did God open a curtain to our future? Would our son travel the country someday and share the story of his miraculous, God-given life? Would he someday act as a living defense for us, telling the world that sexual orientation can change and homosexuality can be overcome?

Had I just witnessed a prophecy, a premonition, or just a father's super imagination? I didn't know—and I won't be certain for several decades. I only know that in those moments—as I stroked Timmy's hair; held his tiny face close to mine; felt his skin warm on my cheek; and heard his soft, cooing sounds tickle my ear—I could not imagine feeling more right with my world, my family, and my eternity.

I felt tears trickle down my cheek. I tried to still my shudders so I wouldn't wake Timmy. Still, I couldn't stop crying altogether. The vision reminded me of other spotlights I myself had once basked in during my old, tiara-pursuit days. I didn't weep now for sorrow but in deep joy, because I knew those days were gone forever.

Tiaras? I laughed to myself. *What man who knows the joy I feel tonight could ever covet one again? After all, God Himself has promised to place something far better—a regal crown—upon my brow. On that final day, I will meet my other children at last; see my Lord's own radiant eyes smile into mine; and then, with all my being, I will embrace Him—my True Love, Deliverer, and King.*

AFTERWORD

In May of 1998, John was offered a position with Focus on the Family as a specialist in homosexual issues. He, Anne, and Timmy packed up once again and moved to Colorado Springs, Colorado, where they now live.

God continues to provide John and Anne numerous opportunities to share the good news: Freedom from homosexuality is possible through a relationship with Jesus Christ.

ACKNOWLEDGMENTS

N O ONE COMES OUT of homosexuality by himself; it takes a community of loving, supportive people. Along my journey to freedom, many people have helped to shape my life and guide me to wholeness.

Foremost, I would like to thank **Bob Davies**, executive director of Exodus International—North America. Bob, you were the initial inspiration for this project and provided tremendous encouragement during the years that passed while this book was being shuffled around to an assortment of writers, publishers, and agents. You edited this book in brilliant fashion. You are a valuable brother, and I consider you as one of my closest friends.

To **Frank Worthen**, one of the founders of the ex-gay movement. If you hadn't listened to the Lord, rather than the other Love in Action staff members, I would probably be dead by now. Words cannot express my heart-felt gratitude and love for you. Your wisdom and experience put me on the path toward heterosexuality. As long as I live, I'll never forget getting off the Airporter at Larkspur Landing and walking into your arms for the first time. I felt like I was home.

To **Mike Riley**, senior pastor of Church of the Open Door in San Rafael, California. Mike, you are like a father to Anne and me. Your door was and still remains always open whenever I need to "phone home." Thank you for the numerous hours you spent counseling us while we were stumbling through the dating process. I'll never forget your tears during our wedding ceremony. I love you.

To **Thor Nelson** & **Linda Hubbard**. God used both of you to lead me back to Him. You taught me the Word and the profound truth that no matter what, God would *never* leave me. You provided me with the initial hope that change was possible. I continue to give honor to you both when I speak across

247

the country as examples of Christians who love gay people even in the face of uncertainty. Thank you.

For his continued faith in me, I'd like to thank **Wayne Ericksen**. Wayne, your nurturing heart, friendship, and support made the writing and publication of this book a reality. Thank you for standing up for righteousness in the face of a society whose morals are crumbling. Anne, Timmy, and I value you and appreciate all you do to sustain us.

These people have been significant throughout the years. I love, value, and appreciate you and the encouragement you've provided.

Chris Corbett	Stan Oakes
Joe Dallas	Kevin Oshiro
Steve Donaldson	Tom Perez
Damon Dyslin	Jeffrey Satinover
Dave Galanter	Bert Savarese
Mike Haley	John Smid
Ross Hayduk	Jay Stone
Dawn Killion	Anita Worthen
Joe Nicolosi	

Much appreciation is extended to **Tony Marco**, the writer of this book. You did a superb job in bringing my story to life with the creative edge it needed. I felt safe and supported by you during the 40-plus hours of interviewing. Remember the relief we felt once we reached the end of "the gay years"?

Thank you to **Les Stobbe**, my literary agent, who shopped the manuscript around to nearly every Christian publisher in existence, only to be rejected by every one. We finally did it, Les!

Thanks to **Rebecca Cain** who spent hour after hour transcribing cassette tapes. Becky, at one point you knew more about me than my own wife!

To **Phil Hobizal** and **Jason Thompson**, the staff of the Portland Fellowship. Thank you for putting up with my idiosyncratic behaviors and ideas day after day. Your input has enriched my life and made me a more humble person.

Appreciation and love is extended to **Summit View Church** and the great community of believers: **Mark** and **Annette Martin**, **Brian** and **Julie Cole**, **Craig** and **Robin Flippen**, the **Mowreys**, **Smiths**, and all who supported Anne and I through our time in Portland.

To my dear **mother.** Few people will ever know how hard you've worked to better yourself and love your family. Thank you for being a great Christian mother, mother-in-law, and grandmother. **Tom,** thank you for your continued encouragement, love, and support. I'm finally having a "Rainbow Day!"

Dad and **Vicki,** thanks for your unconditional love, support, and faith in me. I've learned much about accepting myself and other people from you both. Dad, some of the qualities and attributes I like best about myself have come from you. See, I used the book title you suggested, Dad. Much love.

Hugs and kisses go to **Vicky, Bruce, Jake, Brian, Joe, Jenny, Eric,** and **Trevor.** I love you all.

To my son, **Timothy.** It feels like I waited all my life for you to be born. I love and cherish you with all my heart. I am here for you, Son. I will listen and respond to your needs and cries for help. I will share your triumphs and struggles along the way. I won't be perfect but will point you toward the One who will always be able to provide for you what I cannot. I'm proud of you, Timmy, and love watching you grow up. I hope you'll be proud of me.

I owe my unconditional love and thanks to my cherished wife, **Anne.** Honey, you are my best friend. I knew I loved you and wanted to marry you even before you had a clue about the confusing world of men! You are the best wife for me and a tremendous mother to our son. I appreciate you in a million different ways. You are beautiful. You are competent and smart. You are gentle. You are humble. You complete me.

Most importantly, I thank my **Heavenly Father** for giving me a life I never thought possible. You are the Father Who is always there and never rejects. I love You.

APPENDIX

RESOURCES FOR ADDITIONAL HELP

Organizations

EXODUS INTERNATIONAL is a worldwide coalition of Christian ministries that offer support to men and women seeking to overcome homosexuality. Many of these ministries have specialized services for family members and friends, including support groups, one-on-one counseling, and literature. For a free packet of literature on the work of Exodus, including a complete list of referral ministries, contact:

Exodus International—North America
PO Box 77652
Seattle, WA 98177
(206) 784-7799

NATIONAL ASSOCIATION FOR RESEARCH AND THERAPY OF HOMOSEXUALITY (NARTH) is an organization of nearly 700 professionals across the country who treat homosexuality from a variety of perspectives. Contact them by writing:

NARTH
16633 Ventura Blvd., Suite 1340
Encino, CA 91436
(818) 789-4440

Books

Many excellent books are available to help you understand and overcome homosexuality. Ask for titles at your local Christian bookstore. If you prefer, you can conveniently obtain many of these books by mail. For a free catalog of books on homosexuality and related issues, contact:

Regeneration Books
PO Box 9830
Baltimore, MD 21284
(410) 661-0284

John and Anne Paulk

JOHN is a legislative and cultural affairs analyst with Focus on the Family, specializing in homosexual issues. He and his wife, ANNE, address audiences across the nation and have appeared throughout national and international media on such notable programs as *60 Minutes, Oprah, Good Morning America, The 700 Club,* and *ABC World News.* To arrange media interviews or speaking engagements contact them at:

Focus on the Family
8605 Explorer Drive
Colorado Springs, CO 80920
(719) 531-3400
E-mail: paulk@integrityonline9.com

Tony Marco

TONY MARCO has written extensively on the subject of homosexuality. He is the author of nine books and is considered one of the nation's leading non-profit fundraising copywriters and creative consultants. He can be reached at:

5058 Old Fox Trail Court
Crozet, Virginia 22932

To order additional copies of

Not Afraid to Change

send $12.95 plus $3.95 shipping and handling to

Books, Etc.
P O Box 1406
Mukilteo, WA 98275

or have your credit card ready and call

(800) 917-BOOK